The Faith No More
& Mr. Bungle
Companion

The Faith No More & Mr. Bungle Companion

By Greg Prato

Printed and distributed by Greg Prato
Published by Greg Prato
Front cover photo by Silvio Tanaka [tanaka-foto.com]
Front cover design by Kurt Christensen [kurtchristensen.com]
Back cover photo by Greg Prato
Copyright © 2013, Greg Prato. All rights reserved.
First Edition, November 2013

ISBN 978-1493696666

Foreword

I can't pinpoint Faith No More as the sole reason why I started to venture outside of just plain old heavy metal and to other musical styles. But they certainly were one of the main instigators. While Nirvana gets the lion's share of credit for helping turn the tide away from horrible hair metal and towards more honest/real rock sounds (as they should - Cobain and co. were one of a kind), there were several bands before 'Nevermind' broke that helped prepare the public for the oncoming changing of the guard. And I hereby deem Faith No More as one such contributor.

Out of all the rock n' roll shows I've attended over the years, without question, the first time I ever saw Faith No More live in early 1990 was one of those life-changing experiences, where suddenly, you listen to music and view live performances differently (you will have the pleasure of reading more about this event in greater detail when you reach Chapter 6).

Something that can't be stressed enough about FNM is the group's ability to take on just about any musical style imaginable, chow it down, regurgitate it, and it come out sounding spot-on. New wave, hip-hop, heavy metal, soul, pop, industrial, or Middle Eastern sounds, the band could do it all. *Expertly.*

And we mustn't forget about Mr. Bungle, the band that originally was known to many as merely "Mike Patton's side band," but over the course of a trio of recordings, blossomed into an awesomely unpredictable group, that proved just as stylistically diverse as FNM.

I had the pleasure of interviewing every single darn member of Faith No More for a feature on the band's history for Classic Rock Magazine article back in 2006 (and have also conducted interviews with various FNM and Bungle members before and after for other publications and sites). After several years of careful consideration, I have come to the realization that the time was finally right to go for the gusto…a full-on Faith No More/Mr. Bungle book, that was part historical overview and part analyzation, that left not a single bloody stone unturned.

Enjoy!
Greg Prato

p.s. Questions? Comments? Feel free to email me at
gregprato@yahoo.com.

Contents

"They were really like a spider web, pulling equally in five different directions. There was no de facto leader of the band. If any guy tried to be the leader, the other guys would just say, 'Fuck you.' They would laugh him out of there. It was pretty much the most democratic band I've ever worked with. No guy could lead that thing. [Mike] Patton was really into Sade, as was Roddy Bottum. And Roddy was really into the techno thing, and Mike Bordin was into Killing Joke and studied African drumming at UC Berkeley. And Bill Gould was the glue of the whole thing."

--Matt Wallace, Faith No More Producer

Chapter 1: Introdução

By the spring of 1990, the members of Faith No More - singer Mike Patton, guitarist Jim Martin, keyboardist Roddy Bottum, bassist Bill Gould, and drummer Mike Bordin - had already spent nearly a year touring the world in support of their buzz worthy album, 'The Real Thing.' Understandably, the band was looking forward to a well-deserved rest, and possibly beginning the process of plotting their next studio effort. Although 'TRT' hadn't been an immediate smash hit, it kept its presence on the Billboard album chart, while their most recent single/video, "Epic," was being aired on the weekly late night MTV program, 'Headbanger's Ball.' Additionally, 'TRT' had recently received a Grammy nomination, while the group was receiving steady press coverage in such publications as Rip and Kerrang! And although FNM hadn't broken out of the club circuit Stateside, in Europe, the band was headlining bigger halls, as evidenced by a recent performance at the cavernous Brixton Academy in London, England.

Then, one day, the band received a phone call while overseas. "More than anything, I remember us being in Europe, in this van that smelled like vomit, from the day we got it," recalls Patton. "Our manager [would] check in with us maybe once a week. He called and said, 'Your single is blowing up over here.' We didn't believe him - we thought he was joking. We thought he was kind of buttering us up, so he could keep us on the road, and we all wanted to go home. I remember landing in the airport and going to a hotel, we were going back to the States, and seeing the damn video. Turning on the TV by chance and seeing the video, and going 'Oh shit...the joke's on us'!" Patton also remembers not being exactly thrilled with his recently-obtained stardom - "When a master comes in every day and beats you at 3:00, and one day he comes in with a chocolate éclair, you don't want that fuckin' chocolate éclair!"

Patton's band mates also seemed to feel the same way about suddenly being thrust into the public's eye, and selling oodles of albums. "Our time isn't that much our own anymore," said Bordin. "It's like living in jail, only they take us out to eat lunch at the Ritz. When you see your position on the chart, it's terrific. But it's like it's happening somewhere else. It's demoralizing when you're supposedly doing really well, but in fact nothing has changed, and it's just as fucked as ever."

Gould, on the other hand, saw commercial success as a golden opportunity, but not in the same way many would assume. "I don't see the point of limiting accessibility out of stubbornness. There's always been this misconception that 'commercial' equals 'stupid.' Just because something is accepted by a lot of people, it doesn't mean there isn't some interesting thought behind it, you know? You can actually do a lot of damage on a mass scale."

Still, FNM's singer was having difficulty coming to grips with all the fame and adulation. "Actually, it's kind of...pathetic sometimes, because we really don't have any control over what's going on at all. Right now we're caught up in this huge machine that just keeps churning and churning, and we can't get out of it no matter what. Now that the album's doing so well, we just gotta keep going with it. It's good and all, we all want it to happen, but sometimes you feel really helpless. Completely powerless. That sucks, 'cause I mean, I guess that's what the industry is all about is just other people taking control of you. Pimping you. But you've got to draw the line somewhere."

Welcome to the big-time, boys.

Chapter 2: Faith. No Man

The nucleus of Faith No More - from the band's beginning until its end - was Bill Gould, Mike Bordin, and Roddy Bottum. However, before the trio united as one, there were various line-up switcheroos, as well as related projects. And it was Gould and Bottum to first cross paths. Both were born in Los Angeles during 1963 (April 24th and July 1st, respectively), were the sons of lawyers, grew up in Hancock Park - a well-off neighborhood built around a private golf club (the Wilshire Country Club) - and first met when they were nine or ten years old. Eventually, Gould and Bottum were classmates at an all-boys school, Loyola High School.

Both were bitten by the music bug fairly early, as Gould took bass lessons and Bottum studied classical piano, but the duo would not be band mates straight away. According to Bill, one of his first real bands was the Animated (which Bottum was not included in), which was comprised of pals from Hamilton High School in LA, and musically, was equal parts new wave and jangle pop. "Before the Animated, I was in Boy Scouts when I was about twelve years old, and just started playing bass. A kid in my troop (Roddy was a member too!!), Paul Wims told me that he played guitar, so my mother would drop me and my bass over at his parents' house and we would jam Beatles songs in his living room. Then [drummer] Kevin Morgan, who lived down the street from Paul, joined in. Next came [lead guitarist] Mark Stewart, and finally Mr. Chuck Mosley on keyboards. By the time we were all jamming together as a band and writing songs, I was probably 15 years old."

"At the beginning, Paul and I were into stuff like Yes, the Beatles, probably your garden variety beginner stuff, but Chuck and Stew brought in a much more sophisticated element into the band. I think I heard the Sex Pistols album ['Never Mind the Bollocks...Here's the Sex Pistols'] for the first time at Paul's house, at rehearsal. I also learned about bands like the Fall, Pop Group, XTC, Joy Division from them; to look back on it now, they probably saved my (musical) life! Meanwhile, I got into more aggressive punk stuff too, maybe a bit more than them, but it created an interesting dynamic that made the music part Buzzcocks, part XTC, part 'I don't know what.' It was a very strange band (compared to other bands in LA) and we really had a hard time finding anyone to play with that made sense."

Wims also recounted his memories about the Animated years later. "We were all surprised that a bunch of 18 and 19 year olds could play so well together (1979 or so). We were all on the same page musically. We started out playing cover songs, but then started writing songs ourselves. Eventually we had enough songs to start playing shows. We would rehearse in the Silver Lake (near downtown LA) area and one day a studio engineer named Joel came to hear us rehearse (the recording studio was across the street). He liked us so much that he recorded our first demo for free (five songs), which helped us get gigs. I wish I still had those recordings but I do not."

"The EP ['4 Song EP'] was recorded in 1981. We only had enough money to do four songs. We could have done ten if we had the cash. When that EP was released, I was only 20. I am now 50. 'Edith C. Sharp' and 'Plastic Heaven,' which was a minor hit on KROQ radio station here in LA. They played it for about two weeks before taking it off the air. That's probably the best song on the EP."

The Animated would go on to open for several notable groups (including the Bangles' precursor group, the Bangs, as well as the BusBoys and the Troggs), and perform at then-popular/now-defunct punk clubs (Madame Wongs, Hong Kong Café, Club 88). But like most "first timer" bands, the Animated wasn't long for this world, splitting up in December 1982. By that point however, Gould was long gone from the group. Bill Gould: "I really liked the music, these guys challenged me especially with songwriting in a way that has kept me always trying to keep the bar as high as possible. I left the band when I moved up to Berkeley to go to school when I was 18 (1981), the same year I met Morris, Worthington, and Bordin."

The "Morris, Worthington, and Bordin" in question is none other than singer/guitarist Mike Morris, keyboardist Wade Worthington, and aforementioned drummer, Mr. Mike Bordin. The way that Gould would cross paths with the trio is simple enough, as Gould recalls it occurred upon arriving at University of California, Berkeley. "The first thing I did after I unpacked all my stuff in the dorm room, I walked down to the record store on Telegraph Avenue, and looked on the bulletin boards to get in a new band. There was a phone number for this guy Mike Morris, who was putting a band together. And that was what became Faith. No Man."

While Morris and Worthington would play a part in the eventual formation of Faith No More, the obvious main player to the story was Bordin. Born on November 27, 1962 in San Francisco, Bordin describes his heritage as "My grandfather came from Russia, Kiev. That side of my family is Russian and Welsh. The other side is Italian, Hungarian and I think some Polish too. I'm a real mongrel."

As Bordin entered his teens, he became close friends with a gentleman who would eventually enter legendary status with headbangers worldwide - late/great Metallica bassist, Cliff Burton. Bordin: "I grew up with Cliff and we used to play instruments together before either of us were in bands. We actually knew each other before either of us played instruments. He was my weed dealer, and we'd just talk about music and go to concerts and party - nothing major, just kids, this was in seventh grade. He said one day, 'I'm gonna play bass,' and I said, 'Alright, well I'll play drums.' That's literally how it was. We then joined a band Jim Martin had, because he was from the same area, and Jim and Cliff became inseparable, and this was again about 15 years old, 16 years old, and here we are. That's where our connection really truly started, and then he obviously joined [Metallica], and left us." [Burton would tragically die on September 27, 1986, in a tour bus accident]

During his teen years, Bordin was the recipient of several nicknames - one of which would stick with him to this very day. "I have a lot of nicknames. When I was a little kid, I was called Motormouth, because I talked a lot. Jim [Martin] has given me a nickname, Puffy. It's a long story...I don't like to be called it much because everyone calls me it. It has to do with how I looked as a teenager. I used to have this big, big hair - like afro hair - and when I walked it'd go, *Whooooosh! Whooooosh!* My hair was really puffy. I've never told anyone else that! Serious. It looked like one of those foam things you put on microphones."

It wasn't long before the afroed youngster began taking the drums seriously, and taking lessons to hone his craft. "I learnt how to read music and drum patterns and how to hold my sticks. That was the first thing I learnt. It's a drag and takes time, but it's worthwhile. It's good to have solid training and solid learning, but if you're smart then you'll always try and take it that much further. It's like riding a bike, once you learn the basics you can push it further, and if you're creative and clever, you can figure out the way that you can make it best for you. When I was learning with a regular teacher I used to get frustrated because I would always see people who could play faster than me and there were always people who could play flashier than I could, and in the end, it got kind of intimidating because I knew that it wouldn't end. There are always going to be people who are playing faster or flashier than you."

"Learning African rhythms with a guy from Ghana broke that mould. It taught me how to play things as I heard them. It taught me that if you hear five people playing drums, and you can hear what all those people are playing then you can play that, and you can do it all yourself. If you have the syncopation and the coordination, you can be your own ensemble, except it's an ensemble of toms and snare and hi-hat, you can put those different drums in different patterns together and make a whole new thing. It was like learning how to speak another language. When you can speak one language, sometimes it can only take you so far, but when you learn another language then sometimes that's exactly what you need to get you that little bit further."

According to Morris, it took some time before the new drummer got into the required groove. "Bordin ended up being perfect for the job, even though at first, he seemed to think it odd to play beats without using his hi-hat, instead using his toms. I wanted that low, bass-y, tribal beat and he could play it precisely and not tire out, as many drummers would have."

However, the drummer traces his "off the beaten path" approach to before joining forces with Faith. No Man. "I don't particularly want to contradict Morris, but the fact is that there were several things working together at that time to break me out of the 'normal' style of drumming. Seeing the Sex Pistols' last show [with Sid Vicious] at Winterland really changed everything for me. I knew there was more out there musically, because I had seen it with my own eyes. The guy that introduced me to Morris and consequently the others, Rick Clare, I was in a bad new wave band with that I didn't fit in at all. He knew I was coming from a metal background and consequently into harder stuff like Killing Joke, PiL, etc., and suggested I look into Morris, who he said was also into stuff like that."

"Listening to that style (maybe they called it post-punk?) was hugely influential in breaking out of tradition. Pete De Freitas (Echo and the Bunnymen RIP), Martin Atkins, and Big Paul Ferguson were all both much more musical and rhythmically aggressive in their approaches and very inspiring. Maybe most importantly, I was in a class at school with a Ghanian drum master, CK Ladzepko, who taught Ghanian style ensemble percussion. This was drum (tom) patterns as rhythmic frameworks exclusively. There was a huge group of bands in the Bay Area called worldbeat who studied in this class, the Looters, Big City, Mapenzi, to name a few. Being left handed really helped here, because I hadn't been crossing my hands anyway, and I could get around the drums with ease. Playing like this and listening to the first couple Killing Joke albums, among others, it all really made a lot of sense, and at that time, I was absolutely ready (and looking) to do something different, as were many people."

"There is a lot to this story, it was such a transitional time. Musically, it was wide open, and there were tons of characters in and around the thing. Morris did have specific and precise patterns in mind when he was writing songs, which also began to drive other members crazy after not too long. Bill Gould and I became friends (I remember him being surprised I loved Roxy Music), and that kind of started a connection on the side that wasn't subject to being dominated by a central leader type. We knew we wanted to explore."

According to Morris, the roots of Faith. No Man stretched back a few years earlier, under a different moniker. "The original name 'Sharp Young Men' was a piss-take on all the 'elegant' '80s groups at the time, it was meant to be smart-arsed, ironic, similar to the 'Bright Young Things' of the '20s, whatever. The name 'Faith. No Man' came about during a rehearsal when the others decided that 'Sharp Young Men' was 'too straight' sounding. So I proposed the name 'Faith in No Man'. Bordin responded saying it was 'too wordy' and suggested shortening it to Faith. No Man. The full stop (.) was intentional and always has been a part of the name."

According to Gould, Faith. No Man's sound was far from the all-encompassing sound of what Faith No More would one day become. "It was a little more derivative of what was happening in Great Britain - Theatre of Hate and Killing Joke. And there was a post-punk thing that was kind of new. I was kind of getting out of punk rock by then, because the Black Flag crowd started becoming saturated with football players and meatheads. So this post-punk thing was very appealing." Also, Faith. No Man began playing shows (at such San Fran punk venues as the On Broadway and the Mabuhay Gardens), which Gould doesn't sound particularly fond of by his simple description - "Pretty horrible shows."

Looking to get their sound down on tape, Bordin recounts that producer Matt Wallace entered the picture the same way Gould did. "[Gould] saw a flyer around Berkeley, saying 'Dangerous Rhythm Studios - cheap demos, I'll do anything.' We did some demos with him, and we loved him. A good, fucking fun-loving guy, he was willing to work as hard as he had to." Recording soon began in Wallace's parents' garage, which led to Faith. No Man's debut single, 1982's "Song of Liberty" b/w "All Quiet in Heaven." Gould: "I had pneumonia - a really bad bronchial infection, where I couldn't hear. My ears completely plugged up, so I recorded that record deaf!"

With tensions mounting between Morris and Gould, Worthington bailed, and Gould called on an old comrade to replace him - Roddy Bottum. Not long after, Morris got the boot. Bordin recalls this early line-up shift - "We all just kind of quit. We said, 'We're going to start playing [without Morris]. We like each other, we've got a vibe. We've got an itch that we want to scratch.' So that's why there was keyboard, bass, and drums, and that's why we switched guitarists so much, because it was just us three. The 'Man' was gone - the man was 'No More'."

Which leads us to the birth of the now world-famous band name, Faith No More. As legend has it, it was either Bordin or a friend, Will Carpmill, who helped hatch it. Carpmill: "Mike Bordin and I were in class, trying to come up with a new band name for FNM. Possibly 1983? We were passing the sheet of paper back and forth with our ideas, riffing on 'Faith. No Man.' I think I might have suggested 'Faith. No Morris' with a laugh, and then a few seconds later, one of us had 'Faith. No More.' Not sure if it was me or Mike. A guy sitting behind us in class, who apparently was also not listening to the lecture, told us that 'Faith.

No More' is the exact semantic opposite of 'Semper Fidelis,' which is the US Marine Corps motto, 'Always Faithful'."

And why did the period in the middle of the band's name soon cease to exist? "No reason, we just stopped using it," recalls Gould. "We didn't even have to discuss it. I don't think any of us ever cared for it, it was a carryover from the Faith. No Man days."

Chapter 3: Faith No More

With the Gould-Bordin-Bottum faction now in place, the bassist would soon realize that the trio's surroundings played a part in the creation of their sonic make-up. "I don't think a band like Faith No More could have come out of LA. There are different motivations in San Francisco. Most musicians are really poor there, and there's not much prospect of life getting better for them. Greed doesn't motivate their approach to music as much as it does in LA. It's a rainy city with a lot of European influences. But we were like, 'Fuck you, we're from California. We like the beach.' That was thought of as very uncool."

"I remember we got MTV because that was thought of as uncool as well. We lived in this house which we didn't clean once for a year and a half - clothes all over the floor. But we pooled our money and got cable television and MTV. We did it just to fuck everybody off. We started watching MTV so much that it became this thing that was real. People in San Francisco look down their noses at popular culture, but to us it's a weapon. I remember we played a club in San Francisco once where we did a perfect, note-for-note cover of Van Halen's 'Jump.' People hated it." Speaking about the lack of tidiness in their aforementioned apartment, Roddy recalls, "We had these outrageous pot parties - we had a party the first day, and a year later when we moved out, there were still beer bottles around from that party."

During this wild and wooly FNM era, various guitarists and singers came and went. One such short-lived singer was a gentleman by the name of Walter O'Brien, who had met Roddy while both were attending San Francisco State University during the fall of 1983. O'Brien would later recall preparing for his one-and-only show with the band, at the Fiesta House in Los Angeles, on December 30th. "They had a rehearsal space at a place called the Vats in San Francisco, which was an old Hamm's beer brewery, converted into rehearsal spaces for punk bands. We actually practiced in a 40'x10'x10' beer vat! I rehearsed with them several times in preparation for the show. We would also hang out at their apartment on Shotwell, where Roddy, Bill and a slew of others lived. Friends of the band from the Shotwell house and school traveled to LA to see the Fiesta House show. Even at that time those guys had a musical sophistication that set them apart from other bands, and the drive to be a great band, recognition of which they achieved a few years later. I look fondly upon the time I spent with them. My musical career ended with FNM."

Another singer that signed on for a spell was none other than Courtney Love, who a decade later, would find fame as the singer/guitarist of Hole, and as the wife of Nirvana's Kurt Cobain. Bottum: "She was around for six months or so - quite a while, considering that we were switching around singers a whole lot at that point. [The music] was kinda along the lines of what we did on the first record. We would just play riffs over and over again - we thought we were so inventive, because we thought it was so driving and so heavy. But she was really good. She did a lot of screaming stuff, and we had a lot of slow melody stuff too. When she sang with us, she was punk rock; now she says she's always been punk rock, which is not true at all. After she left our band she was totally into - I mean, with a sense of humor, but really hardcore pop sorta stuff.'" The keyboardist would also recall that Love "Liked to sing in her nightgown, adorned with flowers," but as Gould points out, it just didn't work out. "She was a very chaotic personality - she took a lot of work. It just got too much after a while."

Years later, Bordin recalled that there were elements of FNM's early sound that would be similar to their later, fully-realized direction. "When we started it was much more simplistic, me and Roddy and Bill. There's a song on ['The Real Thing'] that's descriptive of what we were then, the song 'Zombie Eaters', where the bass line starts: 'Bam, Bam, Chk, Chk, Chk,' that was one of the original things we did, we did it for about twenty minutes at a time. That was what we did. Bauhaus used to do it in their day; it was like a skip, it was like a piece of music cycling itself over and over, very simple, just like a small chunk. And that's what we were after, I think, to try and get at something that wasn't really being got at then, with all the...there was Hüsker Dü there, and there was early REM, a lot of that jangly kind of psychedelic Replacements sort of...not really getting at what we felt could be gotten at."

Gould agrees with Bordin's assessment of FNM not being afraid of a little repetition early on, as the band continued to play such local venues as the Mabuhay Gardens, as well as venturing down to Los Angeles to play at the Anti-Club. "We played clubs forever, but we never did covers. Actually, we started off as very inaccessible. We wouldn't have any changes in our songs, they would be like a skipped record that would go on forever. It kind of turned into music somehow. We were very uncompromising. We were young and just having fun. There was a lot of substance to that music and we were getting a lot of gratification out of it. Really, though, what we were doing then is the core of what we're doing now. We still have that musical freedom."

As a result of the group's decision to not compromise their sound, some locals labeled FNM as "anti-hippie." Bottum: "We were established as an anti-hippie band because of where we live, in San Francisco. I mean it's the hippie capital of the world, and in the past what this city has stood for has been this sort of hippie-love environment. So, when we started out, we wanted to move as far away from that as possible. It's what we were working against to get where we wanted to go."

With a name in place and their unmistakable sound rapidly taking shape, the only pieces of business left were to locate a permanent singer and guitarist. Filling the former category would be a one-time band mate of Gould's from the Animated - Chuck Mosley. With a FNM gig set for LA, Gould invited Mosley to give it a try on stage. "He had a couple of 40-ouncers of beer - I don't think he'd ever sang before - he just got on the mic and yelled," recalls the bassist. "I think we had a show in San Francisco after that, and he came up for that and did it. It just started becoming a band thing."

Born on December 26, 1959, in Hollywood, California, Mosley was an adopted child, and would later discover that his birth mother was Jewish and his birth father was part African American and Native American (interestingly, Mosley's adoptive parents were of the same ethnic make-up). He would go on to study classical piano for ten years, before discovering punk rock and going to Hollywood shows. It was around this time that Mosley was enlisted to supply keys for the Animated. Mosley looks back on how he eventually got the gig as FNM's frontman. "They had three shows booked and had gotten rid of [Love]. I did those shows in San Francisco, and I just came out really aggressive.

We might have even practiced for those shows. Their fans liked me, and other people around them told them I was good enough."

Mosley recalls his early days as a singer - "The thing I hear most often is, 'Did you ever think of going into stand up?' I learned early on the devastating effect [of] the in-between song silence and the band trying to talk amongst themselves and tune up. The unfamiliarity of relating to the crowd was always an 'energy black hole,' so I always tried to fill it up with whatever's going on at that present time - just saying really stupid stuff." Despite signing on, Mosley would continue to reside in LA while Gould, Bordin, and Bottum continued to be based in San Francisco (it's a nearly six hour long drive between both towns), resulting in the singer having to receive music by mail, so he could pen lyrics.

And when it came to filling the role of the six-string, Bordin remembered an individual from his past - Jim Martin. Bordin: "I was with Billy Gould eating at a Mexican restaurant in the East Bay, and lo and behold, there's Cliff [Burton]. He goes, 'Y'know, you've got to get Jim in your band, because Jim is working a regular job, it's fucking killing him. You know he can do what you want him to do'."

According to Gould however, Martin's name came with a disclaimer from Bordin, who had previously played with Martin (and Burton) in a band called EZ Street. "Jim and Mike Bordin never really liked each other, apparently. The way it was put to me was through Bordin - 'There's this guy Cliff knows. He's an asshole, he's always been an asshole. I was in a band with him and I quit because he was such an asshole. *But he can play guitar'.*"

Born on July 21, 1961, in Oakland, California, Martin grew up in the nearby town of Hayward. "People say that I'm macho because I'm big and hairy compared to the rest of the guys in the band. I grew up with three brothers. It was pretty rough and tumble. Couldn't get away with being a pussy. I like a bottle of beer. I like girls. But I don't know if that has anything to do with rock. As I remember, I was like this before rock." Eventually, Martin began soaking in the sounds of such classic rock acts as Black Sabbath, Led Zeppelin, and Pink Floyd, which eventually reflected in his playing style. "My influences to a greater extent were Jimmy Page, Jimi Hendrix, and David Gilmour. Mostly Page. His method of using a pick and his fingers at the same time and his way of squeezing the humanity out of a guitar. It's funny how influences work. My influences were influenced by old blues men. Those legendary blues men were influenced by their tribal ancestors. The tribal ancestors are the link back to the beginning; they are the keepers of the essence. Through my influences I am connected to the roots of time and the music that elevates the primordial spirit of mankind. We do not truly compose anything genuinely new, the listeners and the presentation are what is new, and it is the perspective that varies. The ability of expression and improvisation, the stuff of creation that fascinates all life."

When Martin was about fifteen years old, he was a member of the aforementioned EZ Street. Martin and Burton also played together in such additional outfits as Vicious Hatred and Agents of Misfortune, and along with a drummer pal, Dave DiDonato, would often take trips up to a house that the guitarist's family owned, in Maxwell (a three hour ride up north from Hayward). Martin: "We had this property that my folks bought, I think it was in 1969. It's up in the Coastal Mountain Range, in California. And it's well off the beaten path. So you can go up there, and you won't see anybody for the duration of your stay. Guys run some cattle up that way and stuff, but generally, you never see anybody. So pretty much, anything goes. That's where we did most of our exploratory music projects. And we recorded them on the spot as they happened. It's tapes and stuff of just whatever was coming right off the top. So, we did quite a few of them, and it was a good experience. A lot of material came out of it that you might be familiar with - [Faith No More's] 'Woodpecker From Mars' has a section in there. A Metallica song would be 'For Whom the Bell Tolls'."

DiDonato: "Cliff and Jimmy brought all their gear. At night, we'd go out and start jamming. We had a little generator there, that we put up at the back of the cabin, and ran some power cords down to the front. In some of the tapes, when we stop playing, you'll hear the generator humming away. But they would have like six or eight effects boxes on the ground - basically on the dirt or on plywood, in front of the cabin. This is where they did a lot of experimenting on their tones, and what plugged into the sequences, and a lot of the settings. A lot of it was just trial and error, and they would hook up into these pretty huge riffs, tones, chords, whatever, and we would just jam for hours. The tape would catch 30 minutes, [before] someone would go over there and flip the tape back over." Years later, DiDonato put a CD of these aforementioned recordings up on his website, Rotgrub (which has since been taken offline). But as DiDonato admits, those expecting traditional song structures from these jams are out of luck - "At times, Jim did not care what Cliff was doing and vice versa."

With Martin's arrival (armed with his trusty 1979 Gibson Flying V with mirrored pickguard, that he'd play nearly exclusively for the duration of his time in the band), the final piece was in place of Faith No More's musical puzzle, according to Matt Wallace. "I always liked to compare him [to] the guy who comes in with big army boots and stomps - wearing muddy shoes - across your floor. He came from a Black Sabbath and Corrosion of Conformity [background]. He was really into the much heavier stuff. It was an essential ingredient to weigh the band properly."

And in addition to bringing an extra-added musical muscle, Wallace points out that Martin was an unmistakable original. "At the time we met, he looked like the star of that movie 'Eraserhead' [the character Henry Spencer, played by the late Jack Nance]. He almost looked like Kid N' Play, where he had this slightly tallish, curly head of hair that looked really weird, and he had these really thick glasses. He would just say whatever's on his mind - there was no governor between his brain and his mouth. It was kind of refreshing to have that."

Chapter 4: We Care A Lot & Introduce Yourself

With things rapidly coming into focus for FNM, the band's live work became more consistent (although sticking mostly to their San Fran homebase), and Martin remembers these shows as a time when the group looked towards non-musical areas for inspiration and guidance. "We burned a lot of sage at those early shows and some of the band members liked playing on significant days of the Wicca calendar; such as the summer solstice or the spring equinox. These were the really early shows. Once we started in earnest, we left the Paganism behind."

As a result of the group's early interest in all things Wiccan, Wallace was met with apprehension from a few acquaintances when he went to work on FNM's next set of demos in 1985. "Everybody kind of freaked out, because the band were this...a lot of people thought of it as a Satanic thing, but I think they were, for lack of a better phrase, more into the Wiccan thing. We walked into Prairie Sun to record - they were doing these sage smudges. They had this slightly metaphysical thing about them - people were always like, 'Dude, they're into Satan!' But it never phased me, I knew they were creative guys, and that they were going to do what they were going to do."

With several new songs in the can, Gould handed the tape to a friend that worked at a nearby record store - with specific instructions. "'Just play it when people are shopping for records.' It turns out that Ruth Schwartz, who started Mordam Records, was shopping for records when he played the tape, and came up to the desk to ask what music that was. He told her, 'It's just my roommate's band. She said, 'What label?' and he said, 'They're not signed.' And she called us up like two days after that. It's kind of bizarre, but that's what happened."

Recorded at Prairie Sun Studios in Cotati, California, FNM finished off the second half of the album (one half was comprised of the demos Wallace worked on earlier) - the entire record being done in two three-day weekends, with the group earning a co-production credit along with Wallace. But it was during these sessions that a troubling recurring pattern with Mosley sprung up. "I probably 'mental cased' myself into a cold, a sore throat, or [lost] my voice. It just never changed. And I was never fully prepared - I was always working on stuff as we were recording. That's kind of been a trademark of mine - coming to the studio mostly prepared, but not really knowing what I'm going to do on certain parts and having to work them out right there." The singer recalls that when his voice was back in working order, things went a smidgen smoother - "I could croon a little because I liked David Bowie, but I couldn't do much else." Mosley also admits he simply "rapped over the stuff where I couldn't hear a melody." Still, singing in key would remain a challenge for the dreadlocked vocalist. "When it came to the stuff that required more singing, I had to really focus to get in tune. I hear myself out of tune a couple of times on those first two records. You couldn't adjust anything. It was just whatever you could get. Matt was good at getting the best out of me."

Released in late 1985 (the exact date has been lost in the sands of time) via the aforementioned Mordam Records ("More damn records," get it?), the ten-track album would be titled after the album-opening "anti-anthem," "We Care A Lot," which was built around a simple and repetitive (surprise surprise!) bass lick by Gould, and lyrics that poked fun at the day's current events - as well as all the pop star posing and celebrity self-gratification that went along with Live Aid (a highly-publicized two-concert event that took place in London and Philadelphia on July 13th, to raise funds to help fight horrific famine in Ethiopia). The album would contain the least amount of heavy metal elements when compared to FNM's subsequent releases. In fact, "The Jungle," "Arabian Disco," and "Pills for Breakfast" (the latter an instrumental) are the sole compositions that prominently feature Martin's metallic guitar work.

But that's not to say that the album doesn't remain a great, cutting edge debut - especially when compared to all the blah mainstream rock that glutted MTV and radio at the time. Case in point, several tunes that would continue to appear in FNM concert setlists for years afterwards, including "Mark Bowen" (titled after an early FNM guitarist), "As the Worm Turns," and especially, the aforementioned title track. And giving a tip of the hat to such classical guitar compositions performed by metalheads (Randy Rhoads' "Dee," Tony Iommi's "Orchid," etc.), Mr. Martin offers a brief solo/acoustic interlude - the appropriately titled

"Jim." Years later, Bottum admitted to still having a soft spot for FNM's inaugural full-length. "I still like it. There are parts of it that are really amateurish, but I think it's great. It's pretty representative of the time."

Up next would be an album cover design, which featured an eight-pointed star (looking like two squares overlapping in an off-kilter manner) - an image that would become Faith No More's logo, and adjourn t-shirts the band has sold at their concerts throughout the years. It turns out it was the band's bassist who was the brains behind it - "The star was my thing. It's a pretty deep and pervasive symbol that has meaning in several different cultures. What it signified for me at the time was chaos...order through disorder." Gould would also later admit that the star design was inspired by the Chaos Star, from British author Michael Moorcock's 'Eternal Champion' stories. "Well, yes there is an element of that, chaos was the thing that drew me to it originally. In a nutshell, musically as well as personally I think all of us found ourselves faced with certain structures in our lives that didn't really work for us...either through coming of Faith. No Man or just turning 20, living on our own, and wanting to do things differently, and the way we approached this was to try something that had no rules, only the rules we made ourselves. So this meant doing new things and seeing where they would go. The point of this chaos is that we were trying to discover who we really were, and maybe in this recording you can hear a little of that."

With the album finally released, college radio latched onto the album's contagious title track, which would become one of the decade's great underground rock anthems. Gould: "I think that we didn't know how damn good it was until we were actually recording it and heard it on two speakers. We were kind of surprised that we had this song that seemed to have a life of its own." Bottum also remembers what inspired him to pen the lyrics. "I wrote the lyrics to that song after listening to a whole lot of Run-DMC."

A guitarist from a then up-and-coming band - with no notable recordings out yet - took note of FNM for the first time, thanks to "We Care A Lot." Ladies and gentlemen, meet Soundgarden's Kim Thayil. "They had all that buzz on college radio with 'We Care A Lot.' 'We Care A Lot' was *huge* at college radio. I had just come from being a college radio DJ a couple of years before at KCMU in Seattle. I was not generally into the music that got heavy rotation at college radio stations.

These were often indie stations and alternative stations that played a lot of commercial pre-MTV crap...or MTV-ish crap. 'We Care A Lot,' I don't remember ever seeing on MTV. But it got a lot of new wave radio and college radio airplay. I liked the song. I remember I wasn't acquainted with them when I first heard it. Other people were telling me about it - 'Oh, this song is really big. It's all over college radio.' And I heard it, and I was like, 'Oh, fuck yeah!' I remember liking it, but I thought it had an anthemic and gimmicky quality to it. But I knew that there was some credibility this band had with college radio."

"Like I said, I had a bias being a former college radio DJ - I didn't like a lot of stuff we had to play there, and fortunately, my shift was late at night, so I would tend to play a lot more hardcore and progressive music, and experimental shit. But when Soundgarden ended up playing with Faith No More, their musical ability was just superior and the set was full of all kinds of cool riffs and songs. I dismissed 'We Care A Lot' as that kind of college novelty song, and the rest of the set was just fucking strong. I really liked Mike Bordin, and Jim Martin was a fucking hilarious dude. He was a great guitarist - he was a heavy guitar player, and he was fucking funny. He was a man of few words. Every other word probably consisted of expletives, and the expletive of choice was probably the word 'fuck.' It was just great - 'Hey Jim, how are you doing?' 'I'm fucking doing all fucking right. How the fuck are you, motherfucker?' He was quite a character and we liked him. He had those big red glasses - they looked like giant TV sets made by Fisher Price. He looked like a biker wearing some TV glasses. [Laughs] Those guys both seemed to have an interest in heavier music - Mike Bordin and Jim Martin."

FNM also caught the attention of another soon-to-be-renowned musician - Fishbone singer/saxophonist Angelo Moore. "I would see Faith No More in the music scene - the LA music scene. They were good, too. They were all from back in the day. What do I remember about Faith No More? 'WE CARE A LOT!' [starts singing the song and bass riff] I just remember we'd be playing the clubs around town, and they would be a part of the scene. We would just all be there. We played Orange County, San Diego, Eureka, San Francisco - all up and down the west coast. They would just be a part of the scene. Faith No More, Mr. Bungle, the Chili Peppers, Thelonious Monster, and all the rest of those people that were around at the time. I think we may have played a couple of shows with Mr. Bungle and probably Faith No More. We probably played with them at Madame Wongs, yeah. Eventually, everybody broke off in their different directions. All of those bands were just part of a community. They were part of the music community of Los Angeles, is how I see it when I look back."

It was also in late 1986 that then-Metallica bassist Jason Newsted first experienced the powers of FNM, firsthand. "For me personally, Faith No More was one of the very first Bay Area bands that I witnessed live. I was a new, fresh-faced kid. Wide-eyed, spongy-brained, taking up anything I could around me. I was in the band Metallica for maybe seven or eight days at that point. I had an apartment down on the north shore, and I went into the Mabuhay Gardens, to see Faith No More play. The Metallica guys were there - they steered me to it, because of course, Cliff was great friends with the Martin brothers, and Jim was still playing guitar in Faith No More then."

"So they steered us towards the gig, and Chuck Mosley was still singing at that time, and came out with a dress on. And Jim's up there with his Flying V. They were so alive, so vibrant, so honest, and so 'San Francisco.' It was so representative of what was happening on that street, in those blocks, at that moment. It was just incredible the way that that identity was. And consider the individuals that made up the band - it was the Bay Area. Really beautiful representation in that way. So that's my first impression of the visual part of it. Just real wild for a kid coming from a farm in Michigan. Like, *'Holy crap*. This is really crazy!' But the appeal of the music and the liveliness of the music - the honesty of it - was just infectious. There was no way not to like it. It was just so pure and so freaking good...the players were all, obviously. Billy, as a bass player, that's where I always looked first - always got to check that out first and then check everybody else out after that - and he was and still is a monster. Really, really impressive. The propulsion that Billy created in that band is something that not many bands get to reach."

The album's supporting tour was a whole other story, however. Gould: "We got in a four-door pick-up truck, with a little trailer hitch, and just hit the road. Great fun, great tour, very hard work - had no fucking money whatsoever." Martin also recalls this early FNM touring era. "We traveled across the country and had about 30 dates in 90 days. It was brutal. We saw very little money, and as a consequence, we ate very little. Chuck was an asshole. The wheels fell off the truck. We met many generous people who let us stay with them. We lived in the Metroplex in Atlanta, Georgia for a couple of weeks. Rats ate hot and sour soup out of my beard!"

And it was also around this time that Faith No More and Soundgarden played their first shows together, which Kim Thayil remembers quite well. "We didn't even have a record out yet, so it may have been in '85/'86. I know we knew Mike Bordin - Mike had heard some demo of ours, doing the song 'Nothing to Say,' and he loved it. He's a great guy - he's the guy that Chris [Cornell, Soundgarden singer] and I initially took to. He was hugely into us and spoke highly about us. We played three shows in the northwest. Now, we hadn't really toured yet - that was sort of our first tour. We played in Seattle, then we played in Ellensburg, and then we played Vancouver - out of the country. Chuck was singing with them, and he sang at the gigs in Seattle and in Ellensburg. I do not believe he sang in Vancouver - I do not think he could get into the country because of a previous DWI arrest, and his DWI was either in the US so they wouldn't let him into Canada, or the DWI might have been in Canada so he was expelled. I can't really remember the details. He couldn't make it up to Vancouver. So Roddy Bottum did the vocals."

"We did the gig opening for them in an area of Vancouver called Gastown, at a small bar. A couple of things I remember about that was some time during the middle of the set, Chris said he heard someone say, *'Fucking Led Zeppelin crap,'* and then threw a glass ashtray that shattered on Matt Cameron's kick drum. I remember hearing the thud and the crack. Which is kind of fucked up, and whoever did that, could have seriously gotten their fucking ass kicked by the band. But we weren't really the kind of band that would cower, so what we did was we just moved to the front of the stage and played even louder and more aggressively. That kind of shit got us more aggressive and combative. And almost always, we won them over. But then Faith No More came out and did this set that they had done with us on two previous shows, playing it without Chuck." Thayil recalls walking away from those shows appreciating the affable folks of FNM - "They were so friendly. They almost seemed like big brothers. And I immediately got the sense -

especially with Mike Bordin - that he was kind of taking us under his wing. And we got that feeling from Billy Gould, too. Those guys are just great guys. And it was very important to us."

Shortly after returning from their introductory Stateside tour, work began on their sophomore effort (which saw the group jump from Mordam to Slash/Reprise). Recorded at Studio D in Sausalito, California, the album was once again co-produced between the group and Wallace, while Los Lobos' Steve Berlin was added into the mix, too. And it turned out that 'Introduce Yourself' featured a more focused sound and approach than their debut, and also included a re-recording of 'We Care A Lot.'

"One of the things that [Slash/Reprise] wanted when they signed us was to have us do the song over again, because they felt it hadn't fallen on enough ears," recalls Mosley. "They thought it was a hit. Hence the second version. There were two years between the two versions, and we updated the lyrics." While some rock acts would possibly balk at re-doing a signature song, the singer didn't have a problem with it - in fact, he welcomed it. "I always like doing the same song on another album. I actually have two songs on 'Introduce Yourself' where one song set a precedent, in a sense, in a group of lyrics: 'Chinese Arithmetic' and 'R N' R,' where I had the same lyrics repeated. 'R N' R' was almost like a sequel. I elaborated on the line 'Like the time you tried to teach your nephew to ...'. I had originally said 'fart,' but they changed it to 'walk.' So I had a habit of ripping off parts of songs - including my own. It kind of made sense to have a second version, where we were biting off of our own song."

Released in April of 1987, 'Introduce Yourself' would contain several different album covers - the vinyl twelve-incher would sport a blackish/greenish splatter image, the cassette version featured a totally different sideways dripping green blob shot, while the CD release (albeit issued years later) would merely slice the album cover in half.

Musically, 'Introduce Yourself' certainly pushed Martin's metal guitar more to the forefront, as heard on such selections as "Faster Disco" and "Death March." But with Bottum's airy keyboards, Gould's funk bass, Bordin's tribal drumming, and Mosley's unharmonious vocals added to the equation, the album wasn't going to be confused with a Metallica record any time soon. That said, 'Introduce Yourself' does contain one of the band's all-time great gonzoid guitar riffs, in "The Crab

Song." Also included was the furious punk rocking title track (which would soon become a concert standard), as well as the slow-building "Chinese Arithmetic," which would also pop up in setlists for years to come, plus one of the most melodic and accessible tracks the band had penned up to that point, "Anne's Song."

An extremely colorful (literally) video would be filmed for "We Care A Lot," which earned some spins on MTV's Sunday night alternative program, '120 Minutes.' "When we had started on that tour, it had just gotten picked up by '120 Minutes,' and they were playing it all the time," Mosley recalls. "It was the song that brought in a big chunk of the audience at that time. It was obvious by the response. It was almost overnight. We had started the tour, and a week or two later it had gotten on '120 Minutes.' The attendance was totally bolstered by that song coming out." Additionally, "Anne's Song" would receive the video treatment as well, which resulted in a clip featuring Mosley singing into a light bulb, two "Jim Martins" replicating the song's solo, and Bottum showing off a new buzz-cut hairstyle (a sharp contrast to his earlier long dreadlock hairstyle).

As it turns out, the re-recorded version of "We Care A Lot" probably served as an introduction to FNM for eventual HIM frontman, Ville Valo, all the way in Finland. "I think I heard 'We Care A Lot.' I used to be a bass player, and in the late '80s, everybody was into the idea of slapping as much as possible. So it was like the Red Hot Chili Peppers and fIREHOSE, and a lot of those bands that were highly influential. And we had a cassette-trading club, more or less - everybody was trading odd demos of Primus-like bands all across the world, and I think that's the way I heard Faith No More the first time."

The album's ensuing supporting tour saw Faith No More hook up with another up-and-coming band, the Red Hot Chili Peppers. Martin: "We were traveling in a box van with no windows. Drove all the way to the east coast for the first show. [Chili Peppers' bassist] Flea asked me if we liked to smoke weed. When I said 'Yes,' he said, 'We're going to get along just fine.' We did something like 52 dates in 56 days." The tour would run from October through December 1987, and served as the second-to-last-ever Peppers tour with guitarist Hillel Slovak, who would die on June 25, 1988, from a heroin overdose.

Although 'Introduce Yourself' wouldn't exactly do battle with the likes of Def Leppard and George Michael for top placement on Billboard's Album Charts, the album served as further proof that Faith No More was rapidly accomplishing something special - one of the few bands of the day that refused to be tied down to a single musical style...something they would hone and perfect on future albums. And the album has proven to be an influence on subsequent musicians over the years, such as Korn's bassist, Fieldy, who once picked the album - as well as the Chili Peppers' 'Freaky Styley' - as one of his top all-time favorites. "That shit just fucked me up in the head, blew my mind and changed my life. Before that, I was listening to dirthead shit, just straight-up metal like Iron Maiden and Metallica. Then those two bands came up into my life and I was like, 'Fuck, man, that's still heavy, but it's not metal.' I just loved it. I became obsessed by it. I had always known that there had to be a way to take the bass further than just following the guitar, and these two records showed me the way. Actually, they were the last albums to blow my mind, but I'm still searching. I'm constantly looking for that phat-ass band that will rock my world."

It was also becoming clear that a buzz was growing louder overseas for the band, as the UK publication, Sounds, selected 'Introduce Yourself' as one of the "albums of the year." With that in mind, it made perfect sense to schedule FNM's first-ever trip to England. But it was an event (and its aftermath) from one such trek that resulted in a major line-up shake up.

Chapter 5: Goodbye Chuck, Hello Mike

Having played FNM's first-ever UK dates in January and February of 1988 (an advert promoting the dates at the time boasted, "When Faith No More visit the UK in January, move mountains to be there" - Neil Perry, Sounds), the group returned for a more substantial European tour in the spring. And it was during this time that it became clear that Mosley was going to be the next in line to get the old heave-ho. The problems became exacerbated when a roadie friend of the singer's was fired after getting into a fistfight with Martin. Gould: "By the time that happened, Chuck was already kind of out of it for me. I guess Jim and [the roadie] had been drinking and they got in a fight. It came to a point where Jim was our guitar player - he broke his hand fighting the guy. It's the first night of our European tour, and somebody had to go - it obviously wasn't going to be our guitar player. Chuck's reaction...he took it very personally - to stick up for this roadie." On the same tour, tensions ran so high that Gould punched Mosley on stage.

Despite all the bad blood, the shows were still spirited, as then-Frank Zappa guitarist Mike Keneally would reflect years later about a show he attended on May 2nd at the Paradiso Club, in Amsterdam, Netherlands. "The headliner came on, which was Faith No More. Very, very weird, very interesting, and I thought quite good band, and scary, because they did the Nestles white chocolate theme song, and then they rocked it out towards the end. Then, they sang the last part of 'Stairway to Heaven,' and then, later on in the show, they quoted the first part of 'Norwegian Wood,' and Scott [Thunes, Zappa bassist] and I were just aghast. Definitely. They were really funny, and they did 'War Pigs' as the last part of their first encore. Really, very interesting group, and I bought their shirt because I was so impressed."

Keneally would also add, "The night after Scott and I saw them, I wore the Faith No More shirt onstage during the Zappa show, and a couple of the Faith No More guys were there. Years later, after they became huge, they started hanging around the Zappa planet fairly frequently - Z played with them on a festival bill in Europe, and their drummer was going with Moon [Unit, Zappa's daughter] for a time. Anyway, Jim Martin their guitar player, told me at some point that seeing me wearing their shirt at the Zappa gig was a huge morale booster for them, a major help at a time when they needed it. That pleased me to no end."

Although it is difficult to pinpoint its birth, it could quite possibly have been around this time that Martin earned an appealing nickname from the media, "Big Sick Ugly." Years later, the guitarist had a pretty good idea of who the wisenheimer was that coined the phrase - "It was bestowed upon me by the filthy press. I am pretty sure Geoff Barton gets the credit. Steffan 'Cheese Burger' Chirazi, 'Krusher Joule' and Neil 'Greasy Chester' Perry helped magnify and perpetuate it and it was Kerrang!, once again, who rolled that one out there. Thanks to them for some funny times." Another nickname that would be linked to the guitarist would be "Fatso," which is quite puzzling, as Martin always seemed to be a rather slender gentleman.

Upon returning home, Gould recalls the final straw with Mosley. "There was a certain point when I went to rehearsal, and Chuck wanted to do all acoustic guitar songs. It was just so far off the mark - I think I actually attacked him again!" [Laughs] Instead of simply firing Mosley, Gould employed a similar tactic used to oust Morris several years earlier. "The upshot of [the confrontation] was that I got up, walked out, and quit the band. Just said, 'I'm done - I can't take this any longer. It's just so ridiculous.' The same day, I talked to Bordin, and he said, 'Well, I still want to play with you,' and Bottum did the same thing. It was another one of these 'firing somebody without firing them'."

After Mosley's exit, rumors began circulating about the singer's alleged party-hearty lifestyle. "I've never been addicted to heroin," explains Mosley. "But I've done everything from PCP to acid. Had a problem with coke, which I don't touch anymore." Looking back on the split today, Mosley offers his take. "I said, 'I don't want to [leave], I want to work this out.' I even made moves before that to make them say, 'Look, I'm on your guys' team. We're all shooting for a common goal here.' I did a couple things to gesture that I was going to work along them, not against them. But by that point, they were already too sick of me. I felt bad about it, but what can you do?"

It turned out that not all of the FNM members were happy to see Mosley go. Bottum: "At the time I was super close to Chuck and it was sad to lose a friend like that. We'd been through a lot together and him leaving was tough. My affinity, honestly though, was to Billy and Mike. We had a thing going on that was a little stronger than our relationship with Chuck. We had no intention of putting it to rest. We never once thought about breaking up. I think we honestly felt pretty strong about what it was that we were doing."

Mosley also returns the kind words for his ex-band mate. "I've always talked to Roddy forever. Ever since the day that they had him call me to fire me! We were kind of buddies in the band at the time, and he became the godfather of my first daughter. We've always been really tight. We've never gone a couple of months without talking over the last 20 years." Understandably, being asked to leave the band proved to be a huge disappointment for the singer - "I regret making them so mad at me that they felt that the only way to be able to continue on the journey was to fire me." Mosley would later turn up as a singer for hardcore-reggae legends the Bad Brains (although the Mosley-fronted version played live, it never made it to record), as well as a pair of albums as part of another band, Cement (1993's self-titled debut and 1994's 'Man with the Action Hair'). After being away from music for a spell, Mosley would return in 2009, with his first-ever solo album, 'Will Rap Over Hard Rock for Food,' which featured a new rendition of "We Care A Lot," with none other than Bottum guesting on keys.

With Mosley out and a decision made for the remaining members to carry on, discussions began about what their next move should be, which led to an interesting thought. Gould: "We had considered taking over vocals ourselves a couple of times. But, one thing about the way we write music is that everybody kind of has their own job to do, and singing plus playing would be two jobs. We were thinking it would probably be best off to just have somebody do the one job and do it really well."

Eventually, a singer search began, and a name that was being thrown around early on was none other than Soundgarden's Chris Cornell. "We were friends with them," explains Gould. "I think one day, Mike and I went to [Cornell's] house to jam, but I don't think that we had a musical connection." With Cornell now out of the running, it was back to the drawing board. And then…the band remembered a demo they had received at a gig - Mr. Bungle - featuring Mr. Mike Patton on vocals.

"Mike Bordin really liked his Mr. Bungle tape he gave us," recalls Bottum. "So did Jim Martin. I didn't - not my cup of tea." Martin recalls a phone conversation he had with Patton around this time. "We auditioned about five other people, and it was pretty clear that Patton had superior natural ability. We called him and told him to come down; we wanted him to go to work immediately. He was very hesitant like, 'I can't do this right now; it's not a good day. I have a school box social to go to. And tomorrow is show and tell. If I had plenty of advance warning, I might be able to come down for a little while, but today is not good.' I informed him he was at a crossroads in life - one way was to become a singer, the other way was to be a record store clerk in a shitty little town in Northern California. He really was like that. Very clean and shiny, nice kid. Milk and cookies type."

Born on January 27, 1968, in Eureka, California, it sounds as if Patton came from your average All-American family (his father was a football coach), and early musical favorites included Elton John and the 'Star Wars Motion Picture Soundtrack' ("That was really cool and atmospheric" he once remembered about the latter). By high school, he was a member of a group that featured several high school chums, Mr. Bungle. Taking their name from a 1950's film that promoted good manners and hygiene for youngsters (and later popularized when shown during Pee-wee Herman's 1981 HBO TV special, 'The Pee-wee Herman Show'), Mr. Bungle was initially comprised of Patton, guitarist Trey Spruance (b. August 14, 1969), bassist Trevor Dunn (b. January 30, 1968), alto-saxophonist Theo Lengyel, and drummer Jed Watts. Patton: "There's a core of three of us that have known each other since we were 15. That was me, Trey, and Trevor. We met Trey because we went to the same high school [Eureka High School], and he was one of the only other people that played bad heavy metal! We bonded, and met the other guys in college."

"We had all been kicked out of other bands and got pushed into the same corner together," Dunn once explained. Lengyel remembered it a bit differently - "Well, it really started back in '86, when we were in high school. And it was originally sort of just a thrash metal band, I guess. But then these guys asked me to play some horn parts on some sort of goof shit that they were doing, they weren't really very serious about that at the time. But then, we worked more horn shit into it, sort of became a more central part, or more important part of it, and then went away from death metal and a lot towards more, I don't know, varied kind of shit."

"Varied kind of shit" indeed, as evidenced by the material that comprised Bungle's subsequent demos - 1986's 'The Raging Wrath of the Easter Bunny,' 1987's 'Bowel of Chiley,' 1988's 'Goddammit I Love America!,' and 1989's 'OU818' - as well as the band's penchant for plopping such absurd covers as the Village People's "Macho Man" and the "Howdy Doody Theme Song" into their performances. After graduating from high school in 1986, Patton enrolled at Humboldt State University in Arcata and started studying English...and had no clue as to his life's direction. "I had no idea what I wanted to do. I was completely lost," he once recalled. Around this time, Patton landed a job at a record store - which he hated. "I've only had one other job - working in a record store and it was horrible, a nightmare. I hated it so much I stole from my boss almost every day. Half of my record collection is stolen. He was too dumb to realize that his store wasn't working, no one was buying records, so I'd steal them and he'd think people were buying them. Plus he didn't pay me enough so that's how I got my extra payment."

A ten-hour drive south to Los Angeles and a four and a half hour drive to San Francisco, Eureka was once described by Patton as being comprised of "hippies and loggers," while Spruance once elaborated about their hometown, "I'm frightened by a lot of it. There's a lot of pot growers with machine guns and cops running around, not to mention all the rednecks who want to beat you over the head with baseball bats. It's White Trash-ville USA! About ten miles away, this town called Ferndale - which is where they filmed 'Salem's Lot' - almost had a Satanic mayor. He's this psycho-sculptor guy named Hobart Brown, who they wouldn't let run because he was a Satanist." Despite not having an album in the shops nor living in a town that was exactly known for spawning rock bands, Mr. Bungle did manage to open for a few touring acts, including the Meat Puppets, Primus, and according to Angelo Moore, quite possibly Fishbone. "I remember when Mr. Bungle was called 'FCA.' They were out of Eureka, and they were playing speed metal shit - they had speed metal songs that lasted like, six or seven minutes. They threw horns and organ and shit in there after a while - keyboards and stuff - so yeah, I would say they were influenced by Fishbone."

But an event occurred on the evening of October 4, 1986, that would affect Patton's future - he attended a Faith No More performance at Humboldt State University Depot, in Arcata, California, which led to the handoff of Bungle's 'Raging Wrath' demo from Patton to FNM. Patton: "FNM played in Eureka [actually in nearby Arcata, but please, continue Michael...], and I can't believe they came. No bands came there. But here they were, in their shitty van, all rotten and stoned, and I gave 'em a tape of Mr. Bungle."

A little more than a year later, Patton and his Bungle band mates took in another FNM show - on December 28, 1987, at the Fillmore in San Francisco - which was the last date of the aforementioned intense FNM/Chili Peppers tour. Patton: "Eureka is a really small town. So me and the Bungle guys thought, 'Gee, we're gonna go see Faith No More and the Red Hot Chili Peppers at this club in San Francisco. It's like this big event. We have to organize it with our parents.' We drive a few hours down to the city, to the Fillmore. We're just stupid kids, and it's only our second time in San Francisco. We get there, go see the show, and when we come out, our tires are slashed. Then we fix the tires. We end up staying at Mr. Bungle's guitarist's grandma's house. We park the car in someone's driveway, not thinking, and we come out the next day and it's been towed. What an unbelievable hassle. We swore we'd never come to San Francisco again."

The summer before Patton was to begin his junior year at Humboldt, he received the aforementioned fateful phone call from Martin. "When I first got the offer, I was a little hesitant," says Patton. "My first inclination was, nah, I can't do this. I was really tied up in my little 'go to work, go to school' thing. I was working at a record store, *wow...*" After thinking it over, Patton decided to give it a try with Faith No More, only on the condition that he could also keep Mr. Bungle afloat, as well (unlike the multi-project rock band craze of the early 21st century, this was an almost unheard of proposition during the late '80s).

"It was a little weird at first," Spruance once admitted, while discussing the period in which Patton joined FNM. "[Mr. Bungle] were being approached by quite a lot of record companies at the time. But we figured that if he didn't do it, it would have turned out to be something that Mike would have regretted for the rest of his life. We weren't doing anything super important at the time I guess, so off he went. It wasn't that big a deal at the time because back then, FNM weren't that successful. 'Introduce Yourself' had only sold like 80,000 records or whatever."

After making the move to San Francisco to get acclimated with this new band mates, Patton first lived in Bordin's apartment (up until then, Patton had lived with his parents). "I was in my room all alone! I didn't know anybody, I'd just moved to the city and it was just like, 'Oh fuck man! What am I doing here'?"

And while there was no denying Patton's talent, it took a while for the singer and Gould to see eye-to-eye. "I have to say, I didn't like Mike the first couple of years he was in the band, I thought some of the things he did were pretty immature. But he's done really well. When he joined the band he was a fucking brat, an arrogant little baby, a child. He looked awful but he was the only guy we tried that really worked, but we had to take a fucking lot on. Here was this unsophisticated kid who'd never sipped alcohol before, never been in a bar, and we were all these crusty fucking guys. I felt pretty responsible for bringing this nice happy kid into this band, but he sang well. He was a lamb - he didn't stand a chance."

However, Metallica's Jason Newsted saw the effect that Patton had on FNM's music immediately. "When Mike got in to be the vocalist, it took it to a whole other planet. And we had already known Mike from the Mr. Bungle stuff, so we already knew he was out of left field and beyond. When he came into it, that flavor fit so well, it was what that band needed to really take them to that other place. He was the vehicle or the conduit that took that band to the place it needed to, because of his incredible talent. There's only one of him…thank God! A very, very talented cat."

Chapter 6: The Real Thing

With Patton now on board, it was time to see if the new kid on the block could deliver the goods when it came to lyric writing, as all the music for the songs that would comprise Faith No More's third album (to be titled 'The Real Thing') had already been penned by the others. Bordin: "The music was written in shifts on that record, in that that was the first record we wrote and recorded in LA. We were staying down in the Oakwood [Apartments]. Jim and I were sharing a place. We were partying hard, and Metallica was in town - people getting fucked up and drinking Jägermeister. That was that whole beginning of the bad period that [James] Hetfield talked about when he got sober - that was 'Alcoholica'."

"Billy and Roddy were working probably 10:00 to 3:00. Jim was drinking all night with his buddies - he wouldn't go to sleep until 7:00 or 8:00 in the morning. We would get up at fucking 4:00 and go into the studio around 7:00, and work 'til probably 10:00 or 11:00. So we were totally doing shifts. We didn't even have each other's phone numbers! We just went into the rehearsal room and thought we'd see each other eventually. And then one day, Billy stayed late or we came early - 'Hey, where have you been?' And then Billy started getting on our own schedule too. We just started writing shit - we were all working on stuff. And then ultimately, it all came together. It was very fucking fully realized - this is us, this is what we are."

Gould recalls discovering Patton's talent for penning lyrics and vocal melodies early on. "I think sometimes our music takes a few listens to get really comfortable with. Patton just jumped right on it, though. He was completely familiar with it. I think a week after he had joined the band he had written all the lyrics to the songs, which are pretty much the lyrics that are on the record now. He was a real natural, which was lucky."

Patton remembers having to get the hang of working with traditional song structures. "It was strange for me, because I had spent every musical moment with the Bungle guys, and we have our own thing - we're Nintendo kids, so we get into a studio and there are all these little knobs, and we've just gotta play with the dials and push the buttons. [Mr. Bungle] basically doesn't know how to write songs - they're like A-B-C-X! So it was weird for me to try and put something over a song that was really linear, and very verse/chorus/verse/chorus. So I think I did what was really...obvious. That's fine, but since then, I've definitely vowed to spend a lot more time and put a lot more into anything I do." And while some of the veteran FNM members may have looked at 'The Real Thing' as being a "make or break" album, Patton felt no pressure - "It was no big deal, I'd just gotten out of school then so I probably approached it the same way as doing a project."

With everything in place, the "new look Faith No More" entered Studio D to lay down the new tracks (from December 1988 through January 1989), with the production being handled once again by Matt Wallace and the band. Patton has an interesting memory of the location. "The studio had a weird history: apparently, Sly Stone once dismantled the sink in the studio bathroom and smoked crack out of a piece of the plumbing. They found him passed out a couple hours later." But when it came time for Patton to lay down his vocals, Wallace was surprised to hear that Patton had opted to utilize a peculiar singing voice. Wallace: "He was singing really nasally and also, his pitch on record was not as good as I knew it could be. I was just like, 'Why don't you just hit the notes?' And he goes, 'No man, *this is my style.'* Because he'd sing the song on tape, and he'd do this amazing, really full voice. I'm like, *'That's* the voice! Get that on the darn tape!' He was like, 'No man, I don't want to do it'."

"I never asked Patton this directly, but one of two things happened - one, he was trying to keep that kind of snotty, punky, rap persona, and that was important for him to have that snotty attitude on the recording. Or another possibility was that he still had a lot of loyalties with Mr. Bungle, and I think he wanted to separate himself as the singer from Mr. Bungle and Faith No More."

Sonically, Martin was not entirely pleased with his guitar sound on FNM's prior records, and sought some outside advice from two renowned names - Rick Rubin and James Hetfield. "What happened was I drove down to Los Angeles one day, to see Rick. He was recording Wolfsbane [the album 'Live Fast, Die Fast']. So I went down there, and I sat in while he was working on that - they were working on getting guitar sounds that day. He let me see what process he was going through to do it. I talked to other people about it as well. I talked to Big Mick Hughes, Metallica's live soundman - he told me some things also. James Hetfield told me some things that they did in the studio to get the guitar sound. So pretty much, I was checking around to find out how to get what I was looking for - getting more ideas."

Musically, 'The Real Thing' was another unpredictable mishmash of styles - again, a recording that gloriously stood out like a sore thumb amongst all the one-dimensional hair metal and thrash metal that ran rampant at the time. For instance, the psychedelic-prog-thrash instrumental, "Woodpecker from Mars" (a title which Gould once described as "An Indian name for the drug DMT"), the piano/lounge schmaltz of "Edge of the World," such melodic pop rockers as "Underwater Love," serious headbanging fare like "Surprise! You're Dead!," the ambitious title track, and a leftover from the Mosley-era, "The Morning After" (earlier titled "New Improved Song," with different lyrics).

Gould explained that the band tended to employ an interesting technique for all the band members to get on the same page during the songwriting process. "The way we write songs comes not so much from a style, but more like a visual scene that we see in our heads. Then we try to create something that gives us the feeling of that scene. So, rather than just being songs, they also paint a picture, For instance, we had a song called 'Edge of the World.' Before any of the parts of that song were even written, there was the basic, nonmusical idea of the song: Just imagine a sleazy cocktail lounge with a fifty-year-old man trying to pick up a fourteen-year-old girl. Because so much of our music starts from visuals, it's hard to pin down any one person in the band doing the same thing every time we write a song. Every song is different."

Arguably, the finest compositions are the three that kick off the record - the metal-punk rocker "From Out of Nowhere," a tune that would one day be listed as one of the reasons the "rap metal" genre was created (for better or for worse), "Epic," and one of the album's most pop-y numbers, "Falling to Pieces." When asked what "From Out of Nowhere" was about lyrically, Bottum reckoned that it "Seems to be about a chance meeting and how chance plays a role in interaction," while Patton explained it as "Jello shots, Hermetic Philosophy, Ptolemaic

Cosmology...you know, your average commie/junkie jibber jabber."
Perhaps the reason that the lyrics came out the way they did was because
of Patton's "state" at the time. "I think I was on some sort of macho
endurance trip - doing sleep deprivation experiments."

On the album's subsequent tour, "From Out of Nowhere" was
often utilized as a concert opener, as well. Gould: "That song was good
because most of our stuff was so mid-tempo that the set was always in
danger of dragging. With this one, we could at least start things on a high
note and hopefully this spark would keep the rest of the set alive. There
is nothing worse than being on stage for 80 or so minutes when things
are not working correctly. Generally this seemed to work out well, and
we stuck with it as an opener until we hated it so much we scrapped it
from the set altogether."

Regarding "Epic," Patton points to a new wave mega band that
offered inspiration. "Believe it or not, 'Epic' was my best attempt at
impersonating Blondie's 'Rapture.' Lyrically, I was more concerned with
the rhyme scheme than any constant train of thought. The lyrics mean
whatever you want them to mean. They don't belong to me anymore,
they are YOUR responsibility now!" Interestingly, Patton doesn't feel
that the version of the song included on the album failed to live up to the
demo. "I think we may have demoed the song once before recording it. I
remember actually liking that early demo better than the final version.
Sometimes we'd fall in love with the magic of those crude recordings and
the finished version could never quite measure up."

And on "Falling to Pieces," the band offers up one of the album's
most melodious tunes. Interestingly, metal enthusiast Martin wasn't
opposed to the song's potential pop audience appeal - "That song was
written specifically for a purpose. It was meant to be a pop hit." The song
is also driven by a memorable Gould bassline. Gould: "There's a record
out that was produced by Mickey Hart from the Grateful Dead that
features Tibetan monks chanting; I was trying to get that kind of effect
on my bass."

'The Real Thing' was issued on June 20, 1989, and the twelve-
inch vinyl version would sport what would be the group's most trippy
album cover image - a shot of a sun rising from behind clouds,
surrounded by several "flaming splashes" (you have to see it to
understand it), while what looks like a burnt-out/dead planet hangs

overhead. Unfortunately, the CD version contained just a close-up of one single "flaming splash," while the cassette slashed the album version artwork in half. But what the CD and cassette versions lost in visuals was made up for musically, as a pair of bonus tracks were tacked on - the aforementioned "Edge of the World" and a killer cover of Black Sabbath's "War Pigs."

The album would also spawn several singles and/or videos. The first single/video was for "From Out of Nowhere," which was your average ordinary lip-synched performance clip, filmed at a performance at the I-Beam in San Francisco - which features Patton in a nifty pair of spandex biker shorts. However, the filming of the video resulted into a rather serious hand injury to the singer, when shattered glass cut four tendons and the main nerve in his right hand. Years later, Patton would discuss the mishap - "Oh man, I didn't know anybody knew about that. But it's not that big of a deal. There was a period where it was a very big deal, where I had to learn how to do everything with my left hand. Play basketball, brush your teeth, masturbate, all that good stuff. In terms of writing, that's changed a little bit, I still have the movement but the feeling is not there. I'm just so damn used to it now. But let's just say I'll be writing on guitar. I'll be playing and playing and everything will be fine and then maybe I'm recording or something and all of a sudden it won't be sounding quite right. I'll look down and the pick will have fallen out of my hand and I'm playing with my fingers but it feels the same. So that's a little example of how different that can be. You go, 'Oh shit. Whoops,' and I put the pick back in my hand. But I wouldn't say that it's affected my writing in any other sense but physically. It's hilarious because the doctors told me that I wouldn't get the movement back but I'd get the feeling back. They were 100 percent wrong and I'm glad they were wrong because I'd rather be able to move the fucking thing."

The second and third video clips would leave much more of an impression - "Epic" and "Falling to Pieces." Both videos would be directed by Ralph Ziman, and are largely considered to be the finest of the band's entire career. "Epic" would feature plenty of striking images - Patton singing in a rainstorm, an exploding piano, and several interesting shirt choices (Bottum wears a t-shirt that declares "MASTER," Martin is dressed in a long-sleeve with an image of his fallen friend, Cliff Burton, while Patton pledges his continued allegiance to his other band, with a

Mr. Bungle "There's a Tractor in My Balls" t-shirt). But perhaps the most memorable scene is of a flopping fish.

A rumor would later circulate, that the fish from the "Epic" video was on loan from then-Sugarcubes singer Björk, which Ziman would later clear up as mere malarkey. But Ziman's memories of working with the band remain positive - "I remember, the band had one day off from tour, and they were in London. The record company had phoned us on very short notice and asked us to do a music video. They made it sound like a really low priority. I think it was being done for Warner Bros. at the time. I just made a list of a bunch of things I thought we could do. Exploding a piano. A fish flopping around. We literally had one day to pre-produce it. So we handed the fish off to the art department. I can't remember what it was. If it was a carp? It was a fresh water fish. We shot that in London in some studios next to the tour venue. And we wound up letting that fish go in the river when we were finished. We had a couple of them. We would let them flop around, and then we'd swap it over, and we'd shoot another one. I don't remember what kind of fish they were, but the animal handler had brought them in because they were so feisty."

The trippy clip for "Falling to Pieces" would feature Patton in several different costumes (a blood splattered surgeon outfit, a clown outfit, and lederhosen), a singing hand, a skinless face, as well as the singer mouthing the lyrics while fish swam by - which would eventually explode. Bottum would later point out how he was pleased that the peculiar video helped balance things out - "It's good we have a bit of violence and horror, because it's such a poppy and horribly upbeat song." A low-budget, black and white clip would also be filmed for "Surprise! You're Dead!" (directed by Gould), comprised of footage shot in Chile during a subsequent South American tour - including supposedly an image of a chicken getting its head chopped off (it's hard to make out some scenes due to all the jumpy camera work and grainy picture quality). Understandably, the video would never be shown on MTV, but would be included on the 1993 home video, 'Video Croissant.'

It seemed like almost immediately upon the arrival of 'The Real Thing,' Faith No More was tagged as one of the leaders of the "funk metal" movement (which would eventually mutate into "rap metal") - along with the Red Hot Chili Peppers. Other acts from the era that the press would fit into this category would include Primus, Fishbone,

Limbomaniacs, 24-7 Spyz, Living Colour, Mordred, Infectious Grooves, and to a certain extent, even Jane's Addiction. But it was a style that FNM didn't seem to want any part of, as Bordin once explained - "We didn't come up in the funk-thrash thing. Maybe some people put us at the head of it, but it's something we never championed. We never fitted into any category. We weren't even involved in the bohemian clique because we were such a bunch of dirtheads - guys with rotten dreadlocked hair who smoked dope and didn't give a fuck. We liked to put our finger on the sore spot a little bit by not playing up to any clique or group."

Another time, the drummer disclosed that he didn't want to be lumped in with headbanging bands, either - "We're not a heavy metal band, because we don't have jack-off guitar solos every song and we don't have some dick singing fake opera. We're more acid-head dirtbags." Years later, Patton also made it clear that he did not take it as a compliment when subsequent funk metal/rap metal bands listed FNM as an influence - "It's awful I know, we don't want to take credit for any of it. If you're doing something with it, then fucking do something with it - show some fucking balls. That's what really bothers me about that shit, it's pathetic."

And while Kim Thayil could see traces of funk and metal in FNM's sonic stew, he agreed that the band was certainly not a one-trick pony. "Of course, they were the progenitors of 'metal funk' - before Jane's Addiction, and least before we were aware of the Chili Peppers, Faith No More was having some success and touring with this kind of hard rock/metal funk component. The metal funk thing was kind of a late '80s thing, that translated through the early to mid '90s, it started having a genre of success. Before that, I thought of 'funky metal' as Aerosmith. Aerosmith always had these cool metal and hard rock riffs, that had a nice little syncopation and funky kind of groove to it. But with Faith No More, it was less of a funky metal, and more of a metaly funk. But the versatility of the band, I feel like I'm diminishing their musical contribution by just saying that they're a metallic funk. They were far more versatile than that."

Carcass' screamer/bassist, Jeff Walker, also weighs in on the whole "funk metal" tag that dogged FNM. "If you think back, you had that ugly thing around the late '80s/early '90s - the whole funk metal thing. I think that's sadly one of their worst legacies, isn't it? Because they were never really a funk metal band - they just had that one song, 'We Care A Lot,' where they got pigeonholed into the whole Chili Peppers/funk metal thing, didn't they?"

Faith No More hit the road almost immediately upon the release of 'The Real Thing,' revisiting England in July, hitting the States, and then jumping on nearly an entire month's worth of dates with their old buddies in Metallica in September (which also served as the last month of the group's never-ending "Damaged Justice" US Tour). Despite the longtime friendship between both bands, certain audiences weren't feeling the love, especially at a gig on September 8th at the Salt Palace in Salt Lake City, Utah. Gould: "We got a really bad reaction, which really gets us excited. So I did this bass solo that went on for about two minutes on just one note. The spit was flying, people were so mad, hating it so much - it was the greatest feeling, 10,000 people wanting to kill you!"

Patton also recalls this particular hostile gig. "The best shows we've done were under the worst conditions. At places where no one wanted to see us. We were supporting Metallica, somewhere in Utah. It's swarming with Mormons there. They hated us. Threw bottles. Spat at us. Fourteen, fifteen thousand people. Then I made a remark about Mormons and they hated us even more. Then our bass player played a fifteen-minute solo. One note, dang dang dang. Bottles flew over our heads. War. But those circumstances, when you don't feel at ease, are often the most inspiring."

Bottum voices similar memories of the tour. "At that point, no one knew who we were, and we were getting up in front of these huge crowds in these weird little cities. Sometimes people would totally spit on us and treated us like shit, but to get that reaction out of anyone is pretty flattering!"

Despite all the hostility, one FNM performance on the Metallica tour left a lasting impression on a youngster by the name of Brian Welch, who a decade later, would be better known as one of the guitarists of nu metallist hit makers, Korn. "They were the first ones to cross over lots of different stuff, mixing heavy shit with keyboards and rap. It was eerie. I was about 17 when I first heard it, and listening to a lot of Metallica, 24-7 Spyz, Living Colour and Fishbone. I dug them all, but Faith No More moved me in a different way, a way more than anything else. That shit was just so bad. It totally changed my direction. It said to me that you didn't have to follow a certain path, that you could just create anything, go out and mess around with anything, that there were no rules. It showed me that you could just fuck around and come up with your own thing. I remember seeing them open up for Metallica, and everyone started booing them, going 'Rap sucks!' I was so bummed. I felt like screaming at everyone, 'Quit fucking booing them *and listen.*' They all just heard the rap beat and didn't give them a chance."

A show review from that time (at the Cal Expo Amphitheatre in Sacramento) in the Probe mirrored Welch's memories. "The only thing really memorable about this show was that it was raining and it was an outdoor show. Mike Patton came out in scuba gear with the flippers and the mask and everything. After the first song he said God was a major asshole for having it rain on us and we should tell him to 'fuck off.' He then gave the sky the finger and said 'Fuck you God!' a few times. The crowd loved it (kinda interesting seeing thousands of people telling God to fuck off), but there was a chorus of boos when they kicked into 'Epic.' This was before the video came out and very few people there had ever heard of FNM so the crowd had a 'What is this rap shit?' attitude."

Once the Metallica dates wrapped up, FNM found themselves back in their home-away-from-home, England, for much of October, before playing dates in Germany in November - the same time that the Berlin Wall came a-tumblin' down. Patton: "I think the closest parallel that I've ever experienced would be San Francisco when the 49ers won the Super Bowl. It wasn't like a real historical, spiritual thing - just everyone yelling and getting drunk."

Shortly after the dawn of the '90s, Faith No More hit the States again as part of a package tour, which saw them on a bill with their old pals Soundgarden, as well as sci-fi/prog-metallists Voivod, which was jokingly dubbed "The Munsters of Rock Tour" in the press. And according to Kim Thayil, Soundgarden was blown away from their compadres' latest studio offering. "That album, 'The Real Thing,' is so goddamn amazing. When that album came out, of all the Faith No More albums, that one got so much listen in the van and the bus on various tours. It was so strong. The whole thing sounded good, but it was so strong vocally, because of the versatility. Chuck Mosley was more of a 'talk singer' - a little bit of a rapper and a little bit of a frontman/yeller guy. And Mike Patton could actually croon and do ballads and shriek and do punk rock and metal. He just had this versatility that was fucking amazing. I don't want to just emphasize Patton all the time, because all the guys were amazing. We played with them in both incarnations, both singers. It was just a difference that happened when Mike joined the band and the way the songs changed and how they were framed vocally."

Soundgarden drummer Matt Cameron also has fond memories of the tour. "That was probably one of our best tours ever. It was just so memorable. We loved the bands we were touring with - everyone got along great. At the time, Faith No More was just starting to break - Voivod at the time was the biggest draw. During that tour, Faith No More started to just get mega-huge, so we had to flip the line-up around a few times - depending on what city we were at. I just couldn't believe how great Voivod was back then. They would just smoke the biggest fatties before they went on stage - the most technical, most involved music you could ever imagine, and it was just spot-on. So they must have learned it that way, y'know? We got along great. I'm still in touch with Mike Bordin. It was just killer. I think Patton and Chris - the two singers were egging each other on each night, who could sing the highest or who could do the craziest acrobatics. I remember once, Patton played before us and he threw the mic cable over the lighting rig, and he said, 'I predict Chris Cornell will do this tonight!' And he started to crawl up the mic cable and dangle from the lights."

Thayil also recalls the singer still trying to find his comfort zone. "When we started that tour, Mike Patton was trying to figure out his stage persona. He kind of seemed to be working on his identity - trying to figure out who he was. After a while, he was kind of imitating Chris. He wasn't mocking Chris, because he definitely seemed a little bit like 'a freshman' - he seemed a little bit nervous. Here he was, joining a band that was already up and running for a few years - a band that had a history with Chuck Mosley and a number of albums. Mike seemed a little like a fish out of water, trying to get 'land legs.' He was kind of awkward for the first few shows - his stage presence wasn't that great - but eventually, he started jumping around stage like Chris did. And Chris would take his shirt off...and then Mike started taking *his* shirt off. But we didn't think he was mocking, because he seemed so nervous and insecure. He is an athletic guy, he is in shape, he has a great voice, he had this long beautiful hair - like Chris did. First he started flailing his hair around like Chris did, he started jumping around on stage. But he has a great voice - amazingly versatile and powerful voice. It's funny, because he was very 'rock star-ish' then, which is very different from his Mr. Bungle thing and the other stuff he's done."

"If there was any plumbing [in the venue], Chris would climb it or treat it like monkeybars. And eventually, Mike Patton started doing that, as well! And later, in 1992 on Lollapalooza, [Pearl Jam's] Eddie Vedder started doing that as well. So Chris definitely had a 'stage antics influence' on at least Mike Patton then, and Eddie later. But Mike started stomping around and climbing things, and jumping off the stage, and Chris would jump from the stage and stagedive, and do the crowd surfing. When Mike started jumping from the stage and crowd surfing, we were like, 'Fuck dude. We're going to go on after them, and Mike's already doing stuff that Chris does. Is he mocking us?' Because we got wind that he had a smartass, prankster element to him. But he seemed sort of insecure and nervous about his new gig, so we thought he was trying to figure out how to be a rock star in his band that he just joined, that already had a history."

Thayil also remembers two entertaining stories from the tour. Story #1: "Jim Martin was a man of few words and few expressions...facial inflections. He was very even. We were on the east coast somewhere - probably somewhere outside New York/New Jersey. We're on the interstate oasis for food and fuel, and there's a McDonald's. We went in and it was late at night - we had been drinking. I can't remember if I was riding in Faith No More's bus or Jim was riding on our bus - we knew we were going to make a stop for shopping/food/fuel. So Jim may have ridden with us for the short drive. We did that a lot - if someone was planning on watching a movie, the people interested in watching the movie would ride on one bus and watch that movie. Anyways, I was up, Eric Johnson - who now works in some management capacity for Neil Young, he used to work for us - and we jumped out, and so did Jim, and we went to McDonald's. I think Jim walked in with an opened beer. The woman at the counter asked - and these are the events either in this sequence or in reverse sequence - but she asked who was next, and Eric ran right to the front of the counter, stood on his tiptoes, raised his arm as if he were an eager schoolkid wanting to be called on, going, 'Oh! Oh! Oh!.' He placed his order, and then she asked, 'Can I help who's next?' Jim walked up with his beer, and goes, 'Yeah, give me one of those *Egg McMotherfuckers.*' And they didn't argue or ask for an apology - they just took his money, delivered him his Egg McMotherfucker, he stood at the counter, unwrapped it, and started eating it!"

Story #2: "We played the Trocadero in Philadelphia, which is sort of near or in Chinatown, and we were staying at a hotel nearby there. We were up on an upper floor, and there was a suite that was a two-story suite - I forget who had that room, it might have been someone in Faith No More. You walked into the room, and you had a regular nice hotel room, and then there was a spiral staircase. It went up to a second floor, and that floor had a bedroom and windows. We thought it was the coolest thing in the world - a two-story suite. So we were hanging out in there and drinking some beer, and some of the guys that smoked pot were upstairs smoking pot and blowing it out the window. In the course of the evening, we ended up outside that second story window and on a roof. I don't know if we went and climbed out onto the roof or if there was a tiled roof area. I did not go out on the roof - I was at the window. People were hanging out on it - one of whom was Jim Martin. We've got to be at least six or seven stories off the ground. It's certainly not a survivable fall. I remember for some reason, Jim just put his beer down, and stood on the slanted slope of the roof - and there wasn't a barrier or railing - but Jim stood there and just pissed off the roof. We were like, 'Holy fuck!' It was hilarious that he was pissing off the roof, probably onto the adjacent building, the sidewalk below, or the street below...or all three. That was funny. But the other thing was the jaw dropping, 'Oh my fuck! What are you doing? *Get back in here'!"*

It was also around this time that Faith No More received what would be two of their highest "honors" thus far - 'The Real Thing' being crowned the #1 "Album of the Year" in Kerrang!, and it also being nominated for a Grammy Award in the category of "Best Metal Performance." But come the actual night of the ceremony on February 21, 1990, they lost out to Metallica, who won for "One." The same month, FNM returned once more to the UK and Europe in February, and spent March playing more dates with Soundgarden and Voivod Stateside.

Now, if I, Greg Prato, may digress for a moment - there was a fine film from 2002, 'Adaptation,' in which a screenwriter (Charlie Kaufman, played proficiently by Nicolas Cage) is having difficulty writing a film screenplay. So what he winds up ultimately doing is writing *himself* into the storyline…which is what yours truly is about to do in this book. Back in early 1990, I was a senior in high school, and was a long-time fan of heavy metal…but was beginning to grow tired of the same old sounds and looks of metal bands of the time, and overblown, predictable arena shows. A cousin of mine had similar musical tastes, but had begun venturing outside the box, and made the discovery that seeing shows in clubs was in most cases, far superior to stadium shows. He was telling me about Faith No More for some time, having seen several performances of theirs already. But when he played me his vinyl copy of 'The Real Thing' initially, I just couldn't adjust my ears beyond Patton's nasally vocals…although I do recall remarking that their cover of "War Pigs" was quite pleasing to the ear.

Being a major Metallica buff at the time, I noticed that James Hetfield seemed to be a fan/supporter of Faith No More - going as far as wearing a FNM shirt in a photo on the back cover of Metallica's 1987 release, 'The $5.98 EP: Garage Days Re-Revisited' and on the front cover of Rip Magazine (the December 1989 issue, to be exact). I also spotted a small feature on Martin in Guitar World Magazine, in which he sported a vintage Metallica "Jump in the Fire" t-shirt, and a description of the band's music in Rip Magazine stuck with me, which said something along the lines that 'The Real Thing' was "new candy for your stale old ears" (another memorable description I recall was from I believe Guitar World Magazine, stating that the album containing plenty of "high cholesterol guitar riffing").

So with all this data stored, I took the plunge by going to my favorite record store, the sadly now-defunct Slipped Disc Records in Valley Stream, New York, and investing in the CD version of 'The Real Thing.' It turned out to be one of the best musical purchases I've ever made in my life, as everything seemed to suddenly click in my coconut when I gave the disc repeated listens, and realized that all the accolades were spot-on, and that I had a new favorite group on my hands.

When the same cousin mentioned that he and some pals were going to see Faith No More again on March 17th at a metal club in

Brooklyn, called L'Amour (what would also serve as the final night of the FNM/Soundgarden/Voivod tour), I was most certainly in. Arriving early, we were able to get mere feet away from the front of the stage (again, something that was completely foreign to a gentleman like me, who was used to being a mile away from the stage at arenas). When FNM hit the stage, it was also my first time seeing a band in concert that looked no different than its audience (a precursor in some ways to the grunge movement on the horizon), and was devoid of all the posing and ultra-seriousness of most established rock acts of the era.

I remember hopping up and down in unison with everyone else upon the launch of "From Out of Nowhere," and enjoying every moment of the performance, right up until when the final note of "War Pigs" rang out (during which time the stage was completely besieged by the members of Soundgarden and Voivod, as part of the night's on-going "end of tour shenanigans," while Mr. Patton indulged in repeated crowd surfing during the number). Various members of FNM would return to the stage during the sets of Soundgarden and Voivod (to "repay" them for the earlier hijinks) - including Patton returning during Voivod's performance (I believe during their rendition of "Astronomy Domine"), wearing some kind of headband/headgear that featured a dildo sticking out from his forehead...which Voivod singer, Denis "Snake" Bélanger, proceeded to "fellate."

To pledge my allegiance to one of my new favorites, I opted to do the unthinkable - purchasing not one, but *two* Faith No More shirts at the merch booth (one was a black t-shirt that featured a shot of the band on the front, while the other was a white t-shirt with the now-classic eight-pointed star design). To this day, the show remains near the top of my all-time favorites that I've ever attended. A life-changing event? Pretty darn close to it.

And as it turns out, I was not the only individual being affected by Faith No More around this time. Meet the singer/guitarist of the Devin Townsend Project and Strapping Young Lad, Mr. Devin Townsend. "'The Real Thing' was the first time I heard them. The song 'Epic,' of course. And I loved them instantly. It was colorful. The fonts that they used for their logo, the colors they had on the cover. I've always been attracted to things that are part of something established, but radically different. I love that. I love that it's part of the thrash scene, but everything about it is different. That was the thing about Faith No More that I thought was great."

"The sound of it was colorful - there was just reds and pinks and blues and greens and all that sort of late '80s/neon/Living Colour bullshit that we all loved for a while there, and then consequently, felt like an idiot about. I remember seeing some Metal Edge Magazine, and they're all hanging out with Metallica, and Metallica was kind of the 'badass band' at the time. But they weren't like Metallica. I loved that. They were accepted into something, without having to be like it. I also remember reading an interview with Faith No More, saying they hated the sound of 'The Real Thing,' that it was so compressed. But I loved it. It was, again, colorful. It was this big sort of squishy, loud, feedback-y kind of thing."

"But, I think probably the single most influential part of Faith No More for me was that they had a keyboard player. And it allowed them to orchestrate things that are just typically like metal, in ways that were so inspiring for me. And I've had keyboards in everything that I've done since. Whether or not that's a direct result or just a contributing factor to it, it made it OK, and you can still hang out with the cool guys and have a keyboard player - who was gay, to boot. I just thought it was really, really inspiring to see a band that was like, 'Well, fuck you - we're going to do this. We're going to have a gay keyboard player, we're going to wear a bunch of primary colors, we're not going to have a spiky logo, and we're *still* going to be able to hang out with all these bands and be accepted in that scene. I loved that - that sort of under-the-radar thing that gets away with murder."

Also around this time, Limp Bizkit guitarist, Wes Borland, found Faith. "I read an article when I was about fourteen years old. I remember the title of the article - maybe it was in Guitar World - it was 'Metallica's Favorite Band.' And I went, 'I want to know who Metallica's favorite band is,' because Metallica was my favorite band at the time. So I read the article, I picked up 'The Real Thing,' and I just remember listening to it over and over and over again. I just thought it was the greatest." Borland also admits to FNM teaching him an important lesson about the "heavy metal dress code" of the era (which was a pretty darn strict one). "I thought [Martin] was like Metallica meets Cheech and Chong - sort of his look. And just that chrome Flying V - that mirror finish - and those crazy hipster sunglasses. Everybody in the band looked different from each other. That was another 'It's OK for things to be whatever they are.' Like, I didn't have to have a look...I mean, that's insane for me to say I don't have to have a look [Borland is known to perform onstage wearing facial make-up and costumes], but not everybody in the band has to all wear the same blue suit. It was OK to see people being who they are naturally."

Vision of Disorder bassist, Mike Fleischmann, also discovered the band around this time. "I first heard Faith No More in '89/'90, when my older brother brought home 'The Real Thing' on vinyl. I was probably about thirteen, and hadn't really discovered any music that I could identify with. At first listen, I didn't know what to make of it. Was it metal? Was it new wave? For me, initially, the keyboards really set them apart from all the other hard rock bands that were dominating music at the time (Guns N' Roses, Mötley Crüe etc). Plus there was no one who sounded like Mike Patton before."

As it turns out, Madball guitarist, Mitts, was turned on to 'The Real Thing' a bit earlier - closer to its original release. "The first record I heard was 'The Real Thing.' I hadn't heard any of the Chuck Mosley stuff. But a friend of mine that I went to school with, I was in his car, and he was like, 'Check this band out!' And he was somebody that listened to all different kinds of music. He wasn't a metalhead - he was almost the kind of guy you would think would grow up to be a music critic. He was a very well-read, very educated music guy, even back when we were 16 or 17. And he played that record for me. The only reason it got my attention was because it had heavy metal style guitars. Otherwise, back then; I didn't want to hear it. When I was in my teens, I didn't want to hear anything that wasn't distorted, crunchy guitars. What impressed me was the variety on the record. You had songs that sounded like metal, songs that sounded like rock, you had 'Epic' that had a rap-vibe going to it, and the band had a keyboard player. I just remember how it had so many different styles coming from so many different directions, and it was all meshed together by the sound of the band, which was really well-produced, and very heavy. The drumming was top-notch, and all the musicianship was really good."

Also according to Mitts, he was lucky enough to catch an early 'Real Thing' tour date, when FNM performed at a now long-defunct Long Island rock club. "I want to say I saw them twice. One that sticks out is I saw them at Sundance on Long Island here, I want to say right when 'The Real Thing' had just come out. It was before those guys really broke. There were maybe a hundred-something people at a venue, that had a capacity of about 600. It was a big club and there were very few people there. Those guys, you could just hear it, like, 'Man, those guys have a *great* sound. This is not a band that should be performing for 60 kids.' They sounded just like the record - they were awesome."

Lastly, another soon-to-be prominent musician took note of FNM around this time - then-Sepultura (and later, Soulfly) singer/guitarist Max Cavalera. "I think I heard Faith No More...I think we saw a video, actually. I think it was 'Falling to Pieces,' and the bass player was wearing a Sepultura shirt. And that blew me away. I was like, 'That was so cool man - the guy likes us!' I went and bought their album. 'Epic,' that song was blowing up anyway and it was being played on the radio. And I found out they had other records, and went out and bought them. I got to hear the stuff with Chuck Mosley, and I loved it. I thought it was so cool. Jim Martin was a really big part of that band - he did some great guitar stuff. It was a really killer guitar element, and Billy's bass was always really powerful. 'Introduce Yourself,' 'We Care A Lot,' 'Pills for Breakfast' - I really love a lot of the old stuff."

With "Epic" receiving sporadic play on MTV's 'Headbanger's Ball' and 'The Real Thing' occupying the downward reaches of the album charts in the US, FNM returned once more to Europe for dates throughout April and May, including a performance at the Brixton Academy in London on April 28th, which was recorded and filmed, and would eventually see the light of day as separate VHS and CD releases (under the title of 'You Fat Bastards: Live at the Brixton Academy'). Bottum recalls an incident from around this time that demonstrated how FNM had the power to put their fans over the top. "I remember playing in London for like the millionth time on that tour. We were pretty popular in England, but hadn't really taken off at all in the US, and all our American label people came to London to our show to see what all the hubbub was. We opened with that song ['From Out of Nowhere'] and the crowd went bananas and broke through the barrier between the stage and the audience. We had to stop the song midway through because people were getting hurt. We left the stage and came back after the barrier was rebuilt. The American label people were aghast."

Unbeknownst to the band, their homeland was also about to be bitten by the Faith No More bug. *Severely.*

Chapter 7: The Sweet Stench of Success

I can speak from my own memory that it seemed like one day in the late spring/early summer of 1990, MTV was suddenly playing the "Epic" video non-stop, which caused a chain reaction with heavy commercial radio play. In return, the single would crack the Billboard Hot 100 Chart (peaking at #9 and staying on the chart for 21 weeks), while 'The Real Thing' would climb up to #10 on the Billboard 200 Chart (and reside on the chart for an impressive 60 weeks).

Expectedly, the enormous success of "Epic" introduced the band to a whole new wave of fans, such as Coheed and Cambria guitarist, Travis Stever. "I - like many kids in the late '80s - first heard Faith No More because of seeing the video for 'Epic' on MTV. It was a new thing all together to my ears. The piano ending with that poor fish was quite gripping as well. My cousin, Skyler, would come visit every summer for two months. He had 'The Real Thing' and I listened to his copy a bunch. Then when he left I went and bought my own. Oh, the smell of those cassette tapes back then. They were so glorious. That smell gave such excitement. OK, enough creepy smell talk. So yeah, that was the introduction. And of course, there was my stepbrother, who listened to them from the beginning, and he felt like they weren't as good anymore now with a change of singer and sound. Obviously, me and a shitload of people disagreed. Record sales showed that." And you can add Avenged Sevenfold bassist, Johnny Christ, to the list of newly won admirers. "The first time I heard Faith No More was for the song 'Epic' - I remember seeing the video on MTV, with the fish flopping around at the end. I thought it was very unique and just awesome."

Years later, Patton gave an animated answer to being asked if he knew "Epic" would be a hit. "Of course I knew straight away it would be a fucking hit! I already had a down payment on the Bentley and the bachelor pad in [posh Californian coastal resort] Paso Robles! However, I realized it wasn't an international smash when my speed dealer wouldn't even let me score on credit. Did 'Epic' spawn rap metal? Even if it did, I wouldn't tell you. Then again, the rest of the world seems to feel that way, so I suppose apologies are in order. OKAY, I'M SORRY!"

Something else that Patton suddenly had to come to terms with was how his good looks had now caught the attention of many young women, as he entered the realm of "teen idol." Understandably, this was a period of transition for Patton - especially when it came to his public persona. Bottum: "I think it was a weird position for MP to be in initially. He was young and all of a sudden he was very much in the public eye. And he's a good looking guy, I think a lot of focus came from people who looked at him in that traditional rock dude kind of way and it made him uncomfortable. He reacted strongly. And that's totally understandable. It would have made me angry too. A lot of it was him growing into the comfortability level of owning who he is/was and what he did."

Patton's reaction would be to completely reject the "handsome frontman" role, instead of embracing it. Patton: "Goddamn. It's not right. I've never had anyone look up to me and take what I say as gospel. Being so young, I don't know shit; I'm in no position to talk down to someone. The kind of crowd we draw is…I don't know if gullible is the word, but, easy. I step to one side of the stage and they go crazy. It's so simple. It's not as if I'm doing anything important. I mean these kids are like little lambs. All these girls screaming and wanting to sleep with me, it's got nothing to do with sex. It's like vampirism. I'm their transfusion. It's not erotic or sexual, it's cartoonish. I'm uncomfortable with being a pop star. When you walk down the street and people yell at you and try to grab your hair, it's not natural. We were doing an in-store appearance and someone grabbed my hat right off my head. That's not right. You don't do that to someone walking down the street, so why do that to me? And I lost it. Threw hot coffee in his face. He gave me my hat back."

Instead of "living the rock n' roll dream" a la Guns N' Roses (more on them later) and Mötley Crüe, Patton decided to take matters into his own hand. "Masturbation is a lot easier to do than relating to someone. It's like playing a video machine. You can relate to a machine a lot easier than a human being. You can just pound yourself for hours and hours and not think about it. With sex, no matter how great it is, there's always something missing." He was even gracious enough to provide an example - "The only difference now is that I masturbate in front of people. There was this girl in Philadelphia - I hung out with her all day and we ended up in my room. I ended up masturbating while she watched." The singer would then go on to admit, "Masturbation is like this little knot I have inside of me that I can't untie."

And perhaps as a precursor to such bands as Nirvana and Pearl Jam (who rejected the whole notion of partying with groupies), Patton offered up this reason as to why he was abstaining from the pleasures of the flesh - "It all comes down to what your mother taught you. It's not a comfortable thing to deal with. I try to avoid it as much as I can." But according to the singer, at least one of his band mates was envious of all his female attention - "Puffy's the only guy who's jealous. All drummers want to be singers. I think it's a myth that the singer needs to be the focus. Bands perpetuate that myth. With somebody like Sebastian Bach it makes sense. Look at him. He could be in an Avon ad."

'The Real Thing' would obtain gold certification on July 18, 1990 and platinum certification on September 26th, while the "Epic" single would be awarded gold certification on October 2nd. As a result, Faith No More continued touring throughout the remainder of the year and into 1991. And it was during the summer of 1990 that I was able to take in two more Faith No More shows - July 6th at the Ritz, and exactly a week later (July 13th) at L'Amour once again. While the shows were not as mind-blowing as my initial FNM live experience (how the heck could they be?), they were still inspired, sold out affairs, including Patton chucking an entire pizza into the audience at the Ritz (while Martin took a slice and chowed down on stage), and at L'Amour, Patton's stage chatter included touching upon such wide-ranging topics as the then-current NYC menace "Dart Man" (an obviously troubled chap who went around the city shooting darts at women's buttocks - no lie - until he was apprehended by police) and heavy metal manly men, Manowar. I also recall a part of the show (believe during the very end of 'Epic') that Patton hung upside down from the lighting rig over the stage - sleeping bat-style - and almost got whacked in the face by the headstock of Gould's bass, who didn't know his singer was behind him. It was also at the L'Amour show that I caught the band taunting their mostly headbanger audience by encoring with a cover of the Commodores' soft rock hit "Easy" (possibly the first time they ever did so), as opposed to the expected "War Pigs."

And it was at the Ritz show that I plunked down more of my hard-earned clams for a FNM poster that contained a now-classic shot - of the entire band in their underpants, except for one member. Years later, the individual who refused to strip down gave his take on the photo session (the image would also go on to adjourn a t-shirt). Martin: "I remember it was one of the first big photo shoots for us set up by London Records. Ross Halfin, 'famous rock photographer,' was pretty aggressive, barking orders and abusing band members, particularly Puffy. He ordered everyone to strip down. I said 'Forget it' (I thought it was dumb). The other guys did, he snapped the picture and at that moment, I understood why he was famous..."

The rest of the summer was spent finishing up their US club headlining tour, before visiting Australia for the first time. Bottum: "One of the things we've had to come to terms with this year is that the mass audience is not as cynical and bitter as we are. They don't find the same things as funny as we do. I got onstage in Sydney and said, 'Is it true that homosexuality is illegal in Australia? That's a shame, we won't be able to have any fun backstage now.' And the audience was genuinely pissed off, saying shit like, 'Fuck off, you faggots.' I think it's really comfortable for us to confuse our audience rather than leaving them with the feeling that they know what's going on. That's why we do the cover of the Commodores' 'Easy.' We used to do a cover of Black Sabbath's 'War Pigs' but we stopped because that's what the audience expected. Every time we played, kids would yell "War Pigs.' Play 'War Pigs.' The one night we said, 'Are you ready for the cover song?' And the audience went crazy with expectation: 'Yeah! Yeah! They're gonna play 'War Pigs.' Then we launched into 'Easy.'"

Up next was a string of mammoth Euro festivals (Reading Festival, Pukkelpop Festival, etc.). And as reported by journalist Neil Perry, Patton offered up a doozy of a stage rap at one such stop - "At a recent European festival the band were sharing the bill with Lenny Kravitz and Sinéad O'Connor: 'You're a special crowd,' Patton told the audience, 'So I'm going to tell you a secret. Right now, Lenny Kravitz and Sinéad O'Connor are fucking backstage...' (Kravitz, watching from out by the mixing desk, was said to look suitably mortified)."

To satisfy the sudden demand for anything Faith No More related, 'Introduce Yourself' was finally issued as a compact disc, and the aforementioned 'You Fat Bastards: Live at the Brixton Academy' home video was released on August 20th. Martin described where the title came from - "We felt a certain warmth when the crowd started shouting that at us, a feeling of affection." Eight tracks from the performance would be issued as an import album outside of the US (utilizing the same title) on February 4, 1991, with a pair of unreleased studio tracks tacked on - an acoustic guitar showcase titled "The Grade" and a surprisingly strong original, "The Cowboy Song." Bottum was later asked why such a worthy tune as the latter was left off 'The Real Thing' - "I think that song always felt unfinished. It seemed like it missed an integral part. I don't know. I think we threw the towel in on it 'cause it just didn't satisfy."

Upon returning back to their homeland from Europe, FNM got the nod to perform "Epic" at the seventh annual MTV Video Music Awards (hosted by Arsenio Hall), on September 6th at the Gibson Amphitheatre in Los Angeles. The performance featured Patton dressed in one of his more peculiar outfits (with a "hand" sticking out of his crotch), and the singer flopping around on the stage floor at the song's conclusion - in tribute to the little bugger that graced the now-hit video. The "Epic" clip was also nominated for Best Metal/Hard Rock Video that year at the VMA's, but lost to Aerosmith's "Janie's Got A Gun."

The fall and winter months saw the band touring arenas and/or large theaters, first as special guests for Billy Idol, and then for Robert Plant. Patton was quoted as looking forward to the shows, but not for the expected reason "I really want to see what kind of people come to these shows. It's probably just gonna be lame MTV people. And I'm really curious to see how Billy Idol is as a person. He's probably gonna be real easy to torment. We're gonna try to find the quickest possible avenue to torture that fucker."

Years later, Bottum reflected on these two tours - "We actually were fans of Billy Idol. We all loved Generation X and we were kind of into pushing the envelope when it came to pop rock crossover. We appreciated MTV at the time and us playing with Billy Idol made sense. Robert Plant was an amazing guy. Super sweet. Really supportive. A fan of ours. And a legend. It was flattering that he wanted to take us on tour. And he had an idea about playing shitholes in America that was interesting to us. There wasn't a lot of pomp in his presentation, he was straight up a good guy. One day we rode with him in the back of a pick-up truck in some weird city and stopped and had drinks at a gay bar. That kind of blew my mind. At the time it was a big deal. He was very real." The keyboardist also recalls some end of the tour shenanigans with the spiky haired punk rocker - "We went out onstage naked with bags on our heads and did a go-go dance in front of him!"

Also around this time, Faith No More performed "Epic" on 'The Arsenio Hall Show' (on October 22nd) - at which Patton showed off new streaks in his hair, and during the guitar solo, beat the shit out of a dummy that seemed to resemble an unclothed Adolf Hitler. And on November 4th, the band performed a full-length set at Rip Magazine's Fourth Birthday Party, at the Hollywood Palladium in LA. What set the performance apart from the rest of the year's concerts was that several special guests appeared during the set - first off, Young MC (who was riding high at the time with the hit single "Bust a Move") contributing some rhymes to "Epic," while both Ozzy Osbourne and James Hetfield dropped by (on vocals and guitar, respectively) for a set-closing rendition of "War Pigs."

Understandably, having only three albums worth of material to choose from resulted in the band being beyond burnt out on playing the same songs night after night. As Patton explained, "It's very hard to be objective about 'The Real Thing.' How can you not end up despising it? It's very mechanical to play those songs. There was a period of time when I was really happy with it, but I think we lived a little too long with those things." Gould seemed to agree wholeheartedly with Patton - "We were told to tour for another six months at that point. We couldn't do it. We hated those songs so fucking much. But y'know, I guess we're lucky. Nobody died."

Patton: "Every once in a while, I'd throw in a few lines from a cover song or something, but that was the only glimmer of hope! I don't think any of us really got burned out from touring itself - it's just that we didn't have any other material to play. I mean, we were touring on one record, and when you come back to the same place six times and you're playing the same set, it's like, wait a minute! Who's gettin' ripped off here?! I'd be pissed if I came back to see a band that I liked and they played the same thing. We toured for...uh, too long!"

And despite the newfound success, Bottum found himself a tad troubled. "The funny thing about us is, one day we're going to push it too far, we're going to take advantage and it's going to hurt us. I just see it, the way we are, we're going to burn a great big bridge. Things are going great and we like it, but not to the point where it's something we're going to try and hang on to. If anything we'll try to fuck it off a little, just to see if we can get away with it." Patton also offered an unglamorous description of what life on the road was really like - "You don't spend time on tour, you waste time. You sleep, you wake up, it's time to play, everything else becomes very hard to deal with."

By year's end, FNM closed off an incredibly busy and successful year by performing two songs on the December 1st episode of 'Saturday Night Live' (hosted by John Goodman) - expectedly, "Epic" was performed, as well as "From Out of Nowhere." On December 26th, FNM also became one of the few rock bands to ever appear on an episode of 'Yo! MTV Raps,' when they performed "Epic" once more, and the extremely un-rap-like "Edge of the World." Patton showed off a new hairstyle on the program (his long hair pulled back in a ponytail, with the sides shaved stark bald), while the show's co-hosts, Ed Lover and Doctor Dré, provided back-up vocals on the latter tune. The same month, FNM became not only Spin Magazine cover boys, but were also crowned "Artists of the Year" by the publication.

FNM rang in 1991 with a performance at Rock In Rio II, at the mammoth Maracana Stadion in Brazil on January 20th, sharing a bill with old tour pal Billy Idol, as well as arguably the most popular rock group on the planet at that time, Guns N' Roses. The exotic location seemed to leave an impression on Patton, as evidenced to his response when he was once asked, "Can you imagine living in another country?" Patton: "Yeah, South America, even though it's a strange police state. In Brazil, the police are bored out of their minds, they can do pretty much anything. Who's to say what you or I would do if we were given a gun? At one gig, our drummer was wearing a police vest, which they made him take off. I said something in Portuguese about 'Shove it up the police's ass' and they came looking for me later, so I was sort of in hiding."

The singer also admitted to be taken aback by how so intensely Brazilian fans had taken to the band. "Once Roddy and me were walking to the beach, and a couple of Brazilian kids ran up to our faces and were like hyperventilating with tears streaming down their faces. I was really disarmed. I had no idea! It was like someone cutting off my arms and legs and taking out my vocal chords. I didn't know what to do. I just stood there and looked at her like she was an alien. And then you're thinking about it the whole next day, like, 'How did I react? Was that an exchange of any kind? What happened?' It's kind of like getting in a fight, in a weird way. It's this huge burst of...something. And then it's over with, and you have no idea what just happened."

Sepultura's then-singer/guitarist, Max Cavalera, recalls catching FNM's performance at this gargantuan concert. "We actually played with them at Rock in Rio. It was a great show - they tore it up. It was fantastic watching them live. So much energy from that band live. And they were funny, too. They would crack jokes between songs, and I had never heard a band doing that before. To me, metal was always serious. And when you go see Faith No More, they'd start asking *'Who farted?'* between songs. I'd never seen that kind of shit! So that was really cool. They became quite good friends with us."

Looking back a short while ago, Bottum was surprised how much things had changed in such a short time. "The other day at a soundcheck, Bill was shouting, 'Where's the soundman? Where's the fucking soundman?!' That was pretty funny - two years ago we were just glad to have a stage to play on. I'm sure we're all developing our own little attitudes, we're probably taking a little more advantage of what's given to us. When we started we were really pompous, pretty arrogant. We were deliberately offensive, and I think we still are. Shock value, it's always effective...and anyway, it's exciting. We've never had limitations before, but it's gotta happen sometime." Martin on the other hand seemed to revel in the thought of the group becoming a cash cow. "Big money is great. We're in among it right now. But all big money is a conversational topic, nobody comes into the room and opens the fucking briefcase. It's all swirling around us."

While the majority of 1991 was spent recuperating from the road, there was some FNM-related activity sporadically throughout the year, as the band received their second Grammy nomination - "Best Hard Rock Performance" for "Epic" - but on February 20th, lost out once again to Metallica (for their rendition of Queen's "Stone Cold Crazy"). On June 12th, FNM appeared at the International Rock Awards at the Dockland Arena in London (performing..."Epic" - surprise, surprise!), while the sci-fi comedy film 'Bill & Ted's Bogus Journey' was released on July

19th, which featured a cameo from Martin, as "Sir James Martin, Head of the Faith No More Spiritual and Theological Center." As for the film's soundtrack, Faith No More offered up a previously unreleased tune, "The Perfect Crime," which like "Cowboy Song," could have easily fit stylistically on 'The Real Thing.'

Come September, Faith No More offered up their longest string of live dates for 1991, when they returned to Brazil for an entire month's worth of performances (and premiering two new songs, "RV" and "The World is Yours," with Patton going with a new shorter hairstyle, in case you were wondering). And on September 5th, FNM finally won a bloody award they were nominated for, when they claimed "Best Special Effects in a Video" for "Falling to Pieces" at the MTV Video Music Awards (the clip was also nominated in two other categories, but did not win - "Best Art Direction in a Video" and "Best Heavy Metal/Hard Rock Video").

By October, the band found themselves in the Land of the Rising Sun, playing their first-ever shows in Japan. Bottum described FNM's maiden voyage to Japan - "To me that was fun in a different way. They weren't wild at all, they were just sitting there but it was fascinating. They just sit there and when you stop it's like clap, clap, clap and the minute you walk up to the microphone everyone just stops - they're so attentive. I started to get into it the second night, just walk up to the microphone and go (opens his mouth) and silence." The final show of 1991 turned out to be a homecoming of sorts for the band, as they performed at the Day on the Green Festival at Oakland Coliseum Stadium on October 12th, on a bill that also featured Soundgarden, Queensrÿche, and headliners Metallica.

Looking back, Metallica's Jason Newsted explains that the FNM-Metallica bond had grown stronger, which resulted in more gigs between the two bands, now that the thrash metal outfit was very good pals with a certain Flying V-wielding gentleman. "As years went on and I got to be close friends with Jim, we did shows with Faith No More and they became gigantic when they had the 'flipping around fish deal,' we took them around for quite a few shows as I recall. That was always praising Jim and wishing the best for him, because he was one of 'our circle.' He was one of 'our boys.' So of course, we herald them and put them up on a mantle, because it's personal in that way."

Soundgarden's Kim Thayil recalls the Green performance - but more for a career standout that Soundgarden experienced that day. "We got to meet [legendary rock show promoter] Bill Graham. He came and posed for photos with us. And the people that worked there were like, 'Holy shit dude. *Bill Graham just posed for photos with you!* When he comes out and poses for photos with a band it's because he likes the band, and the bands he likes end up being huge.' And then it was maybe a month after that he died in the helicopter crash [actually, less than two weeks later - on October 25th]. But that gig at the Day on the Green, Faith No More figures very prominently in Soundgarden's history."

Despite all the success, a statement from Patton during the summer of 1990 seemed to sum up how burnt out the singer had become on the road (and keep in mind, this was before FNM continued to perform non-stop for nearly another half a year). "The only thing on my mind right now is vacation...I can't help wanting to go home sometimes."

One can only imagine where Patton's mind was at when the year-and-a-half long 'The Real Thing' tour finally ground to a halt.

Chapter 8: Mr. Bungle

Mike Patton was 21 years old when the tour in support of 'The Real Thing' commenced, and would turn 23 a week after the Rock in Rio II appearance. So it would have been understandable for the singer to take an extended breather and slowly begin to focus on the all-important follow-up to 'The Real Thing.' Not a chance. He was as serious as a heart attack when he stated earlier that Mr. Bungle was not breaking up, as plans were now afoot to finally get the band in the studio to record a proper album. With all the music media hubbub about Bungle (and Patton sporting his Bungle shirt at seemingly every opportunity for FNM-related business), it didn't take long for the band to find a label that was eager to take them on - Warner Brothers.

Rather than trying to ease any thoughts that Patton may be bypassing FNM for an extended period (or permanently) in favor of Bungle, the singer seemed eager to fan the flames in the press - "In Mr. Bungle, it's more like a family thing, more like incest. It's not such an employee kind of thing. In FNM, I kind of get the sense that it is more like five separate jobs that need to be done. There's a 'we' in Mr. Bungle. In FNM there's not really one collective 'it'." Another time, Patton stated about his FNM mates, "I'm gonna need some time away from those bastards."

When asked if there were any issues when it came to juggling Patton's schedule with FNM while Bungle was recording, Spruance claimed it was a non-issue. "It's funny, FNM don't slow us down at all. It only affects us when it interrupts something we're doing - like in the middle of recording Mike had to go and do that Rock in Rio thing. He just leaves and comes back. That's fine, we're not a full-time band anyway - we're in college. Mike's doing his thing. I think if we were doing this 100 percent of the time we'd lose our momentum to make things the way they are. FNM just gives us a schedule to work with."

Instead of penning all-new compositions for their full-length major label debut, Bungle combed through their previous demos for material - every song from 'OU818' would be re-recorded except for one

("Mr. Nice Guy"), while "Carousel" and "Egg" originally resided on 'The Raging Wrath Of The Eastern Bunny' and 'Goddammit I Love America!', respectfully. And when it came to finding a producer that could fathom the band's unpredictable, all-over-the-place style/approach, veteran avant-garde saxophonist/composer, John Zorn, got the nod. Although based in New York City, Zorn agreed to record the band at Different Fur in San Francisco.

"Actually, we just got into him pretty recently," explained Dunn. "And we, or actually our drummer, saw him down in the city and he gave him a tape and asked him if he wanted to produce us. It was actually a shot in the dark for us, but he said he'd do it and it kind of blew us away." Spruance saw similarities between the two factions - "Zorn could lend a lot of definition of parts; his music moves in pretty much the same way ours does. We wanted every part within a song to have an entirely different character and he really brought that out." And with Patton, Zorn found a partner in crime, as the two would work together on various post-Bungle projects throughout the years, with the first being Naked City, which the singer once joked (?) came about because Zorn "Pinched my ass, ripped out a couple of butt-hairs and asked me to sing for Naked City. I guess he liked the way I screamed. By the way, I'm leaving both Faith No More and Mr. Bungle for Naked City." Bungle would be listed as "co-producers" on the record, along with Zorn.

To Spruance's surprise, Warner Brothers embraced the very un-mainstream nuttiness of Bungle's debut. "As extreme and sometimes inaccessible as the album is, the people at Warners seem to really like it. They tell us things like, 'You guys are great! It's really Zappa!' In LA record company talk, Zappa is the pinnacle of 'out there' and the standard against which everything else is judged against. The further out there you go, the closer you're getting to Zappa. Not to denounce Zappa, of course!" Patton also once touched upon the media's desire to often compare Bungle to Zappa. "I haven't really got a good answer for the Zappa question yet. And, boy, we get that question a lot. The funny thing is, I mean, I *like* Frank Zappa - I like some of his records - but he never really blew my head off when I was young, or even now. I'll listen to certain records and they're really great, but none of us are really huge Zappa fans. I don't think we're anywhere near where that guy got; I mean, he worked with everybody in a thousand different genres, and he had his own thing going. I don't really know if what we're doing is like what he did or what. I don't really have a good answer for that."

Mr. Bungle's self-titled debut was released on August 13, 1991 (fascinating factoid - it shared the same birthdate as Metallica's mega-hit 'Black Album,' as I recall purchasing both compact discs at the aforementioned Slipped Disc Records on that date). Featuring illustrations of grubby/grumpy clowns inside the CD booklet (and a single sleepy clown on the cover), upon closer inspection of the CD's back cover, any hope of publicizing the FNM/Patton association was quickly dispelled, as Patton was listed under an alias on the back cover - "Vlad Drac." In fact, most of the Bungle band members were listed under either aliases or truncated names - "Scummy" (Trey Spruance), "Bär" (Clinton McKinnon), and "Heifetz" (Danny Heifetz) - while "Trevor Roy Dunn" and "Theobald Brooks Lengyel" were far easier to spot. And to add to the mystique, Bungle's members hid behind outlandish masks and costumes in publicity photos from this era, as well as for live performances (something that the similarly-attired metal band Slipknot obviously took note of). The band was well aware what the affect of this unorthodox approach would have on the average schmo buying the album. Trey: "People will buy the record, some for the right reasons, others for the wrong reason. Regardless, they're definitely going to hear the difference immediately. Look, you can sell the CD back for about four or five bucks. See ya in the used bin!"

But the real reason why there was little hope of cashing in on the FNM/Patton connection was because while there were a few stylistic similarities between the two acts (metal guitar riffs, funk bass, airy keyboards, etc.), 'Mr. Bungle' did not feature traditional song structures like FNM had on their albums. Let alone that the album was slapped with a "Parental Advisory" sticker due to lyrics contained therein that would make even a sailor blush. But that's not to say that the album doesn't offer up some worthwhile compositions - case in point, the album-opening "Quote Unquote" (which originally was listed as "Travolta," before having to be changed - to avoid a potential lawsuit from actor John Travolta), as well as the surprisingly melodic "Carousel," the frantic "My Ass Is on Fire," and the rubbery funk of "Egg." Also of note is Patton's vocals, as his nasal whine of 'The Real Thing' was quickly being replaced by his natural singing voice (wise move!).

A video would be filmed for the aforementioned "Quote Unquote," which features such scenes as what appears to be Patton singing lines of the song while hiding behind a black leather S&M mask and several dead (or merely napping) gentlemen hanging from a ceiling while wearing masks. Hardly surprising that MTV never played the clip. In response, Patton would point out, "Real art has never been shown on MTV." As for the song's album version, Bungle indulged in an "audio trick" on the listener, as the tune begins with over 30 seconds of mostly silence (especially if you don't have headphones on), before the sound of a glass shattering finally leads into the song.

'Mr. Bungle' is far from a perfect recording. Sonically, the album suffers from a late '80s-sounding production, despite being two years removed from the "me decade." Heifetz would also agree with this observation, as he later admitted, "I didn't know shit about recording drums at the time. I guess I was convinced that gates, new drum heads and shitty reverbs were really great things. I hope I'm not still that stupid."

It was probably best to just simply let a few of these compositions reside permanently on early demos, and not revisit them for your major label debut. A glaring example being the woefully sophomoric "The Girls of Porn," which sinks to the lowest depths of fratboy humor - lyrically, Patton name-checks everything he enjoys about viewing pornography, and how excited he is to "bop the baloney" (while sound samples of adult film stars doing the deed are detected at several points in the tune). And if that wasn't bad enough, the tune that immediately follows is the Shakespearean-ly titled, "Love Is a Fist," that mines almost the exact same type of bird-brained lyrics. And Patton's lyrics and vocal-delivery on "Squeeze Me Macaroni" are probably the closest he's ever come to a true Anthony Kiedis rip-off on record - resulting in a tune that sounds like a sub-par 'Freaky Styley' reject.

Still, the album had a significant impact - as expected, mostly with FNM devotees. "That was just fucking insane," remembers Limp Bizkit's Wes Borland about discovering Bungle. "What Mr. Bungle did to me as just a kid that was first playing guitar was so left of center of the other things I was listening to, which at the time was mostly thrash, like Metallica, Testament, and Megadeth. And Mr. Bungle all of a sudden opened the possibilities. It's kind of like living in a box, and then going,

'Oh...*you don't have to live in a box.'* It was this inspiring realization, through the whole Patton thing and all the things he was involved with. And then to know that he was involved in both bands, which were so different from each other was kind of like, 'Oh, it's OK to do that.' It taught me a lot of lessons as a kid, of just how to be and sort of gave me the thumbs up to approach music in really whatever way I wanted to. Then it eventually wore off on me who the producer was of the first Mr. Bungle album, and that's how I found out about John Zorn, who *completely* blew my mind. Because John Zorn has released...I don't know, just dozens of albums. So I went and started getting into John Zorn."

Borland also thanks Bungle for opening up a whole new musical world for him, and steering him away from mainstream rock music. "It's just so cinematic and schizophrenic. It's like a band that has Tourette's syndrome...it's like the musical equivalent of Tourette's syndrome. I'm a little bit all over the place and a little bit ADD, so that really appealed to me - the adventure of the music. Because the music and the guitar work was incredibly adventurous. There is no other way to describe it, than it's just like, 'Wow. This is heroic. It's the opposite of 'guitar hero' type of playing.' I'm glad I got exposed to that at a young age, because it completely turned me off to anything like Mötley Crüe or Poison. Because I was at this place where I was starting to listen to Steve Vai and Joe Satriani albums a little bit. And Bungle and that whole vibe - which then got me into Primus and all this other stuff - it steered me away from guitar gymnastics, into weirdness. And I'm really glad that I took that turn. Not that I'm disrespecting Steve Vai or Joe Satriani or Mötley Crüe, but those bands and that style of flashy metal playing falls into these certain parameters, and I'm not really interested in being that kind of a player."

HIM's Ville Vallo also shares Borland's enthusiasm about the Bungle-Zorn union. "That was a time we were listening to all that kind of stuff. I think I even played some Bungle stuff back in the day, and I was listening to John Zorn and a lot of breaking limits of genres. You'd have disco, jazz, and black metal in one song. When we were young, that was exciting, because there were no rules, and it just felt...today, some of it might feel dated, but at that time, it was something new. It was like 'Captain Beefheart was back alive and in his heyday' kind of thing. It was like 'everything goes'." Devin Townsend also voiced a similar opinion of Bungle - "It was a big deal as it was for all of us at the time, because between Primus, Jane's Addiction, Mr. Bungle, and Faith No More, there was this almost sense that the more creatively out there you were, the more cred you were going to get as an artist. And as a 19-year-old kid, that was all that was important at the time."

Vision of Disorder's Mike Fleischmann was suitably impressed with what he heard, as was Avenged Sevenfold's Johnny Christ. Fleischmann: "When the first Mr. Bungle came out, it was a lot of fun because they created some controversy with Patton denying he was in the band. It gave people something to talk about. Mr. Bungle was Mike Patton unleashed, really demonstrating how intense and talented he is. The band are all amazing players - it's insane how they are able to jump from death metal to doo wop and make it sound so easy." Christ: "The first time I heard Mr. Bungle was actually from [late Avenged Sevenfold drummer] the Rev. He was the first one that introduced me to Mr. Bungle...and [guitarist] Synyster Gates - all three of us grew up loving it. 'Travolta' was probably the first song I'd heard from Bungle, and I later go into a lot of the other tracks - 'The Girls of Porn,' 'Stubb (A Dub),' and stuff like that. They were just unique and awesome musicians and great songwriters."

However, Mr. Bungle's far-out sound was certainly an acquired taste, which wasn't for everybody - a view shared by Madball's Mitts. "Not a Bungle fan. I had friends that loved Mr. Bungle. To me, there was just too much going on. And that might be the reasoning right there actually - I liked Faith No More because you could hear chugging riffs going on with their stuff. And Mr. Bungle, the riffs are just a lot more freestyle and kind of all over the place."

Several months after the release of the album (which would not even register a position on the Billboard 200 Album Charts), Bungle set out on their first-ever US tour, which saw the band crisscross the States for much of March and April 1992. When asked what fans should expect from Bungle on the road, Dunn offered up a typical "Bungle" reply - "Expect a really shitty band. Wait - don't even expect a band. Just expect really shitty people. I wouldn't even call us a band in the first place. I don't even think that music has anything to do with what we're doing." Additionally, the bassist expressed both hopes and fears for the tour - "I have both, actually, combined into one ambiguous feeling. I mean, we all know it's going to be really painful, we're all going to hate each other, we're going to be sick and dirty and smelly. But I am really interested in seeing the country."

Perhaps the most obvious thing that Bungle and FNM had in common was displayed during this tour - the knack for laying an uncommon (and sometimes unrecognizable) cover tune on their befuddled audience. For example, a plodding doom-noise metal version of Billy Squier's "The Stroke" and a oh-so-serious reading of John Sebastian's "Welcome Back" (i.e., the theme song of the '70s sitcom 'Welcome Back, Kotter'), as well as more obscure material, like DRI's "I Don't Need Society," plus "Third Floor Dungeon," a ditty from the 1953 Dr. Seuss-penned film, 'The 5,000 Fingers of Dr. T.' When asked about how Bungle decides on what covers to inflict upon their audience, Patton explained, "Pretty much, that ball kinda ends up rolling in my court most of the time, 'cause I just listen to a lot of shit and I always keep my ear open for something to do with covers. So you can mostly blame that on me."

From various reports, the supporting US tour certainly had its standout moments, including a performance in San Francisco, during which Patton treated himself to an enema...while on stage. "I heard the crowd got a nice little spray, but I didn't see it because I was bent over." When asked why he committed such a dastardly deed, he responded, "Hey, it was a nice, dirty show, a lot of dirty people, everything was dirty. So why not have a little clean segment - wash out myself, wash out the audience?"

After experiencing life on the road with Bungle, Dunn was flabbergasted when it came to why the opposite sex wasn't attracted to such eccentric individuals on stage. "Actually, to tell you the truth, we don't get groupies. We get letters and stuff, but we've never been on a huge tour or anything. But when we play here, it's funny: no girls ever come up to us. I don't know what the fuck is going on! Once we had this huge banner that we put behind us. It said: 'FREE COCK.' But still, nobody came up." The bassist also explained how Bungle was all about giving fans a show to remember. "We're into big chaos levels. Our tunes are kinda screwed up enough as it is. When you go see a live show you want a little extra, so we try and provide that. We have a whole suitcase full of props that we use. Every show we used to do, we used to have something to throw out in the audience, like used underwear...or loaves of bread. We haven't done that in a while now. Now we mainly use Halloween masks and chew up fake blood. The main thing we see when we look into an audience is people laughing at us. It's perfect. We laugh at them, we laugh at ourselves. They don't dance. They just have this look on their faces like they're watching a cartoon or something."

Even a member of Patton's *other* band was dazzled by the Bungle live experience. Bottum: "I've seen them live a couple of times and I really respected what they were able to pull off. I was always surprised that they could play live what they recorded. That takes a lot more memory than I'd ever have."

Devin Townsend caught a performance on this tour, which turned out to be a life-changing gig...but not because of the headliner. "Mike Patton I think chose this band, Grotus, to come out on the road with Mr. Bungle, and open. They were this independent band from San Francisco. I went to the Bungle show because I was obviously really big into that vibe at the time. And then when I saw Grotus, it just changed everything for me. In fact, I enjoyed it so much more than Bungle that that night, my whole direction changed. I think as a byproduct of what Bungle did and the creative liberties they were allowed to take based on Mike Patton being as forceful with his visions as he always has been, it allowed bands like Grotus to come into my radar, and ultimately, just sort of change my world."

And despite all the shenanigans and the attempts at being anti-listener friendly, Bungle did leave a lasting impression on some - especially Korn guitarist Brian "Head" Welch, who recalled, "We liked that creepiness of it live. They used to stand there and stare at the crowd, Bungle did, for ten, fifteen minutes before they even played one note! Just like, 'What are you doing? *Perform!*' But it was so weird that we ripped that off from them, too, and did that live a little bit. They were really important to influencing us. And also Rage Against the Machine was. I don't know if they get mentioned a lot with Korn, but that anger and that rage that they had and the energy was just so intense. No other band had that when I was younger."

Welch would also later talk to guitar publications about a certain chord that he and the Korn's other guitarist, James "Munky" Shaffer, utilized, dubbed "the Bungle chord" [a chord that has two notes three whole steps from each other]. "Bungle, just the weirdness of it, was totally an influence. That chord, just the weird dissonant chords, and also their stage presence where they would wear the costumes and stuff." When pressed to list Korn songs that utilize the Bungle chord, Welch explained, "The song called 'Divine' off the first record ['Korn'], 'Faget' we use it. Man, we use it a lot on that. We use it on the song 'Need To.' So many."

The tour in support of Bungle's debut would wrap up in the spring, but the group would reconvene for a one-off show at the end of the year, sharing a bill with Primus and the Melvins at the Bill Graham Civic Auditorium on New Years Eve. As Dunn recalls, "After our last tour, we took some time off, about six months. Then, after that we ended up doing this New Year's Eve show with Primus in San Francisco, which was terrible, and we really got screwed by the sound system." No one knew at the time, that this would be the last Bungle live performance for nearly three years.

Around the time of Bungle's debut, Patton was asked for a message to their fans. "Thanks for not supporting us, not coming to our shows and not buying our t-shirts. Oh, and whoever's spreading those rumors about us, keep doing it - they're beautifully erotic."

Eloquently stated, sir.

Chapter 9: Angel Dust, Part 1

Somehow, someway, while Mike Patton was recording and touring with Mr. Bungle in 1991 and early '92, he found the time to focus on helping create the highly anticipated follow-up to 'The Real Thing,' which would go by the title of 'Angel Dust.' Recorded at two separate San Francisco recording studios from January through March 1992 (Coast Recorders and Brilliant Studios) and co-produced once more between the band and Matt Wallace, 'Angel Dust' is largely considered as FNM's finest hour, and was certainly their most daring, challenging, and versatile release. But it wasn't the band's least turbulent recording experience. Quite the contrary, in fact.

"There were times when everyone was really worried," admitted Wallace. "There were a lot of childish games among the band members." Patton agreed with this assessment of the situation - "Everything this time was a lot different. A lot more vicious, a lot more ugly, bitter and deceptive." Ditto Gould - "People who were assholes in the past were bigger assholes this time around."

"Jim wasn't stoked on a lot of 'Angel Dust'," recalls Bordin. "I think in some ways, maybe he just wasn't ready to accept something different, like, 'Here's this formula we hit on that works, let's work on that for a while.' But that's not how we work. That was never the idea. I mean, think back on 'Angel Dust' and 'Real Thing.' Faith No More was a band that started out that was writing a particular set of music for a show. And you can even look at those albums as particular sets of music. They weren't going to be the same - they were never going to be the same. Even the album itself was always incredibly varied within the album - making it a satisfying fucking listening experience."

"But Jim's contributions, I got to say, between 'Real Thing' and 'Angel Dust,' dropped off. I mean, I can think of 'Jizzlobber' on 'Angel Dust,' but I can tell you half of fucking 'Zombie Eaters,' a good portion of that whole middle section of 'Woodpecker from Mars,' the whole of 'Surprise! You're Dead!' He was all over that album, y'know? Those were all parts that he brought, and all of a sudden, those parts weren't there. It was like, 'What the fuck is this? What the fuck is that'?"

"We came into the studio and there were [guitar] parts that weren't written," adds Patton. "So we had to fuckin' scramble, really think on our feet. It's like, you've gotta leave town on Wednesday, and Saturday you're sitting around the house going, 'I'll do it tomorrow, I'll do it tomorrow,' until you've finally got one day to do it all - pack, rent a car. There's no way you're gonna get it all done. You just can't do an album that way."

Years later, Martin looked back on the recording sessions for 'Angel Dust,' and explained things from his side. "My publicized 'not being into' 'Angel Dust' was all about the way the whole process went down. There was a lot of weird pressure to follow up 'The Real Thing,' and as a consequence, the album 'AD' was more contrived musically than I thought was necessary. I wanted more of the record to happen in the studio and Bill wanted every last tack nailed down before we went in. I wanted to spend time with it, management and the record company wanted to rush it out the door. There were a bunch of journalists in the studio. We were paying for a bunch of sampling that we could have created. Matt Wallace was calling me on the phone complaining about Mike Patton's performance. Management and record company were calling me complaining about Mike Patton's performance and desire for outside projects."

"The record company president came in the studio and said: 'I hope nobody bought houses.' All the air got sucked out of the room. That was one of those great moments when reality slaps you in the face. Some of my associates (had) bought houses. The pressure was on, and everyone wanted to be in the studio with me while I recorded, endlessly tinkering and fucking with me and fucking with Matt, and Matt is a really fucking wound up guy already. Prior to 'AD,' I would work alone with Matt and his assistant engineer, period. I had to kick everyone out, and even though it was not a new concept it really pissed everyone off."

Patton on the other hand, offered this not-exactly-complimentary description of Martin's guitar work on 'Angel Dust' - "It sounded like Guitar Center, somebody playing just to get themselves off. It came together after some primitive intimidation tactics. It's kind of the way we coexist with each other. We give each other lots and lots of trouble. We

all believe that everyone deserves equal torment, except for Jim."
Wallace also remembers Martin's dissatisfaction with the material. "He
kept referring to the music as 'gay disco.' He just hated the material on
the record. And I kept saying, 'But we really need you - your guitar
playing is what's going to keep it from being 'gay disco.' We need your
big army boots in here.' He couldn't get his head around it, and the band
was furious."

Rumors and speculation have surfaced over the years that Gould
supplied bits of guitar on the album due to Martin's disinterest, which the
bassist later cleared up. "I did play some guitar on that record, but not as
much as what is generally believed. Jim wasn't around much for
rehearsal, but was around for the recording, and played the lion's share of
the parts. I was more involved in the writing and arrangement side of
things."

Perhaps to make up for the lack of input from the guitarist this
time around, FNM's keyboardist attempted to recover Martin's fumble.
Bottum: "Yeah, there's not a whole lot of guitar on it, is there? In
addition to the E-Maxes, I also used piano, Hammond organ, even an
accordion on 'Midnight Cowboy.' There was a lot more room to do
different things. We were on the road a long time with our last record, so
we had a lot of time to decide what we would do for our next one, and it
only made sense to expand technologically."

While there may have been some friction on the six-string side
of things, Bordin on the other hand was quite pleased with how his
drums came out. "We worked on everything with [Wallace], and it's
gotten better every time, it's much closer than it ever has been to
sounding the way we feel we sound, it's not easy with the keyboards and
guitar and a lot of bass and a lot of drums, it's not easy balancing them.
We try to get a realistic sound, we don't want a super human sound by
any means, we don't want it to sound like...that kick drum that sounds
like that [clicks fingers]. Everything on that album drum-wise is real,
there's no samples, there's no digital effects. We made our own reverb,
we ran all of our tracks through an extremely live room and mic'd the
ambiance; we made our own ambiance. It was really important. It's
extremely organic; it's an extremely real sound, what you hear is what we
did, and I'm very proud of that also. What I was going to say about Matt
and getting better at sounding like us, it also has to do with the way you

write songs. The parts that you construct have got to leave enough room for everybody to breathe, and that's also the progression of hopefully writing better songs, getting better at what we do. It's all kind of interconnected."

Despite all the pressure and mudslinging, Billy assumed a "is the glass half empty or half full?" outlook - "When we did 'The Real Thing', we had a tiny budget, we were broke and on top of that nobody really gave a shit about us. Nobody knew what kind of music we played and nobody could classify us. We were at a real disadvantage in those days, but now we're at a real advantage."

Also during the 'Angel Dust' sessions, it became apparent that Patton had developed an unusual fetish. Wallace: "He was into this weird, twisted porn stuff. I remember he was showing me some of these videos he got from Japan. I was like, 'Dude, why are you watching that for?!' Crazy shit." Some of Patton's pornographic preferences came to light in this exchange that was overheard by a reporter for Creem Magazine, between the singer and Gould during the album's recording:

[Patton takes a phone call and then returns to tell Billy that they've been invited, along with former Mentor/resident LA sicko El Duce, to Tom Araya's (vocalist/bassist for Slayer) this evening.]

BG: (laughing) Why don't you tell her what's going on!
MP: We're gonna swap video tapes, have a taping party.
BG: Sick fucked-up tapes.
MP: Great things.
I'm almost afraid to ask, but, what?
MP: A lot of shit-eating and stuff like that; dicks on meat hooks. El Duce has a lot of animal porn, which is fine by me.
That's disgusting!
BG: (laughs) Plus you get to hang out with cultural icons! Heroes!

When photographs began to surface of the band circa the release of 'Angel Dust' (which dropped on June 8, 1992), it became quickly apparent that Patton was now almost unrecognizable compared to his pin-up worthy good looks circa 'The Real Thing.' Gone was the long locks, in its place was greasy, collar-length hair, with a long strand pulled down on each side of his face, to replicate sideburns, and instead of being clean-shaven, a clump of whiskers now resided on his chinny chin chin. And fashion-wise, it seemed like he had rummaged through a yard sale, while black worker boots had replaced the white high top basketball sneakers of yesteryear (Patton - along with Bottum - would also briefly sport an eyebrow ring).

And now, we finally get to the music. It's been said that turmoil in an artist's personal life helps create their best work. While some have contested the theory, this was certainly the case with Faith No More and 'Angel Dust.' As its members have clearly just stated, it wasn't effortless, but the end result was certainly worth it - 'Angel Dust' is one helluva listen. The "most valuable player" of the recording has to be awarded to Mr. Patton. As stated earlier, the nasal whine of 'The Real Thing' had been replaced with his natural singing voice, and as a result, Patton gets to showcase his wide range of vocal skills (anything from a croon to spoken words to a grindcore screech can be detected at various points).

And lyrically, Patton truly came into his own. "Last time around, all I could do was slap on some stuff at the end, like peanut butter on toast," explains the singer. "This time I was there for the whole thing. To me, we've all gotten better at playing what we hear in our head. That may sound like a load of rock star shit, but I think it's actually true on this record." And according to Patton, the lyrics and varied subject matter are closer to the real him - "This time it's more like me writing. Before I'd hear like 'From Out of Nowhere' on the last album, and I'd say, 'Oh, OK, this should be a bitter lover song' and I'd invent a scenario that had nothing to do with me at all. This time, I didn't do that at all." It also turned out that cruising and observing played a part in the singer's lyric penning - "I drove around a lot in my Honda. Drove to a real bad area of town, parked and just watched people. Coffee shops and white-trash diner-type places were great for inspiration."

And Patton's vocal talents weren't lost on both his peers (and listeners who would eventually become his peers). "He's got a really eclectic range and character," points out Fishbone's Angelo Moore. "Different characters. I like a singer and a performer when they can have a veritable plethora of different characters to display. Good theatrics, good theater - he's got good theater." Soundgarden's Kim Thayil could also hear a change for the better in the singer - "When he got his confidence in his position with Faith No More, he let his assets fly - which was really his voice, which is amazing."

Devin Townsend remembers being impressed by Patton's singing…and also jealous. "He was effortlessly in pitch. And that makes me hate him as a singer, just because being in tune for me is just a life-long chore. It's never something that I just open my mouth and I'm in tune. I don't know if it's just as a person I'm insecure or whatever, but it's like being in tune for me is a lot of work. And I'm able to now for the most part, but it's taken concentration and in-ear monitors and a bunch of shit just to get that straight. I remember seeing Mike Patton with a bunch of shitty wedges in a shitty club, acting like a jackass, and being perfectly in tune. And I remember thinking to myself, 'Oh…*fuck you'.*" [Laughs]

Carcass' Jeff Walker also gives props to Patton's vocal abilities…sort of. "He's in a world where there aren't that many great singers, besides your Halfords and your Dickinsons. He's also not your typical histrionic-singing metal singer. He probably was a metalhead when he joined the band, but he's obviously matured into some kind of leftfield artist. But then, I don't know - is it a case of any given day of any given week, you can walk into a karaoke bar in North America and maybe find someone just as talented? I don't know."

I remember the first time I heard 'Angel Dust' was via an advance cassette copy provided by the same cousin who had turned me on to FNM in the first place. My initial thoughts were that the album made little sense. But as with quite a few of my all-time favorite rock records, after a few listens, the music found the right receptors in my brain, and I was hooked - resulting in an album that I can honestly say I still go through intense periods of listening to, to this very day. And as with most classic albums, you hear something new each time you listen to it (especially if you listen on a good pair of headphones).

Musically, the album-opening "Land of Sunshine" sounds like the perfect soundtrack while one navigates through a treacherous rollercoaster ride, as Gould's funk bass and Martin's metallic guitar seem to be battling for center stage…but somehow, it all works. Lyrically, we get our first glimpse of the "new and improved Patton," as he described the tune as "A grotesquely positive song, so I watched a lot of late night

TV to get in that frame of mind." Also, it turns out that part of the song's lyrics were pieced together from phrases Patton spotted from inside fortune cookies. The following composition, "Caffeine," would be a slamming rocker that served perfectly as the set-opener when the band launched their own headlining tour later in the year. Bottum would later explain, "Mike wrote those lyrics, they're pretty much based on caffeine, it's the only drug he does." The singer would later confirm this - "I also wrote some songs when I was experimenting with myself. I was doing some sleep-deprivation experiments, staying up with coffee for as long as I could."

"Midlife Crisis" would go on to become an instant FNM classic (and like "We Care A Lot" and "Epic," is a tune that has been performed at every FNM show since its initial release), while the lyrics are a kin to the style that Kurt Cobain was rapidly popularizing at the time - offering a set of seemingly nonsensical lyrics that when strung together, create all sorts of images in one's noodle. Musically, the song features a sample from the beginning of the Simon and Garfunkel classic, "Cecilia," which is then combined with Puffy's hard-hitting drumming. "It was one of the first songs I heard when I was a kid," reminisces Bottum, "And I think I sampled it 'cause I had a funny relationship with it. The song was kind of built around the rhythm of that sample." Another familiar sound occurs in the middle of the tune - the sound of a descending whistle - which turns out to be a sample of the Beastie Boys' "Car Thief."

On the tune "RV," Patton assumes the role of a down-on-his-luck white trash fellow, who seems to relish his demented thoughts. Patton: "RV means recreational vehicle. A typical part of American culture: people live in holiday caravans. We call them white trash. In America, everyone knows someone who lives in an RV. These people are looked down upon, while everyone knows they're part of society. These people are usually fat, watch TV all day, and eat TV dinners. The song 'RV' is almost a mark of honor to those pigs. My family's like that. The kind of people who stay inside these caravans all day and complain: nobody speaks English anymore. No one listens to them, they're only talking to themselves. The song is a profile of the average redneck mentality."

The song "Smaller and Smaller" was the one and only tune off of 'Angel Dust' to never receive a live airing over the years. Gould explains why - "'Smaller and Smaller,' while pretty grandiose in concept, always felt too long and too...plodding...to even consider doing live. And truth be told, we were never quite as attached to that one as some of the others." Perhaps most memorable about the song is the use of what sounds like aboriginal chanting. Patton: "We decided to take an Indian chant and fuck it up, sort of a 'Dances with Wolves' aesthetic."

Looking back on the melodic "Everything's Ruined," Bottum recalls, "I think at the time Mike was talking about his dealing with being in a successful band. Musically we like to think of the Carpenters as an influence on that one." Patton would admit, "One thing I've been doing is listening to a lot of mood music, easy listening. And I've taken a lot from that. The chorus of 'Everything's Ruined' reminds me of Sinatra, Jackie Gleason." One of the heaviest tunes on the album turns out to be "Malpractice," which was composed entirely by Patton, and is sung from an extremely peculiar viewpoint. Patton: "There's this one song I wrote about a lady who goes to a surgeon and she's getting operated on and she realizes she likes the surgeon's hand inside of her. She doesn't even care about being cured, she just wants someone's hands inside of her - she gets addicted to that."

'Angel Dust' is all about contrasting, so from that statement, it makes perfect sense that one of the album's heaviest and extreme ditties would be followed by one of its most melodic - "Kindergarten" - which appears to be about a person returning back to their old elementary school's playground as a grown-up, and wondering if they will be able to graduate or not (perhaps something a kin to a seemingly popular nightmare that us grown-ups seem to have - you're back in school, missing classes or not having studied sufficiently, and in danger of flunking out).

Certainly some of the liveliest lyrics on the album reside within "Be Aggressive." But surprisingly, Patton had nothing to do with the words - Bottum is the sole author of the rockin' tune, which features haunted house organ sounds at the beginning. But the extreme subject matter - which is best described as celebrating the act of, er, *swallowing* - was inserted on purpose, according to the song's creator. Bottum: "What'd you think? Pretty fuckin' extreme, isn't it? Did you think it was a homoerotic song or something? That's what's gonna be good about it. I think certain people are gonna be really vocal about it, like 'What the hell is that?!' And others'll be so weirded out by it they won't say anything.

As long as we make a few people squirm, our job is done." The song also includes a recurring chant from "cheerleaders" (Bottum: "They weren't really cheerleaders, they were friends of ours, loud, obnoxious girls") and a raw guitar solo by Martin, best remembered for a flub in the middle of it, that went uncorrected. "I was surprised that I was allowed to go on as long as I did," Martin admits about the six-string break. "The band doesn't really like guitar solos that much. It was a part of the song where it really belonged, but that hasn't stopped the band from chopping a guitar solo apart in the past."

Following in the alternating extreme listening/easy listening pattern of 'Angel Dust,' the very pop-friendly "A Small Victory" falls into the latter category, which appears to be a clear attempt at scoring another hit with the mainstreamers. And it turns out it may have been the tune that included the most samples on the entire album. Bottum: "Yeah, they just fit the song. It's the most radio-friendly song we've ever done. So we looked for samples along that vein. I think that it went really well."

It appears that the song on the album closest to catching the attention of funk/rap metal fans that were introduced to the band via "Epic" would be "Crack Hitler." But with such an excessive title, you could forget about potential mainstream radio spins or MTV airings. Patton: "'Crack Hitler' is like a sleazy version of the 'Emergency!' theme, like a '70s TV action show. It's got like a 'Shaft' guitar line and siren samples. You picture five cops with guns chasin' a guy through an alley! It's like bad, bad disco - bad! Horrible!"

Up next would be the album's most curiously-titled tune, "Jizzlobber." And just what is a jizzlobber? "'Jizz' means sperm, and 'to lob' means to throw," explains Patton. "The title is comic, but hasn't got anything to do with the rest of the lyrics." The track begins with sound effects of the outdoors (once on the ensuing tour, Patton introduced the song by saying, "Imagine yourself during this next number kneeling down to a country stream - yes, a babbling brook - and taking a long, nice drink"). "Jizzlobber" would turn out to be another one of the album's heaviest tunes (featuring distorto-static vocals and heavier-than-hell guitar riffing), and is the only tune on the album that Martin had a heavy hand in writing (the only other tune on the album he helped create would be "Kindergarten").

And how do you wrap up such an unpredictable, all-encompassing, tour de force of an album? With a heartfelt rendition of the all-instrumental theme song from the once-upon-a-time-controversial 1969 film, 'Midnight Cowboy,' of course! Gould recalls how the John Barry-penned tune worked its way onto FNM's "to-do list" - "I went through some strange period where I was listening non-stop to an old SF pop radio station called Magic 61, that played stuff like the Mills Brothers, Gogi Grant, Tony Bennett...'Midnight Cowboy' was a byproduct of this, as was the later covered 'Greenfields' and 'Spanish Eyes'."

If the album's thirteen tracks weren't enough, there were even a few leftovers lying around. A studio rendition of "Easy" and a re-recording of the Mosley-era classic "As the Worm Turns" would both appear on the Japanese edition of the album, while a song that was premiered live the previous year, "The World is Yours" would remain unreleased until its inclusion on the bonus second disc of the 1998 compilation, 'Who Cares a Lot?' According to Bottum, the song featured a sample from the 1987 on-camera suicide of American politician, R. Budd Dwyer - "I think that was a video snippet that Billy and Mike P kind of were obsessed with at one point. The delivery of what he says before he pulls the trigger was super disturbing. It might have been a little dark, even for us." And one other track, "Seagull Song," has never been released (as of this book's release) in its entirety. According to Gould, there's a reason why this track remains shelved - "We really don't like this one (!!!). We don't always agree on much but we do seem to agree on this...in our minds, it was a noble attempt but didn't really work."

A total of three singles would be released from the album (of which videos would also be filmed for) - "Midlife Crisis," "A Small Victory," and "Everything's Ruined." The "Crisis" clip would be directed by Kevin Kerslake (best known for his work for Nirvana and the Smashing Pumpkins), and continued the band's string of striking clips that began with "Epic" - slo-mo images of the band playing in a dimly lit room with flashes of light, Patton having fun with a shovel, and the most memorable of all scenes being in the middle, in which an unlucky gentleman has his limbs tied to horses, pulling in different directions all at once. What should have been the album's big hit single, "A Small

Victory," wound up falling flat on the charts - no doubt due to an indulgent, hard-to-follow video (directed by Marcus Nispel), which mixed re-enacted scenes of war with shots of the band (not playing instruments), as well as a lady dancing in leather and Patton lip-synching the lyrics behind big thorn-y things, while covered in some sort of baby powder/baking soda substance. One of those times that a director forgets that they're merely shooting a music video and not an epic full-length motion picture, I guess. As a result, MTV didn't air the clip much, resulting in a potential hit single flushed down the toilet (although it would earn a nomination for "Best Art Direction" at the 1993 MTV Video Music Awards, where it would lose to Madonna's "Rain"). "Everything's Ruined" on the other hand, is certainly a charming clip due to it being the complete opposite of its pompous predecessor. Gould: "Warners spent the video budget on 'Small V' and 'Midlife' so that when it came time to 'Everything's Ruined,' there wasn't much left (!!). It was our idea to take this further and make a video as cheap as humanly possible, in one of those video booths like they had at county fairs, where you sing and dance in front of a blue screen. We didn't quite get to do that, but we got it as close as possible."

Regarding the album's title (which is slang for the drug PCP, or in pharmaceutical speak, "phencyclidine"), it would lead to some debate over the years as to what it was supposed to represent or signify. But according to Gould, it was chosen for a reason you wouldn't suspect - "It's two beautiful words but a real ugly thing. It's kind of what the record's like; it's got some real beauty in it and it's got some real ugliness in it. It's like the balance thing." Patton adds, "We were delighted by the idea that angel dust is a horrible drug that makes you aggressive and paranoid. And the title together with the picture of a beautiful, restful bird, that you would normally see on an easy-listening sleeve. That contrast has a disturbing effect on people. The average rock fan will put a sleeve like that aside: bluh, I don't want to listen to this. That's what we like best."

As Patton mentioned, the album cover art was also part and parcel of the entire 'Angel Dust' experience, as well - featuring a white bird (an egret, to be exact) against a dark background on the front, and on the back, pieces of meat (and a severed cow's head) dangling from hooks, inside what appears to be a meat packing plant. "Roddy had the idea of a white swan to go with the title," recalls Gould, "But we had a hard time finding something. At the end, a mutual friend knew a photographer [Wernher Krutein] and we went over to look at his stuff...and the bird was right there. We knew then and there that was the cover." As it turns out, the striking 'AD' cover photo left a lasting impression on Kyuss singer (and soon-to-be FNM touring partner) John Garcia. "The cover of that was a new level of class for rock n' roll bands. Just an awesome, awesome picture. And the cursive font on that. All the way around, just a classic record - that's got to be my favorite."

Bordin was once asked if the grizzly back cover image had anything to do with a "vegetarian statement," to which he replied, "It has nothing to do with that. It has more to do with: the band itself, the sound of the band, the sound of the record, the songs on the record, the title, and the cover, going from wide to narrow. The band I think has many elements, some heavy, some beautiful. The record is balanced I think between some things that are really aggressive and disturbing and then really soothing." Or as Bottum explains, when viewed as one piece, the front and back covers go hand in hand with the music - "We were going for the beauty and the horror - it kinda works with the theme of the record."

You would assume that with work on the album now completed, there would be a collective "Ahhh" between the band members. Not so, according to Patton - "It's the same cycle each time. Kinda depressing actually. The day you finish the album, you must start thinking about the next one. Forget the songs, those songs are dead. As soon as they're on the album they're dead. Little corpses. Point is: you have to live with these corpses every day. Then you're going to dissect and cut into them a little differently each day. That's fun: to see how the songs develop. For the rest it's boring."

With such a struggle in the studio to complete the album, the prospects of peace, love, and understanding between all five band members on the ensuing tour didn't look particularly swell...

Chapter 10: Angel Dust, Part 2

Circa the release of 'Angel Dust,' hair metal was dead as a doornail (thankfully), as such styles as grunge, punk, and alt-rock had infiltrated the mainstream. However, there were a handful of bands that came out of the "big hair/cowboy boot scene" that were still thriving - Guns N' Roses being one obvious example. With their latest studio offering, 'Use Your Illusion,' having just been released in September 1991 and spawning such mega-hits as "You Could Be Mine," "Don't Cry," and "November Rain," Guns was in the midst of a worldwide tour - big enough to fill stadiums all on their own. And while there may have seemed to be a world of difference between the two bands both stylistically and with their public personas, Guns had been very vocal in the music press about being big-time FNM fans. So it shouldn't have come as a complete surprise when Guns invited FNM to support them on a European tour of outdoor stadiums during May and June 1992 (with FNM's old tour pals, Soundgarden, rounding out a three-band bill). Additionally, FNM would get the nod to tour similar mega-venues in the US from July through September, on a co-headlining bill between G n' R and the merry men in Metallica.

"Better than I thought," was Patton's description of how the tour was going early on. "I'd thought our presence there would be totally misplaced. We said: we may not like G n' R, we may not like playing in open air stadiums in broad daylight, where we sound like shit and look like shit on a much too large stage that wasn't built for us, and we may not like the fact that people are paying too much money for a ticket...that's all true. But the fact is: it's a very good opportunity to reach a large audience that otherwise wouldn't have come to see us. And that's good. The other side of it is that we want to headline again. It will happen in October. Playing with a roof over our heads. We're at our best like that."

One bright spot was crossing paths once again with Soundgarden, who were riding high with their commercial breakthrough, 'Badmotorfinger' (which had spawned such MTV/radio hits as

"Outshined" and "Rusty Cage"). As Kim Thayil explains, "This was weird - our first gigs with Faith No More, we opened for them, our next gigs with Faith No More they opened for us, and then our next gigs with Faith No More, we're opening for them again. That was before 'Superunknown' blew up [in 1994], so it might have turned all around again! We've toured with Faith No More probably more than anybody…well, I don't know, we played a lot of dates on Lollapalooza with Metallica and the Ramones [in 1996]. We also toured with the Ramones on the Big Day Out in Australia - they became fast friends." Soundgarden's drummer, Matt Cameron, remembers being awestruck by FNM during the tour. "That's when Faith No More was at their full, mighty power, and they were just incredible. Oh my God. They were just one of the most stunning live bands I've ever seen in my life."

Then-Guns N' Roses guitarist Gilby Clarke recalls FNM winning over the crowds. "I thought they got a great response. From the shows that I saw…I honestly don't remember how many times I saw them, but it was probably around ten times or so. I always thought they got a great response - they were extremely good at performing live." That said, Clarke admits to not exactly being a FNM fanatic. "No, I wasn't. [Laughs] Look, they were a great band. It's a matter of taste - it just wasn't my taste. It's kind of the same thing with Kid Rock for me. When he's got a great song, I love it man. It's just as a whole, the great songs were few and far between for me. So I wasn't really a fan of them. I watched them quite a few times on the tour, and I really loved Jim Martin - I thought he was a fucking fantastic guitar player. But yeah, I wasn't such a fan."

However, it didn't take long for FNM to voice their dissatisfaction with the G n' R traveling rock n' roll circus, which turned out to be one of the few (possibly only?) instances in rock history where an opening band continually unabashedly badmouthed the headliner both from the stage and in the press - and still finished the dates. And according to Bottum, the backstage area wasn't full of the hedonistic exploits that the Gunners supposedly indulged in. "It's like, seriously, the most boring backstage scene I've ever seen. Because there's so much security around. There are so many rules and so many regulations happening, it's just boring more than anything else. But I think that's the way they like it, honestly. Their security is so intense everywhere…it's hard to imagine that people would get away with anything without their permission." Patton agreed with Bottum about the backstage boredom level - "These are the most boring shows I've been to. The crowd is so safe. Backstage is so boring. All we do is eat..."

"G n' R and their management are like a small government," added Gould. "Axl [Rose] is the president, and his manager's a personal advisor. A couple of the other more visible band members are vice-presidents. Then there's the little guys who come underneath, to make sure only the right information is leaked out. They're dependent on the band for their living, so they will police themselves. Support bands are like other countries with whom they maintain a diplomatic front. Like, keep your mouth shut, enjoy the ride and everything will be cool. Open your mouth, and jeopardize your own position. It's an interesting thing to experience first hand." At another point, Gould compared G n' R's frontman to another peculiar bloke. "Touring with Axl has been like touring with Michael Jackson - although I think I've seen Michael Jackson more times on this tour that I have Axl!" Also, another bad habit of Axl and company - going on stage well past their projected start time, for reasons unknown - stuck in the bassist's craw. "We wouldn't do it, so I don't know why it is. I'd like to know myself!"

"I always feel a need to provoke, especially if we're supporting some band like Guns N' Roses and people aren't really listening," said Patton. "By insulting them, you make them at least look: it's the lowest common denominator." Even playing at the prestigious Wembley Stadium (famously known as the site of one of two Live Aid concerts in 1985) didn't seem to move the FNM singer - "I wouldn't go to the show. It's a spectator sport. If we can be annoying, then we've accomplished something. I think." But it was on stage that Patton saved his most outlandish comments for Axl. "I've seen Axl Rose every day," Patton told an audience at the Hamburg Marquee Club on June 2nd, during a rare FNM headlining set on a day off from the G n' R Euro jaunt. "I wanted to tell you something, ever since I first saw him he has this little piece of dried sperma right here on his lip. Wanna know what? It's mine!" And during an interview with a reporter, Patton pointed out that Mr. Rose had teleprompters on stage that flashed the song lyrics, in case his mind wandered mid-concert, and that his goal was "To take a shit right on top of those TV screens, in front of tens of thousands of people." Lastly,

Patton dropped this bombshell - "A juicy tidbit I heard the other day was that Warren Beatty was fucking Axl's girlfriend. I think he knows because we had a show cancelled the other day and maybe - just maybe - that had something to do with it."

Patton's band mates continued to air dirty laundry, as well. Gould: "Every band in the world might think they want to open for G n' R, but lemme tell you, it's been a real ugly personal experience having to deal with all the shit that surrounds this fucking circus. I've always hated that aspect of rock music, and I've never wanted to be part of it; so to find myself being associated with a tour this big kinda sucks." Roddy: "Besides, I'm getting more and more confused about who's who in Guns N' Roses, and it's blowing my mind. There's Dizzy and Iggy and Lizzy and Tizzy and Gilby and Giddy. Shit, man, onstage now there's a horn section, two chick backup singers, two keyboard players, an airline pilot, a basketball coach, a coupla car mechanics..."

A few weeks into the G n' R/Metallica Stateside trek, FNM appeared on the show 'Hangin' with MTV,' and provided one of the more memorable appearances of a rock n' roll band on an otherwise stinky show. The appearance (which aired on July 20th) included such standouts as an interview segment in which Gould picked his nose for an extended duration, as well as performances of three ditties - "Midlife Crisis," "Caffeine" (which would be included on the subsequent home video, 'Video Croissant'), and "A Small Victory" - the latter of which ends with the band confusing the show's host, as they continuously repeat blasts of noise in place of where the song's ending should have been.

But as Patton alluded to earlier, both the Euro and US dates that FNM shared with G n' R were chock full of cancelled dates. Gould explains a possible reason. "There was a rumor that Axl brought his psychic on tour with him, and it would be bad luck in any city that started with the letter 'M.' So he cancelled Manchester, Madrid, and Munich. He did Montreal, and that's when the riot happened."

The Montreal riot was certainly the low point of the tour. At a tour stop on August 8th at Olympic Stadium, Metallica singer/guitarist James Hetfield was accidentally burned by pyro during a rendition of "Fade to Black," which led to the band having to cut their set short (drummer Lars Ulrich got on the mic afterwards and promised they would return at a later date, to make up the show). With the crowd already on edge, G n' R decided to go on earlier than usual, which according to Clarke, didn't turn out so well. "I remember that *clearly*. That was another one which I didn't find out that there was tension between the bands [Metallica and Guns N' Roses] until like, years later, because we all got along really well on the road. I mean, every party after the show that I remember going to, Lars was there. I can honestly say, I think he hung out more with us on that tour than his own band! I thought we all were getting along great, until we all saw the same piece, where James was making fun of the band [an interview with Hetfield, in the April 15, 1993 issue of Rolling Stone]. But yeah, that night when that happened, we were backstage when the rioting happened.

The show, when what happened with James went down, we tried to get on stage early - we were trying to be the good guys, going, 'OK, let's not make it two hours after Metallica is done. Let's get right on stage, before they get uneasy,' and we went up there. But there were real problems - they didn't finish the staging on time. The monitors weren't finished. We went up there and every song was getting worse and worse, and it was just like one of those calls you have to make. It's like, 'Look, this isn't getting better. This is getting *worse.'* And it was like every song we do, things are feeding back, they're squealing. If we went off stage and said, 'Let's take a half hour break so they fix it,' that riot was going to happen. It's like, everybody was just on their edge, and because of the St. Louis riot before that [on July 2, 1991, when another G n' R performance was cut short], it was almost like it was doomed to happen. And that's what I remember about it when it went down. We went off stage and we were still in the arena. We didn't run to the hotel or anything - we were there when it was going down."

"I watched a lot of it. I watched police cars being turned over and people smashing windows. There's just no reason for destroying a perfectly brand new arena, just because you didn't get the concert you want. It was a little scary...there was a lot of adrenaline flowing. You're a person just like everyone else, and you're watching this go down, and you're going, 'I don't understand this.' It just really reveals humanity when you're seeing people acting like animals. It's like, 'How is this even possible to happen?' We were all at a rock concert a half an hour ago, and the same very people are destroying this venue and endangering people's lives. I don't know if 'scared' was the right thing, because I wasn't scared, like fearing for my life. I was just very confused. I was trying to get a handle on the situation. It was just a very dangerous situation."

The New York Times reported at the time that "The Montreal police said rioters among the 53,000 audience members smashed stadium windows with an uprooted street lamp, looted a souvenir boutique, burned a sports car and Guns N' Roses t-shirts and set dozens of small fires. About 300 club-wielding police officers chased rioters through the streets and fired tear gas to regain control. The police sealed off the area and shut down four nearby subway stations to prevent the riot from spreading to the transit system."

And to add to all the FNM vs. Axl shenanigans, the rift between Martin and the rest of the band appeared to be growing wider by the minute. "[Patton] had some weird mind control over Bill and Puffy," recalls the guitarist. "There were many embarrassing displays of megalomania expressed in the music press. Our presentation became very undignified, and as a result, I began to lose interest." Years later, Martin blamed the band's inability to turn down interviews during this time as another contributing factor to the rift. When asked if he could go back and do anything differently, he replied, "Number one thing: limit journalist access and impose more control over the interviews. Almost anyone could get an interview at that time. It was a free for all, and it hurt us."

When Axl finally caught wind of all the insults in the press, he called a private meeting between himself and all five FNM members. As Gould recalls, "We got busted one day, and we had to go apologize. It was like getting in the principal's office. We went and met Axl in his room, and to tell you the truth, he was super-cool and super-gracious. Then some guy comes in, and says, 'Now that everything's good, come over here.' We went into some trailer where there's some 'lesbian love act' going on. It just blew the whole thing. It was so fucking gross that we were just like, *'Oh God.'* We thought that we came to some kind of meeting of the minds, and obviously, we hadn't."

Martin also remembers this peace offering that ultimately fell flat. "Axl Rose and management confronted Bill and Patton for their awkward remarks in the press concerning Axl. Puffy denied association, Bill said it was something else, Patton was excused because he was an idiot. I began to avoid interviews and photo shoots, you know, all the things you need to do when you're in this business. It was exhausting. The band became more hostile because they didn't think I was pulling my weight, and they accused me of being one of 'them.' There was also a dishonest attempt to realign our business agreement. My disinterest deepened. We became estranged."

Additionally, Clarke recalls witnessing a "talking to" that Patton received backstage, from G n' R guitarist Slash. "The controversial part about the Guns N' Roses tour with Faith No More was the fact that Mike, the singer, used to talk a lot of shit about us while he was on stage. He'd have to answer for himself - his opinion of why he was doing that. But I was actually there with Slash when he had to tell them to knock it off. Slash's point was, 'Look, you're out here because the band wants you to be out here. If you don't want to be out here, don't do the tour.' But to bag on Guns N' Roses while you're opening for them as you're asked for a guest is not cool. I was actually with Slash once again when we had to play with them in Slash's Snakepit at some festival [in 1995], and we had to take a boat ride with them - myself, Slash, and the singer Mike - just by ourselves in a boat ride. After some of those uncomfortable incidents, it was not that much fun." Clarke also remembers Patton's "distance" during the Slash talk. "Mike didn't say anything. He didn't say, 'I'm not going to do it anymore.' He was just kind of listening, and he kind of agreed, 'OK, I won't say anything to the audience.' But he didn't really reveal anything."

Kim Thayil seems to side with the point that Slash was trying to get across to Patton. "Faith No More had more of a problem, because they had to go on right before Guns N' Roses. What I remember about that is what cool guys Slash and Duff [McKagan, G n' R's bassist] were - what friendly guys those guys were. We met Duff on a couple of occasions; we got along great with those guys. I talked to Axl a couple of times on the tour, and he specifically came and sat down next to me on occasion. He was a friendly guy - he was cool to me. I know Chris went and hung with Axl and got to talk to him, and Axl was very friendly to Chris. I don't think that Guns N' Roses is to blame, is one of the points I'm making. I'm saying specifically, Axl might have been a little bit dilatory in his arrival on stage. But that would probably cause more of a problem for the band Guns N' Roses than anyone else, and more for Faith No More than for us. Least for us. So I think it's unfair for Faith No

More to make fun of Guns N' Roses, when Guns N' Roses' hospitality was wonderful. By having us on tour, they really took care of us - the guys in Guns N' Roses' crew were really cool to our guys and crew. If someone wasn't cool, then he was having a bad day. And the guys in the band were really friendly and supportive of us."

Three years after the tumultuous FNM/G n' R dates came to a close, Patton still had words to say. "We care about our music. G n' R is just a show. They care more about their rock n' roll lifestyle than their music. You can see all that with Axl and Slash. They haven't talked with each other for months now." Once, when asked what his "worst moment on stage was," Bottum's response was quite telling - "All moments from the Guns N' Roses tour." Lastly, perhaps it was this Gould quote that best summed up his group's experience on the tour - "For these gigs, it's more like I finally get to the head of the line in the Department of Motor Vehicles."

With their G n' R association now over, FNM finally set out on a headlining tour of US theaters, to support 'Angel Dust,' which surprisingly, despite being largely considered by fans as their best studio album, turned out to not exactly be a blockbuster in their homeland. While 'Angel Dust' remains FNM's all-time best seller in just about every part of the world (peaking at #2 on the album charts in the UK and cracking the top ten in Austria, Norway, Germany, and Switzerland), the album peaked at #10 on the Billboard 200, going gold (compared to the platinum status of 'The Real Thing') and spending 19 weeks on the chart (compared to the 60 week chart residency of 'TRT'). Patton: "Our manager sent us a fax the other day, saying that since our record isn't doing so well, we better start hanging out with groupies to boost sales."

Bordin still felt that it was "mission accomplished" with FNM's fourth studio effort overall. "I honestly never thought it was commercial suicide. Lou Reed puts out 'Rock N' Roll Animal.' It was a nice hit record. Got him on the radio I'm sure. Then he puts out 'Metal Machine Music' and expects the same result. That I think is commercial suicide. The definition of insanity, even. When we released 'Angel Dust,' we didn't want the same result we'd had with 'The Real Thing.' I don't think any of us could stand to go through another photo session with Mike Patton expected to play the role of 'Hunk of the Month' for 12-year-olds."

But despite the album's underwhelming chart performance Stateside, it would go on to become probably the group's most influential release on other artists. Case in point, Devin Townsend - "'Angel Dust' ended up being one of the most influential records in my life. It was creatively willing to go to places that were uncompromising in an environment where they had commercial success. So there was an element of fearlessness to it, that was acceptable, because it had the right aesthetic. And that I thought was just such a great loophole for doing things that were out of the ordinary. It's like, as long as it looks and has the right logo, you can get away with almost anything. You make it look like what's commercially acceptable and you can say anything you want. And I hadn't recognized up until that point that that was truly like this way of getting away with things that you couldn't get away with if you made it as out-to-lunch as Bungle or whatever." That said, Townsend also offers some criticism - "I hated the sound of it. Still do, to be honest. I never liked the sound of it. And I was never a big fan of the drummer's tone. But just the combination of circumstances personally in that band created something that really opened my mind for a lot of things that allowed me to do whatever it is that I do in some ways."

Others agree with Townsend's earlier praise of the album, including Coheed and Cambria's Travis Stever - "Definitely 'Angel Dust' [is Stever's favorite FNM disc]. It is front-to-back a powerful record in every way. I love the guitar playing the most, obviously. Jim Martin had this classic style and grace in his playing that was the missing link between Tony Iommi and any guitar player in heavier music that's worth mentioning nowadays. All the right classic moves and notes, but at the same time, his own style twisted in it. The combination of the keyboards and where Mike Patton would go vocally was - and still is - a sound that can't be recreated. Many have tried, though." Ditto, Vision of Disorder's Mike Fleischmann - "At the time 'Angel Dust' came out, I had just started playing bass and was obsessed with learning every track on that album. I probably played along to it every night that summer. That album has these super heavy songs like 'Jizzlobber' and 'Malpractice,' but they also mix in some country with 'RV' and 'Midnight Cowboy' - they took chances. Following up a multi-platinum album with rotting animals on meat hooks in the record inlay was insane!"

HIM's Ville Valo also credits 'Angel Dust' for helping shape the singer/musician he would later become. "The big deal for me was 'Angel Dust.' That was at the time when I started taking music more seriously. I was skipping school and I basically learned how to sing to 'Angel Dust,' and 'Ritual de lo Habitual' by Jane's Addiction. The early '90s was a crazy good time - there were a lot of bands doing very original stuff. I was into Bad Brains and stuff like that. So yeah, they were hugely influential. And I never got to see them live. They only played Finland a couple of times - at a festival or something, and I was broke, so I didn't have the opportunity. And that was before YouTube. So that was a big thing that I missed."

"'Angel Dust' was something unheard of," continues Valo. "Not dissimilar to Type O Negative - they had a very peculiar sense of humor. And you didn't know, there was a lot of aggression in the music, but there was a lot of beauty in the music - and a lot of really 'bonkers' sense of humor. The cool thing about them was you weren't really sure what the hell they were about. At times they were danceable, at times they were funky, at times they were pop-y, at times they were headbanging to the max. And being at that age and listening to the remnants of the '80s stuff, it was something totally unheard of. And then I love the cover artwork and the videos. It was just so different. And yet at the same time, it was accessible. It wasn't odd for the sake of being odd. Kind of like a David Lynch movie - strange in a beautiful way, that you can't really forget. It was a big deal. And then the fact that all the musicians in the band are great. And Mike Patton as a singer is one of a kind."

Soulfly/ex-Sepultura mainman Max Cavalera was also particularly touched by 'Angel Dust.' "When they did 'Angel Dust,' they had reached the peak. That was the best thing they'd ever done. That album to me is still one of the best records ever made. That's a masterpiece of noise and weird-sounding stuff. It's heavy, it's melodic. Mike Patton is at his best vocally on this record."

House of Pain rapper and solo artist Everlast was also impressed - "'Angel Dust,' that album is amazing to me. I can't get enough of that record. It was just heavy. It was like the funky part of 'Epic' and all that stuff that became…there were a few imitators of that style, and they went hard with it. I still listen to 'Angel Dust' all the time. It's always in the rotation - working out or even before shows, I'll throw it on and vibe out. That's part of my 'comings up' music. So that's going to be stuck with me until I'm gone."

It also turns out that the album has become Mitts from Madball's go-to FNM disc throughout the years. "I would say 'Angel Dust.' It was definitely a lot darker album that 'The Real Thing.' When you're 18, from our culture of music, you almost didn't want to see bands you liked be commercially successful. You wanted them to still be underground; you kind of wanted to have it to yourself. I remember on 'The Real Thing,' they were all over the radio - top-40 radio was playing those guys. And then 'Angel Dust' didn't have that same success like 'The Real Thing.' That was actually a plus to me back then, when I was a rebellious teenager. I was kind of happy that all of a sudden, it was back a little more underground. But 'Angel Dust,' I really enjoyed that record - even nowadays, I can go back and listen to that album."

Across the pond in England however, 'Angel Dust' was always recognized for what it was - a masterpiece. This was confirmed once and for all in 2003, when the disc was crowned numero uno in a "50 Most Influential Albums of All Time" list in Kerrang!, beating out such all-time classic titles as Nirvana's 'Nevermind' (#2), Black Sabbath's 'Black Sabbath' (#3), Metallica's 'Master of Puppets' (#4), Sex Pistols' 'Never Mind the Bollocks' (#10), AC/DC's 'Back in Black' (#12), and Guns N' Roses' 'Appetite for Destruction' (#19).

Despite sagging record sales Stateside, it turned out FNM was still an in-demand concert attraction - hitting the road with the up-and-coming Helmet, who had just scored a hit with their major label debut, 'Meantime' (and its popular single/video, "Unsung"). However, they were not FNM's first choice as an opening band, according to Patton - the beefcake dance act Right Said Fred (who had scored a smash with "I'm Too Sexy") was. "We wanted them to tour America with us, but when we shopped the idea around the promoters - which is what you do when you set up a tour, throw some bait in the water - the reaction wasn't too good. It's too bad, 'cause I would go to a tour like that, out of morbid curiosity. It would be great! Oh man, there'd be brawls. But that's the beautiful thing. People like that should be fucked with, they should have one arm behind their backs. They would be perfect for that. I don't know why we like Right Said Fred so much. Maybe it's the baldness - they're so slick.

They're crass, commercial and goofy at the same time. They're amazing. Also the fact that they worked in a gym is great. I love that."

And as evidenced by a performance in the early morning hours of October 2nd at the Impaxx Night Club & Theater (at a "97 Rock appreciation party" in Buffalo), the band was still stirring up controversy - with a performance that would have made GG Allin green with envy. The Buffalo News reported that "Patton enjoyed the show - during which, witnesses claim, he took off his clothes, exposed himself and then performed lewd acts with a microphone - and would like to come back and repeat those antics. 'I loved it and would do it all over again if I could,' Patton and FNM said in a statement to the Buffalo News released Sunday by the metal band's record label, Slash/Reprise. Barbara Balchick, a representative of the Cleveland record label and Faith No More, told The News: 'Mike said he had a great time in Buffalo and the band did, too. They view the performance as a total rock n' roll assault. No malice was intended. They'd love to do it again if 97 Rock would let them'."

The article went on to explain of the incident - "A spokesman for the Southside Station said that two complaints were filed after the show, and four witnesses have spoken to the police. Witnesses have said that Patton removed his clothes, exposed himself, turned his back to the crowd, bent down, and then performed lewd acts with the microphone. Also, witnesses said, another member of the band used his guitar neck to perform lewd acts with the singer. 'I've been to many rock shows, but I've never seen anything as sick and disgusting as this," John Ganter said. 'Everybody there was appalled at what Patton did. They just wanted him to get off the stage and get out.' Ms. Balchick said that Patton was injured when several patrons threw beer containers at him. 'Mike got hit and cut in the head, and had to have several stitches,' she said."

"Mary Baker, who also attended the event and filed a complaint with the police, said that Patton grew angry with the crowd and hit her friend, who was standing near the stage, with the microphone. She said Patton also vomited and spit at the crowd. 'That guy is just plain sick, and his whole act was a disgrace,' she said. Jay Desiderio, part owner of the Impaxx, has said that after the incident, the club's security people threw Faith No More out of the club as soon as possible."

A little more than a week after the Buffalo debacle, I witnessed a far less controversial FNM performance, on the first date of a two-nighter at NYC's Roseland Ballroom (October 9th). Wiggling my way as close to the front of the stage as possible for FNM's set, the band hit the stage to an instrumental recording of Europe's 1986 cheese metal tour de force, "The Final Countdown," while four of the five band members jogged around the stage, before breaking into jumping jacks and push-ups (the same member that refused to strip down into his skivvies for the Ross Halfin photo shoot a few years earlier choose to stand off to the side of the stage). The set-opening one-two punch of "Caffeine" and "Death March" was spot-on, but I soon realized I had bit off more than I could chew, as the crush of bodies at the front of the stage was far too much to bear - as well as numerous numbskulls crowdsurfing and several times almost providing a Dr. Martens boot to the skull of yours truly. Retreating back, I took in the show from a much safer vantage point.

Something that became clear immediately from the performance was that Patton's on-stage shtick had changed dramatically from earlier performances I had witnessed. Gone was the bratty personality that would spit water and offer spastic dance moves and animated facial expressions - in its place was a stance he now utilized often on stage, in which he squatted down to sing, and during the more intense parts that required hollering, he would violently throw his body forward, to cause the mic cable to fling over his shoulder. And one more acute observation - from this tour onward, the days of Patton regularly going shirtless on stage had come to a close.

Overall, one of the best FNM performances I've ever witnessed, which is also remembered for the band leaving the stage after their encores (one of which I recall was a cover of the Dead Kennedys' "Let's Lynch the Landlord"), the house lights going on, then after a while, the lights being shut back off, with only Patton, Martin, and Bottum returning to the stage. With Patton sitting behind Puffy's kit, the trio launched into "Edge of the World," while a young lady from the audience came up on stage to sing the lyrics.

It was also around this time that FNM's cover of the Commodores' "Easy" was released as a single (December 4th in Europe, April 4th, 1993 in the US). The single would turn out to be a smash throughout Europe - topping the charts in Austria, while peaking at #2 in

Norway and #3 in the UK, among other similarly high placements. In the US, a four-track EP was issued, 'Songs to Make Love to,' which featured "Easy," as well as a song sung entirely in German, "Das Schutzenfest," the aforementioned "Let's Lynch the Landlord," and a reappearance of "Midnight Cowboy." The most curious of the tracks, "Das Schutzenfest," was a tribute of sorts to German pop singer Heino (and was *not* a Heino cover, as some have assumed), of which Patton explained the lyrics being about "The October festivities in Munich [Oktoberfest]. It's a love song: an old man and his friends are hunting for game and he sees a big fat woman and falls in love with her." Even with such delightful selections on the EP, 'Songs to Make Love to' would reach no higher than #58 on the US charts.

A video would be filmed for "Easy," which combined footage of the band in concert with shots of the members lip-synching the tune while relaxing in a hotel room, surrounded by drag queens. Bottum: "When we first started talking about doing the video, we were toying around with doing a low-budget realistic perspective of the band. Someone - not in the band - thought it might be nice to get shots of us hanging around in the hotel room with girls. My mom saw the video and told me she couldn't believe that we had used real girls. When I told her that they were really drag queens, she was shocked." The video also left a lasting impression on Everlast - "And then they do the weird cover of 'Easy,' with the transvestite video. They were just wild motherfuckers, man. And after meeting and spending some time around Mike, I can see how much of that was his madness!" In addition to the arrival of the "Easy" clip, another FNM release hit the racks on February 2nd - the band's second-ever longform home video, 'Video Croissant.' Collecting all of the band's promo videos up until that point (including the rarely-seen "Surprise! You're Dead!" clip, and various humorous tidbits in-between the videos), the tracklistings varied from country to country.

FNM would end 1992 by touring arenas and large venues throughout Europe (with L7 as support), before returning to the US in early '93 and headlining a triple bill that also included stoner rockers Kyuss and the all-female punk trio, Babes in Toyland. According to Kyuss' John Garcia, the tour remains a standout. "I just remember all those guys being extremely gracious and extremely awesome and cool. Jim and Mike, all the guys. Holy shit, what an amazing band. And we saw them I think in their prime. It was a great bill too - it was Kyuss, Babes in Toyland, and Faith No More. What an eclectic tour - three individuals, no styles were similar. It was just awesome to be a part of. I'll be honest with you, back in my early to mid twenties, I don't really - intentionally - remember a lot, because of just my 'state of mind.' But I do remember that being an awesome tour and those guys being extremely gracious, and so calm, cool, and cordial."

Right around the time that the FNM/Kyuss/Babes triple bill would kick off, Faith No More got the nod to perform a pair of tunes on 'The Tonight Show,' whose host, Jay Leno, had just replaced the program's long-standing successor, Johnny Carson, less than a year before. The appearance (broadcast on January 13, 1993) would include renditions of "Midlife Crisis" and "Easy," and feature Patton sporting a Colorado Rockies baseball cap, while Gould was clad in a black t-shirt emblazoned with a humongous image of Gene Simmons' mug, complete with demon make-up. Gould's appreciation of Kiss could be detected once again the following year, when he and members of Tool and Rage Against the Machine offered up a rendition of "Calling Dr. Love" (under the name of Shandi's Addiction) for a tribute disc, 'Kiss My Ass: Classic Kiss Regrooved.'

1993 would also prove to be a most memorable year for Bottum for two completely different personal reasons. First, his decision to come out, via an interview with the gay publication, The Advocate. Bottum: "I'd like to say that I'm totally together about it, but it does kinda freak me out. From now on anytime my name will be brought up, my sexual preference will be one of the first things discussed. It's a way of categorizing people that seems kind of creepy to me. I mean, it shouldn't be like that, right? How many aspects of a personality are there? So many." He went on to say that one of the reasons for his decision to go public was because "Kids who are into hard rock and who may be dealing with the possibility of being gay themselves don't see a lot of positive role models." Bottum also was asked how his band members handled the news - "My singer and I talk about our sexual exploits. When he joined the band, I said, 'Listen, you know I'm gay, right?' And he said, 'Yeah, I kinda figured.' From there on out we would tell each other what we were up to." And finally, in response to being asked

"Which rock stars would you like to sleep with?", Bottum responded, "Kurt Cobain, of course."

More than ten years after giving the Advocate interview, Bottum gave more insight as to why he made the decision at this point. "I don't know, it happens at different times in all gay people's lives. To the rest of the band I think it might have come out of the blue and was awkward - but only initially. We were all free thinkers, independently motivated and proud of who we are and it's never been an issue with any of the band members. Including Jim Martin, the guy who you'd typically think would have issues regarding such." However, it turned out that at least one of Bottum's band mates had no idea about his sexuality before going public. Gould: "I found out by reading it in a music paper. I really hadn't known he was gay. It was never discussed. So it kinda pissed me off. It's not that him being gay is an issue, but hearing about it that way, I guess that I felt personally insulted."

And the second item regarding Bottum during this period was the fact that he had developed a problem with heroin. As Gould explains, "It was hard because when he was on heroin, which was through the end of the 1993 tour, he was not the guy I'd known for 20 years. He was somebody else who I really didn't like. That's really horrible. It sucks. Roddy dealt with the problem. He's doing great now. But I'm definitely still working it out with him personally. It'll probably take a couple of years." Patton sounded sympathetic towards Bottum and his troubling situation...at least at first. "Well it was a while before I realized what was going on. I didn't know what dilated pupils meant back then. I was a clean boy. But well, yeah, you start feeling sorry and you try to help, and then you get really fucking angry - 'You fuck me in the ass and I'll fuck you in the ass. If you're gonna fucking die, then die. Fuck you'!"

Years after his struggle with substances, Bottum admitted, "Yeah, I got into a lot of drugs during one phase of the band and went to a hospital to get help. The band was ultimately really helpful and kind of pushed me in the direction that I needed to go. It's funny, when you're doing drugs, for the most part you think you're getting away with it and no one knows you're doing it. It's only later that I realized that everyone knew all along. It was one of those life things. Didn't have so much to do with the band but circumstantially, we were doing the band at the time and it got in the way of our art and our business."

The 'Angel Dust' tour finally wrapped up (after a springtime trek through Japan, Australia, and New Zealand) with a summertime European festival jaunt, during which time Gould's death metal side project, Brujeria (Spanish for "witchcraft") issued their debut album on July 6th via Roadrunner Records, 'Matando Güeros,' which featured a very disturbing front cover image, of someone holding a severed human head. Gould would be listed under an alias on the album credits - "Güero Sin Fe" (the bassist would also appear on a follow-up release, 'Raza Odiada,' two years later). The final date of the 'AD' tour would be a headlining spot on the second night of the Phoenix Festival, in Stratford-Upon-Avon, England, on July 17th, on an eclectic bill that also featured House of Pain, the Young Gods, and Björn Again.

Little did the public know, this would be the last FNM gig to feature a long-time member in its ranks.

Mike Patton. New York, 1990 [Photo by Steven J. Messina]

Mike Patton. New York, 1990 - Note the Mr. Bungle "There's a Tractor in My Balls" shirt, which was worn in the "Epic" video [Photo by Steven J. Messina]

"Big Sick Ugly" Jim Martin. New York, 1990 - Note the "A Tribute to Cliff Burton" shirt, which was also worn in the "Epic" video [Photo by Steven J. Messina]

On-stage bedlam at L'Amour! New York, 1990, L-R: Bill Gould, Voivod's Denis "Piggy" D'Amour, Mike Bordin, Soundgarden's Chris Cornell, Mike Patton, Voivod's Denis "Snake" Bélanger (masked), Jim Martin, Soundgarden's Kim Thayil (masked), author smooshed somewhere in the crowd [Photo by Greg Fasolino]

Mr. Bungle. Georgia, 1995, L-R: Trey Spruance and Mike Patton [Photo by David Hornbuckle]

Mike Patton at Maquinária Festival. Brazil, 2009 [Photo by Silvio Tanaka - tanaka-foto.com]

Roddy Bottum at Maquinária Festival. Brazil, 2009
[Photo by Silvio Tanaka - tanaka-foto.com]

Bill Gould at Maquinária Festival. Brazil, 2009 [Photo
by Silvio Tanaka - tanaka-foto.com]

Jon Hudson at Maquinária Festival. Brazil, 2009 [Photo by Silvio Tanaka - tanaka-foto.com]

Bill Gould and Mike Bordin at Maquinária Festival. Brazil, 2009 [Photo by Silvio Tanaka - tanaka-foto.com]

Bill Gould, Mike Patton, Mike Bordin, and Jon Hudson.
New York, 2010 [Photo by Greg Prato]

Mission accomplished. New York, 2010 [Photo by Greg
Prato]

Chapter 11: Exit Martin

After the completion of the 'Angel Dust' tour, rumors began to circulate once more that FNM was on the verge of splitting up. And quotes such as this one from Bordin didn't exactly throw water on the fire - "Who knows what's gonna happen? I don't know what's gonna happen. I expect a journalist to wanna try to fucking peek under the curtain. But I'm honestly not going to help you do that, because I know nothing. I know nothing."

On the other hand, Gould sounded more hopeful about FNM's future, post 'AD' - "I think it was more a question of why do we stay together after 'The Real Thing.' I don't think any of us were prepared for that two year period on the road. 'The Real Thing' tour I look back on as a lotta hell. The record wasn't successful right up until the end. When the success came we were too tired, too shell-shocked to be able to appreciate it and, God, we hated those songs so fucking much. I really didn't want to go through it again. 'Angel Dust' was hard to write. And it was even harder for us to get ourselves together to go and tour again. But we knew the record had the potential to really do something, and this time I think we've all played well, and really enjoyed the songs. Now I think we're all feeling a need to reinvent FNM. But it's a natural thing, like equilibrium I guess. The boat rolls to one side and you have to counteract to the other. I think we all feel a need to shift again." Bottum also saw a promising future ahead. "I think everyone felt pretty confident on this tour. And now I'd like to see us really stretch. I'd like to see FNM do something real experimental, like writing a classic top-40 pop single."

Even Martin seemed set on staying put - "Take into consideration the prestige of the band. The power to attract women and a reasonably pleasurable lifestyle. You've gotta be out of your nut to throw something like that away. You can be sure Jim Martin will see this thing through. No matter how long it takes." That said, by the time a video was filmed for "Another Body Murdered" (FNM's best-forgotten collaboration with Boo-Yaa T.R.I.B.E. for the 'Judgment Night Motion Picture Soundtrack') in late 1993, Martin was nowhere to be seen - Gould had played six-string on the song's recording, and also in its rarely-seen video clip.

There were always hints in the press that Martin was the "odd man out" in the band, as evidenced when Patton once selected the guitarist as "Most Annoying Band Member," and explained, "'Cause he's 66 years old. It's really hard to live with someone that old. He's cranky, late and slow. He's Grandpa. He can't do anything like us, his bones are brittle, he's gonna die soon." A similar sentiment was offered by a FNM roadie, who was quoted as saying, "Jim Martin is so old it takes him three hours to shit." And when the guitarist offered such quotes as "The main thing in life is to eat food, occupy your time and have somewhere to bury your bone" to the press, it wasn't exactly in line with the more progressive train of thought that such thriving bands as Nirvana were championing, but more a throwback to the days of party hearty metal. Still, Martin didn't seem eager to fly the coop - "There's no way that any of us can swim out of this unscathed. If somebody left the band now it would take 'em years to get free of the web. Perhaps a lifetime..."

However, in December 1993, Jim Martin was handed his walking papers from FNM...via fax. As Bordin explains, "We really gave it every attempt. The last gig we did was the Phoenix Festival. When we came home, especially me, Bill, and Mike realized that what we'd done on 'Angel Dust' was actually pretty cool and it worked really good. There was stuff we could continue doing. We wrote some songs, and a couple months after that we played them to Jim. We asked him, 'Hey, what are you gonna put on this?' It's always been us writing a framework and he's thrown parts on top of it. It was obvious that it wasn't working. It was impossible, but we gave it a chance to see what would happen. Because we knew it would be a big hassle to do this, not only legally but time-wise."

Gould: "Jim had a real big image. He had a cowboy hat, a cigar and a beard. In a way we had to make a decision, because he had an image, and a lot of people associated the band with his image. You have to choose if you wanna put up with this fucking shit for the style or sacrifice the image for the substance. You're gonna be like Whitesnake and Poison, or you're gonna be real? A lot of people were telling us that we were doing a lot of stupid things. We had a hard time convincing people that we knew what the fuck we were doing."

Patton on the other hand, pulled no punches - "We voiced our opinion, years before all this happened. We always hated each other, and finally we decided to do something about it instead of griping like fucking children." Although the singer would also admit that openly showing his dislike of the guitarist on stage may not have been the right thing to do. "You fuck someone and you have an orgasm. Then you fart and cry and everything just kinda comes out. That's what it's like sometimes on stage. It feels good to talk shit on stage, and afterwards, I'm going, 'Oh shit, what did I do? That was really stupid.' This definitely worsened our relationship. But you gotta do what you gotta do. We're not so good at communicating. We're getting better, because it used to be really bad. You hear things and there was never any real confrontation. I think towards the end we should've had more of that. The stage was almost this playground where anyone could say anything and it would be OK. That's bullshit, because you're supposed to be up there playing, not fighting."

And despite the earlier quote that "Jim Martin will see this thing through," years after his exit, Martin offered a different appraisal of the festering situation - "I actually felt relieved; a great pressure had been suddenly removed and the pain began to leave my body." Interestingly, the last FNM member to be fired before Martin was disappointed to see the guitarist go. Chuck Mosley: "I thought [firing Martin] was as big if not bigger a mistake than getting rid of me - just because he had a lot of pull with the big part of their crowd at the time. And he was 'the personality,' y'know? There was something people could identify to. That Jagger/Richards, Plant/Page thing was gone."

Years later, Gould had a slightly different take on his former band mate. "Jim was a really interesting guy. Smart guy, but different. I don't think he accepted our kind of lifestyle, if that's the right word. His was more traditional...like a back to nature, rock and roll, truck driving, Ted Nugent-listening kind of guy. We were kind of a weird band anyway, but putting him in my band was kind of an experiment to see 'What if we had this and we mixed that?' and it worked. But the maintenance gets hard. After a couple of years, everyone wants to do something for themselves, and what he wanted to do for himself was more guitar, more guitar solos and things like that. There was nothing wrong with what he wanted to do, but it wasn't what we wanted to do, and we couldn't explain that to him. It also has to do a lot with us growing up. I mean, we were in our twenties…you get to a certain point where you have to communicate with other people. You either do or you don't. Bands go through that. Everyone does, for whatever reason."

After departing, Martin took the classy route, and refused to continue mudslinging with his former band mates in the media. "There has been much negative rhetoric in the press, and it was my choice to either play their game, fight with them and let the press spin it, or leave them to play with themselves and allow you to make a decision based on the work I left behind. In an effort to avoid the negativity, I chose the latter."

After leaving FNM, Martin would go on to issue a solo album, 'Milk and Blood,' in 1997 (which featured a re-recording of "Surprise! You're Dead!"), would join punk rock veterans Fang for their 2001 split release (with Dr. Know and the Hellions), 'Fish & Vegetables,' and appeared on recordings by Metallica ("Low Man's Lyric" off 1997's 'ReLoad' and "Tuesday's Gone" off 1998's 'Garage Inc') and Primus ("Eclectic Electric" off 1999's 'Antipop'). Martin would also gain notoriety as being a "champion pumpkin farmer" (seriously!) and spoke about his old pal Cliff Burton on the third night of Metallica's four night stand at the Fillmore in San Francisco, to celebrate the band's 30th anniversary, on December 9, 2011. As evidenced by Martin's appearance nowadays, he looks absolutely nothing like he did during his "Faith No More days," as the long curly mop and Zappa-like facial hair have all been shaved off, and his trademark red tinted glasses have been stowed away.

On June 8, 2013, Martin supplied guitar for Infectious Grooves at Metallica's multi-band Orion Festival, which saw the guitarist cross paths once more with Kyuss singer John Garcia, who was also performing at the festival (with Vista Chino). "I recently ran into Jim in Detroit at the Orion Festival - what a cool guy. He had his kids running around and was playing pinball. I didn't recognize him at first, but went up and gave him a big hug. It was awesome to see him."

To this day, Martin has quite a few supporters on his side, and you can certainly make a claim that musically, there was a "Jim Martin era" of FNM, as well as a "post-Jim Martin era." As one-time Guns N' Roses guitarist Gilby Clarke explains, "What I liked about him is I think without Jim, that band would have been - in my opinion - like a top-40, almost rap band. He brought that great, classic rock guitar playing to it. He had a great tone, he had great parts. To me, he is what made the band a 'rock n' roll band.' Where I think without it, I don't know what direction it would have went in. What I did like about the band was what Jim brought to it, and like I said, brought in that guitar and really fused together that modern hip-hop kind of thing, but with a rock guitar player in it. Which to me, created the sound of the band."

Devin Townsend offers similar thoughts to Clarke's, and recalls meeting Mr. Martin once upon a time. "I met Jim a bunch of times. I was doing some work with Jason Newsted at Jason's house years ago. I guess Jason and Jim knew each other, and I met Jim. I think I was a little young and a little standoffish, and he was definitely a little bizarre, so the combination of it, I remember thinking to myself, 'I don't know if I have much in common with this cat.' But I guess it's telling to me that after 'Angel Dust,' I didn't listen to them anymore. There's something about 'The Real Thing' that I loved - it's often the case with bands that you get that tension in the band, where there's that one guy that doesn't pose in his underwear and whatever. And within the band, everybody is like, 'This guy's an asshole. I hate this guy. I can't wait to get rid of him.' But then when he's gone, that tension that came from being this awkward situation made the music a little less interesting to me, to be honest. There's an element of Jim Martin just being sloppy that was different than Metallica and it was different than Anthrax."

Soulfly/ex-Sepultura's Max Cavalera was also a "Martin man," too. "I think he had that metallic sound - almost thrashy in some songs. And then he'd do super-melodic solos and complete heavy metal-influenced kind of stuff...and then he'd go into a whole jazz section, and then a blues section. Completely amazing. I don't know how they could change from a heavy song into a slow ballad, and into a blues song...or 'Midnight Cowboy.' How the hell do they do that? I always thought Jim Martin was a great character - even the way he looked, with the big puffy hair and the glasses. He looked very iconic. They were never the same after they lost him. They could never really get back to that original state. They did great records, but it wasn't as good as with Jim Martin."

Lastly, it turns out that Carcass' Jeff Walker is a member of "Team Martin," as well. "I'm one of those sad losers that when Jim

Martin was no longer in the band I felt they lost something. They would argue against that, but there was something about the character of Jim Martin in the band that made it kind of cool."

Chapter 12: King for a Day

Around the time period of 'Angel Dust' and 'King for a Day,' two members of Faith No More married their respective girlfriends - Mike Bordin to Merilee (a chef and who does food styling for photographs), and Mike Patton to Cristina (an interior designer and architect). Mike B and Merilee remain married to this day (and even appeared on an episode of 'Who Wants to Be a Millionaire?' in 2001), while Mike P and Cristina (who resided in both San Francisco and Italy, as Cristina is a native of Italy) appear to no longer be an item, as Patton explained on an appearance on the Lovelines radio program in 2006. "I got married when I was 24 - I'm 38 now - and I've been separated for five years. But it's a good thing - I feel like it had to happen. But it's for those reasons you talk about - two people wanting different things. Even though we knew each other really well when we got married, hey, it doesn't get easier."

Soon after, the two then-former bachelors (along with Gould and Bottum) had to endure what is probably the least fun part of being in a long-standing rock group - a band mate leaving and conducting a search to locate a suitable replacement. Some bands take the "cattle-call route," but in FNM's case, they didn't have to resort to placing an ad in the paper. In fact, they had someone in mind early on, who seemed like a logical choice - Geordie Walker of Killing Joke. Bordin: "He was a member in my mind. I really wanted him to be in the band. We all really liked [Killing Joke], that was a great band. In their day, that was the fucking shit! It was really cool to play with him." But according to Gould, the potential Walker/FNM union fizzled out. "It's weird. Geordie hasn't played with a lot of other bands, and he came into a situation where we had a lot of songs already written. It would've taken a lot of time to work things out, and we just wanted to move ahead and get a record out."

Ultimately, it turned out that Martin's replacement was right under Mr. Patton's nose - Trey Spruance from Mr. Bungle. However, Patton was surprisingly not exactly thrilled about the idea. "I was actually against it," Patton admitted. "You don't wanna be too much with someone. It gets a little incestuous. It was like we'd been married for a few years and now we could go and fuck our brains out and play with some other people. It was like being reborn. It was liberating. I'd had some bad water under the bridge with him and I didn't wanna be in another aggravating situation. But you do what's best for the music." But once Spruance was welcomed into the FNM fold, it sounded as if Patton had changed his tune - "Trey came in kind of half-way through when a lot of the songs were already written. Some of the stuff he helped with writing as a lot were gearing towards guitar. It was nice to have a guitarist who could play and had some input. It was like being reborn."

With Bungle refusing to follow any traditional verse/chorus/ verse song structures, it would have been understandable to assume that Spruance would struggle to refine his approach for the FNM album that would be titled 'King for a Day...Fool for a Lifetime.' But according to the guitarist, this wasn't the case. "Well, I've played in straightforward kinds of things before, but never anything where people's livelihoods depended on it. Musically, the hardest thing was just relating to their vision, because the guitar parts are cake - they're easy. I used to listen to old FNM and I wanted to hear the guitar do certain things and possibly strengthen the band, but they weren't really interested."

But as Patton pointed out, a good portion of the material on 'King for a Day' was written before Spruance entered the picture, which Gould also confirmed - "I had a lot to do with writing these songs. About two weeks after resting from our last tour, Puffy and I went into the studio and just started playing - getting grooves together and writing. We wrote the record without a guitar player, from the ground up, so the riffs were written on the bass first. That way, the record was anchored from the start."

The recording of 'King for a Day' would mark several "firsts" for the band. Firstly, it would be the first FNM studio album that had no production input from Matt Wallace. This time, Andy Wallace (no relation between the two Wallaces) took sole production credit - and had previously worked with the likes of Nirvana ['Nevermind'], Slayer ['Reign in Blood,' 'South of Heaven,' 'Seasons in the Abyss'], and Jeff Buckley ['Grace']. "He's a dry sort of guy," explained Patton. "Really just bone dry and not having too much of a personality that he was forcing on the band or a certain trademark stamp that he could slap on us was nice.

With our last producer, there wasn't a whole lot of professional respect. We were more like friends, so if we would make a suggestion or he would make suggestion, we'd both tell each other 'Fuck off.' For this, there was a little bit of distance so he was easier to work with."

Bottum agreed that a change was required in the producer's chair. "I think we pretty much needed an overhaul in our sound. There was a lot going on in the last couple albums. There were a lot of changes. I think what we tried to do is strip down the sound and make things sound a little bit more basic. We've always been a band that's prided ourselves in doing new things and not ever repeating ourselves, so with that in mind, it's kind of ridiculous to keep using the same producer." Bordin weighed in, as well - "Andy really helped us get what we wanted rather than impose how he does it. That was the real attractive point. When you hear Soul Asylum or White Zombie or all the beautiful Slayer albums or Nirvana, they all sound unique unto those bands, and that was real important for us, because after so long playing together, we gotta know how we sound."

And the second "first" for FNM was the fact that 'King for a Day' was their first studio album to not be tracked in California, but rather in Upstate New York, at Bearsville Studios. Gould: "We usually record in San Francisco, and there's always distractions. I have to pay my parking tickets or some bullshit, show up late, people are running in and out, friends come over...but this was cool. The studio's out in the middle of the fucking forest. It's on this dirt road, there's just this studio and a cabin for two miles. It's just like sensory deprivation. But the good thing about it was we had nothing else to do but record. We actually tried to stay in the studio as much as we could, because if we left the studio there was nothing to do."

Nothing to do...except get into what sounded like a pretty gnarly car accident. "We had these rental cars, right," explained Gould. "And we kept bursting the tires on these cars on the dirt roads outside the studio. So we had the guy drive out an hour to fix it every time. We did it with three cars, and he finally gave us a nice car thinking we'd take better care of it." Bordin picks up the story - "So the day we got it we were out driving and got clipped by a smaller car, and we flipped upside-down and skidded for like 100 feet, with sparks and everything." Thankfully, everyone survived intact, but FNM were banned from renting any more cars from the rental company, which as Gould points out, actually helped the band focus more on the task at hand - "Once we ran out of cars, we had nothing else to do but stay in the studio."

Looking back on the 'KFAD' sessions years later, Patton had plenty of positive memories. "Probably I can say that 'King For A Day' was the funnest one to make, so that may be my favorite. 'Cause it was a pleasant experience making it, a lot of the others had dramas going on and really left a bad taste. I'm not even talking about the music, I'm just talking about looking back and remembering the experience of recording the record. I would have to say 'King For A Day,' probably."

While 'KFAD' may have been the most fun FNM album for Patton, it was not for Bottum. Gould: "Roddy wasn't really into the music, so that was difficult. Roddy was just coming out of rehab, and I guess this is common with people with substance abuse and quit - they reevaluate all of their relationships, to see what put them there in the first place. And I think we were one of the biggest things that were occupying his life, and I think he saw us in a very negative light. He definitely wasn't carrying his weight. We wanted him to - he just wasn't there." The keyboardist also remembers that the death of Kurt Cobain (with whom Bottum had forged a friendship with) on April 5, 1994 was another distressing event, as well. "I was friends with Kurt mostly through Courtney. We became close fast. His death was really a serious blow to me - but reinforcing, because I'd stopped doing dope myself and it was a reminder of where I could have gone with it."

"I knew the situation was bad, they were arguing a lot," Bottum added later. "I went to see him a week before he killed himself, hoping there was something I could do to help. When it became clear that there really wasn't, I left. Knowing...knowing what would happen. It was clear where he was going. The last thing I said to him was, 'You're going to die.' I felt pretty guilty, but there was nothing I could do. When somebody really wants to die there's really nothing you can do to stop them." But this wasn't the end of tumultuous events in Bottum's life during this period, as he also lost his father to cancer, split up with his longtime boyfriend, and endured the suicide of another friend (besides Cobain). "My first impulse was to leave the band," admits Roddy. "But I couldn't just let it go, it was something I helped start, it's very important to me."

Despite it being the latest line-up's "honeymoon period," FNM's new addition didn't exactly see eye-to-eye with his mates during the recording process. Spruance: "It was at Bearsville, it was a fucking amazing studio. I thought Andy was in a weird position - he's being told to make this band that usually sounds like they're made of diamonds and has a billion dollar production, to make it sound like a garage band. And here we were in Bearsville, the one place where Puffy's drum sound sounds like his drums - that huge fucking sound of his. But, 'Nah, get rid of the room mics, we're tightening this thing up to make it sound like a chunky Black Flag record.' I'm like, 'What the fuck'?" But the others were quite content with the final product, especially Patton, who stated at the time, "Doing the record was kind of like taking a really satisfying shit."

Stylistically, 'KFAD' followed the last two FNM albums' lead - there was not a single style that FNM wasn't afraid to take head on, and make their own. As Gould explained, "Some bands, like the Ramones, can do the same record over and over again. That's totally cool - I really admire the Ramones. But we just aren't built like that." Or as Bordin clarified, "Instead of putting everything into every song, we wanted to take things out and make them a bit simpler. Perhaps that's what you'd call a 'pop' or lighter feel." And finally Patton offered his thoughts - "This time we actually followed our impulses. We did what was in our heads. I don't know if we should've done it, but at least we did it. I think this is a pop record."

Pop record? Certainly, such tunes as "Evidence," "Caralho Voador," and "Just A Man" coulda/shoulda crossed over to the mainstream (of course, they didn't, as the pop charts were clogged at the time by such blah schlock as Hootie and the Blowfish, Alanis Morissette, Bush, Live, etc.). But elsewhere, 'KFAD' featured some of the most brutal/heaviest compositions of their entire career - especially "The Gentle Art of Making Enemies," "Cuckoo for Caca," and "Ugly in the Morning." I recall the first time I heard 'KFAD' was when it was broadcast in its entirety over the radio shortly before its official March 28, 1995 release, via local Long Island "alt-rock" station, WDRE. And I can honestly say that out of all the FNM albums I heard around the time they were first issued, it was the one that I latched onto the quickest. So in a way, I suppose Patton's belief about 'KFAD' being a "pop record" was correct.

Something else that should be noted about 'KFAD' is that it was the first FNM album to clearly turn its back on guitar solos, as quite a few of the tunes included no traditional lead break (the absence of Martin obviously factored into this). Fast forward to the "nu metal" movement circa the dawn of the 21st century, and many bands were following FNM's lead vis-à-vis the "anti-solo." In fact, this anti-solo craze became so widespread that even the mighty Metallica was affected, as their 2003 sonic stinkbomb, 'St. Anger,' featured barely any Kirk Hammett leads. Limp Bizkit's Wes Borland agrees that FNM played a role in this shift - "Yeah, I think so. Them, and also the 'noise solos' of Helmet - they're guitar solos, but all the stuff that's a lead on 'Meantime' is all over the place and noisy. It sounds like someone's pulled the plug out of the amp and smashed it into the drum set, a lot of the time."

As with every Patton-era FNM recording, the band had selected an explosive opening number to kick off the proceedings - "Get Out" - which would be the only track on the album to be completely composed by Patton. As Bordin pointed out about the tune, "[Patton] definitely has come into his own. 'Get Out', he wrote drums, bass, guitar - that's his song. To me, that sounds like a FNM song, and it's supposed to work that way. That's real gratifying and that's a big part of why we're still here." "Ricochet" continues with "the rock," before the album's first real sonic treat - the smooth soul ballad, "Evidence."

The next few tracks alternate between hard-hitting and much more melodic fare, with one of the album's more peculiar-sounding tracks being "Star A.D.," which features horns, and sounds like a theme song to an awards show of some sort. Lyrically, it has been alleged that it was about Bottum's late friend, Cobain, but Patton denied it. "Kurt? God no! It's about a phenomenon. And if that guy happened to be one, I don't know. It's one of those things that happen; it's a Vegas thing. What could be more shameful than having to change your colostomy bag on stage?! Vegas is great, though. I love it. Welcome to America." Musically, Gould described the tune as, "The guitar solo is like 'Saturday Night Live,' that's the vibe. It's so funny because we try to explain to people that we write songs visually. We think of scenes and that's exactly what we wanted to do. We kind of amuse ourselves and that's cool because it means we're growing as musicians."

Probably the album's most curiously-titled number is "Cuckoo for Caca," which Bordin (whose nickname is incorporated in the song's finale) explained "That song is about the shit that we've gone through in the past five years," while "Caralho Voador" caught the lads in a "bossanova mood." Patton: "I think we're just getting better at imitating, because that's what it is. Us hearing a bossanova thing, that's not bossanova. You gotta make that distinction." Bordin adds, "It's just a function of what we've eaten over the past five years coming out. You shit what you eat...we spent time in South America, we loved it." And when asked what the song was about lyrically, Patton responded, "Just picture a guy who's a really bad driver, that's kind of what it's about." And as for the Portuguese song title, its English translation is "Flying Dick," while the spoken word bit in the middle of the song when translated in English means, "I cannot drive and now it shows. My finger buried up my nose."

Another fierce rocker, "Digging the Grave," would serve as the set-opening number for at least part of the album's ensuing tour (of which Bottum would ditch the keyboards momentarily in favor of a six-string), while "Take This Bottle" is probably the closest the band ever came to penning a traditional country-western tune. Bordin recalls that the song's main author, Gould, wasn't sure that it fit in with the scheme of things. "He was uncomfortable bringing it to the table and showing it to us because he thought we'd laugh at it. To me, it's refreshing to hear this band doing something like that." Patton saw the tune a bit differently - "It's like a Guns N' Roses song! Maybe Hank Williams lyrics, but definitely G n' R music."

'KFAD' also includes a pair of tunes that border on proggy territory (the title track and "The Last to Know"), while the album-closing "Just A Man" served as a pleasant surprise, with its gospel music-leanings (including a choir!). Gould: "There's also some stuff that sounds really tolerable because it's deliberately tacky. Like 'Just A Man,' that's a tacky song. There's things there that when we were first doing them it felt like we were swallowing a big pill. Like, 'Oh my God, who would do something like this?' But that's the fun of it, too." FNM's newest member, Spruance, felt 'KFAD' could have been even stronger, as he explained when asked if he thought the album was "a failure." "If it is, it would be in the sequencing. I think that the last song on the record ['Just A Man'] was one of the best songs they've ever done, and there were a couple of other songs near the end of the album that were really good. I would say that the weakness of that record was the emphasis on the more mediocre music."

Chart-wise, the album's #31 peak in the US was obviously a disappointment, but it fared much better elsewhere, including a #5 placing in the UK (where it was certified gold). A total of three singles would be plucked from 'KFAD' - "Digging the Grave," "Ricochet," and "Evidence." And while none of the 'KFAD' singles registered on the US charts (fools!), "Grave" did crack the UK top 20, peaking at #16. Gould offered his theory as to why US radio had developed an aversion to FNM, post "Epic" - "Radio will say that our song 'Digging the Grave' is too hard for them, too metal. If we do a song like 'Evidence', then none of the metal stations will want it!"

This certainly proved baffling, as just a few years earlier, MTV and radio offered their full support of FNM. Gould: "I tried to figure out why [FNM were blacklisted]. And it's almost like we are willfully ignored. Those people have been around, and they know who we are." Another head scratcher was why the group was never invited to perform on the then-traveling US alterna-festival, Lollapalooza. "No idea, we've never been asked," said Patton. "If we were approached, we'd probably do it. But there's no obligation. I don't think it's that special anyway." Gould would admit, "We have been deemed uncool for Lollapalooza. We *asked* to be on it actually. We don't have the cool factor though."

While the unwise may consider 'KFAD' to be a flop judging solely from its sales and chart performance, it was not due to a shortage of inspired/quality material - in my opinion, it remains one of my top two most underrated rock releases of the '90s (my other pick being Blind Melon's 'Soup,' in case you were wondering), and along with 'Angel Dust,' has become the most-listened to FNM album by yours truly throughout the years. Gould would go on to defend the album, as well. "I'm proud of that record. I think the biggest criticism that it gets is that it didn't sell. It's really ironic. If you judge a record by that kind of logic, then the Ford Taurus would be the greatest car ever made in the history of mankind because it's the highest-selling car ever sold." Point well taken.

The UK versions of the three aforementioned singles were chock full of non-album b-sides, including a Patton-penned rocker that failed to make the cut for 'KFAD' ("Absolute Zero") and a version of "Evidence" sung in Spanish, plus several cover tunes which ran the gamut from GG Allin ("I Wanna Fuck Myself") to the Bee Gees ("I Started A Joke"). As Gould explained about these extra tracks, "The b-sides that we did were three cover songs that were actually recorded at my house. There's 'I Started A Joke' by the Bee Gees, there's a song by a band called the Brothers Four called 'Greenfields,' and 'Spanish Eyes' by Al Martino! They all sound really good, I'm really into it!"

"We were in this bar in Guam. God, it was so twisted! You see, Guam is like a rock in the middle of the ocean; they have like two million snakes per mile -- they have so many snakes that they have killed all the birds, they have no more birds in all of Guam. So, we're sitting in this bar and they have posters of hardcore porn videos all over the wall. It was a regular bar, and they had animal porn on the wall! And we're like, 'What the hell is this?!' And in the corner of the room they had this karaoke machine and they were all singing the words 'I started a joke...' and there was this bouncing ball so they could follow the words. The lyrics were so pathetic and depressing that we just said 'We have to do this song!' It's the most miserable song I ever heard in my life!"

Videos would be filmed for all three aforementioned singles - "Grave" combined clips of the band playing the track with a hard-to-follow storyline, "Ricochet" was comprised of both performance and backstage footage, while "Evidence" was the best of the bunch, as its lounge-y visual vibe fit the music perfectly. "The video is something you shit out at the last minute," offered Patton at the time. "That's how tied into our egos a video is." And as seen in the clips, Patton was now going with an interesting short hair/mustache combo - in an era when a young male wearing a furry upper lip was as "hip" as sporting a mullet. Journalists at the time offered interesting descriptions of his appearance - "Wiry in his White Castle t-shirt, ragged jeans and worn sneakers, with a scraggly moustache and greasy brown bangs, he eerily resembles some rough-trade 'Midnight Cowboy'-type hustler," while another pointed out that "Mike Patton looks absolutely dreadful. His teeth are yellow and covered in plaque and he seems to be quite beat." Quite a contrast to his pin-up worthy looks of just a few years earlier.

As for the artwork for the album cover and accompanying singles, artist Eric Drooker supplied sketches (the cover of 'KFAD' featured a barking dog and a police officer aboard a subway car, only utilizing the colors red, black, and white). Drooker is best known for his artwork for The New Yorker, while he also later supplied the animated bits for the 2010 film, 'Howl,' starring James Franco as poet Allen Ginsberg (Drooker had collaborated with Ginsberg on the latter's last-ever poetry book, 1996's 'Illuminated Poems').

With a tour booked that included non-stop dates from March through September (and saw the band hit both Europe and Australia twice a piece, the US, Japan, and South America), Spruance suddenly had second thoughts and abruptly jumped ship. According to Gould, "I think he freaked out about the touring, how much commitment the band requires. Touring is what really made our band, and the way we see it, it's not going to come easy doing the music that we do, so we gotta make it work. When you tour the way we do, it's not for everybody. It's hard fucking work." Subsequently, Spruance would continue to work with Bungle, as well as with such additional projects as Secret Chiefs 3, Faxed Head, and Weird Little Boy.

However, there were still fans that seemed to long for the metalloid guitar stylings of Jim Martin, such as Devin Townsend. "They had a whole slew of guitar players after [Martin's exit], that I wouldn't be able to recognize on the street. I think Trey Spruance played for a while there, but again, without the fact that I saw him in Bungle and he had a bunch of shitty dreadlocks hanging down, I wouldn't know the guy. I wouldn't recognize the guy. There was something really identifiable about Jim Martin that I think that in my real surface appreciation for Faith No More, contributed to it greatly."

But then there were people like Madball's Mitts, who could hardly tell the difference. "I remember hearing Jim Martin wasn't in the band anymore, and thinking, 'Oh, this record is going to suck.' And then when I heard the record, it was awesome. That's a great, great album. What it sounded to me was that the guy that replaced him tried to emulate what they had done before he was in the band. He tried to write songs that were in the vein of Faith No More - unless, it just happened that that guy was in that style anyway, who knows? But it definitely sounded like a Faith No More record. If no one had told me, I wouldn't have known that Jim Martin wasn't on that. If you listen to it and analyze it, [Spruance] is a little different sounding than Jim Martin, but it's really more of a tone issue. The riffs are still...those are *Faith No More riffs* on that record. I think that's a great album. When he left, it didn't make as big of a change that I thought it was going to make."

So with Spruance suddenly out of the picture, it was time to locate another suitable replacement. Again, FNM didn't have to look far, as their former keyboard tech (and roommate of Gould's), Dean Menta, got the nod. As Bordin explains, "He spent this time on tour watching the guitar and saying, 'Goddamn, I could do that better.' It's so funny because I thought, 'What's the matter with Dean? He's not being part of the crew.' And I asked him one day and he said, 'I don't want to be a tech guy, I'm a musician. I like you guys a lot and it's very frustrating for me to see something I think I could do better.' Shortly thereafter, we started playing together at soundchecks because we didn't have a guitarist there a bunch of times - he didn't show up - and Dean played great. It's a comfortable fit, everybody likes him."

Born on June 23, 1966 near San Francisco, at the time of joining FNM, Menta was composing soundtracks for videogames, and was a member of the group Duh, which was signed to Jello Biafra's Alternative Tentacles label, and issued an album, 'The Unholy Handjob,' the same year that 'KFAD' dropped. Also, Menta was dating Jennifer Finch - the bassist of former FNM tourmates, L7. When asked how he first crossed paths with FNM, Menta replied, "A friend asked me whether I'd like to tour with them as a roadie. I said YES even though I had no clue what kind of music they were doing. On the last tour I had to play guitar for Jim, and I was so good that they called me up one day and asked me to become a member of the band."

So with Menta now on board, FNM hit the road in support of 'KFAD.' And the newest member recalls that his new band mates "Talked shit behind each other's backs constantly and avoided each other...pretty much as they always did." And as a result of the underwhelming chart-performance of 'KFAD' Stateside, the size of the venues that FNM performed at were either the same size as their last tour, or scaled back a bit. Patton: "Maybe we could play places that are a little bigger, but we're not really a stadium band yet. Plus, we haven't really played in a couple of years and we've got a new guitar player, so it seemed natural to go places that were more familiar."

By the time the tour rolled back into Roseland in NYC on May 13, 1995, I of course was in attendance. Somehow, for a protracted period of the performance, I wound up standing exactly at the side of the stage (to Gould's right) but at audience level. A fine gig overall, I remember being pleased to see that there were still many fellow FNM fans willing to support the band Stateside, despite a lack of MTV/radio support. The next night, FNM played a now-defunct venue called Malibu on Long Island. Why I did not attend this performance as well (which was oh-so-much-closer to where I reside than Roseland), shall remain a life-long, unsolved mystery.

A performance on this tour has been heavily bootlegged (I know this because I convinced a friend to purchase an over-priced VHS dub of it at a local record store in the pre-YouTube era!) was one of the last dates of this world trek, when FNM played South America as part of the "Monsters of Rock," opening for Ozzy Osbourne. The specific show, filmed on September 9th at the Teatro Caupolicán, in Santiago, Chile, remains clear in Bottum's mind, to this day. "In Chile, one time when we performed before Ozzy we encouraged the audience to spit at us because it felt like they really hated us and it made us play all the harder. Now that I look back on it, I don't really think that they hated us. I think the spit was a form of flattery. But usually when we were getting kicked off of stages we'd play a lot harder. That used to happen a whole lot."

If you ever want to watch some truly nauseating FNM footage, be sure to point your peepers at the middle of the group's rendition of "Midlife Crisis" from this show (just before the "Car Thief" sample), as gobs of spit are flung at a newly buzz cutted Patton, who opens his mouth, exposes his tongue, and dares the audience to "hit the mark." And feel free to carefully inspect when the band offers up a cover of Portishead's "Glory Box," during which worm-like globs of saliva quickly cling to a close-up shot of the singer's face. Other Patton "standouts" include the singer proudly displaying an opened prophylactic at the beginning of "We Care A Lot," and proceeding to sing briefly into a can of an unidentified beverage during "Easy," before taking in a few mouthfuls to spit out onto the audience.

Shortly after the Chile performance, the supporting 'KFAD' tour would conclude, with its members enjoying some well-deserved r and r. However, with his FNM schedule now clear, Patton immediately reunited once again with some old chums...

Chapter 13: Disco Volante

Throughout the course of rock history, there are select artists that manage to "knock it out of the park" on their first try - the Ramones (1976's self-titled debut), Guns N' Roses (1987's 'Appetite for Destruction'), etc. But there are other bands that you cannot simply judge from their debut album, as it took them a while to find their footing - Rush (1974's self-titled debut), Radiohead (1993's 'Pablo Honey'), etc. Mr. Bungle certainly belongs to the latter category. Perhaps since there was such a long layoff between their first two albums (four years had lapsed from the release of the band's self-titled debut and when 'Disco Volante' appeared), the lads had a chance to assess the situation. But really, the main difference between the two releases is that the debut was full of re-recorded compositions from early demo cassettes, whereas 'Disco Volante' was comprised of fresh material, which were, dare I say, more "mature" than the largely goofy bits that comprised the debut.

"I'm not really sure," admitted McKinnon, about why the band's first two releases were so different. "I think it has more to do with the amount of time that had passed since [the first album]. Because since the last album, everyone was shifting around as to where they were living. The way this one came together was a lot different than the last one. With the last one we had old tunes that we were throwing back together and revamping, and this one was kind of snakes basically. We'd kind of throw things together over time. This isn't really coming out as articulate. [Laughs] Yeah, it's just a lot of time since we did the last thing and the way the ideas came together was a whole lot different."

Dunn on the other hand, had a clearer explanation. "When coming together after a long time we realized that our material was kind of old and lame. It even existed long before we recorded it for the first album. No one wanted to play this kind of music anymore. We knew that we had to write completely new material. But we're not the band who makes endless discussions of how the direction should be, we just made lots of noise until we kind of heard new compositions. The more we heard those sound shapes the more we worked on it. Several demos have been recorded, but we continued working on our songs. Luckily we had no deadline and were able to continue working with our speed, while we also worked on our own projects. The recording itself took another several months. We needed almost one day for the mix of each song. Hard work!"

The bassist has a valid point - while Patton was off resuming his Faith No More duties after Bungle's last tour in '92, a few of the Bungle boys had kept busy playing in other projects, including the psychedelic roots-rock band Dieselhed (Heifetz), jazz composer/pianist Graham Connah (Dunn), and death metallists Faxed Head (Spruance) - not to mention the latter's brief association with FNM, as well. So maybe, just maybe, playing with other artists that were quite different from Bungle strengthened their chops and broadened their compositional skills. Whatever the reason, 'Disco Volante' is where it all first came together for the band. McKinnon: "I think [side projects] have enriched it more than anything, because they give us a sense of freedom. And just, like, more ideas to use, rather than there it is right here. Boom. That is a good question, though, because some ways you'd think it would almost take energy from it, but with people as oddly creative as these guys, it's been nothing but good for it." Another factor that made collaborating easier this time was that the entire band was now residing in the San Fran area. But according to Dunn, just because all of Bungle lived in the same town didn't mean they were best buds - "We all live in San Francisco, but usually don't hang out with each other. An exception is when work with Mr. Bungle has to be done, then we spend our whole time together."

But even with everyone in a central location, schedules had to be carefully synchronized. As Heifetz explained, "We really need to know a couple of months in advance what's going down." "We really have to have something that brings us together," adds Spruance, "Like say we have to get ready for a tour or do a recording, we don't just get together to be Mr. Bungle, it has to center around something we're working together on."

Spruance also explained that the band's music listening habits had affected the new material. "Well, within the band, the interests have diversified; Trevor has gotten further into jazz, I've gotten into movie soundtracks from 1955-75 - Italian movie soundtracks especially. Actually, I've been getting into the music of Romania - it's really amazing. There's a couple of gypsy ensembles there that will blow your mind." And according to the guitarist, the band relocating to San Francisco made it easier to discover such exotic sounds. "University libraries are a pretty good resource. It's where I learned everything. We were living way up in the woods, and moving to San Francisco, which is a little more of an information center, provided an opportunity to explore things a little more in depth. We had a pretty good introduction there at the University - it lit a fire under all of our asses."

Spruance also listed a few specific artists that stuck out. "That's what's so amazing about Romanian music; it's such a fucked-up situation there, both politically and economically, that happiness is a matter of this manic energy that gets so exalted that it takes on this nightmarish quality. On the other side of the coin, there's this avant-garde music from Romania by a group called the Hyperion Ensemble, which was founded by Iancu Dumitrescu. It's a new phase of 20th century music that has to do with the recording processes and electro-acoustic sounds. They're not tape-manipulated, they're actual performances, but it's just the most powerful, thundering, frightening fucking music on the face of the planet. It makes anything else seem like ants. It's so unbelievable because of the way it's recorded - it's all these subtones, this incredible violence, this incredibly cold and doomish feel, but eternally powerful. It's transcendental new age music that explodes your fucking head apart. Then there's musique concrète, which is electronic tape recordings of acoustic sounds, which are then spliced and put together. The stuff from Finland and Sweden is usually the shit."

As a result, Bungle's funk metal freaky stylings of the debut album were - thankfully - kept at bay on 'Volante.' McKinnon: "The band gets tired of doing any one thing for too long; it's constantly evolving. It's never pigeonholed into any one thing, other than it's going to be annoying. And we rehearsed and recorded the first album all together as a band, but the new album was pieced together."

Songwriting for the disc supposedly began shortly after Bungle's aforementioned 1992 New Years Eve show with Primus in San Francisco. And according to Dunn, the band then embarked on a very easygoing, Jeff Lebowski-esque schedule - "After that, we just took our time, assembled riffs and got this record done." As McKinnon explained, two specific members played an integral part in the creation of 'Disco

Volante,' and interestingly, it was the exact same two gentlemen that were probably the most busy doing double-duty at the time - "A lot of times I'll have a part but I won't know where to put it, so I'll throw it to Trey and Mike. They're really good at arranging stuff. So you can blame it on them." However, according to Spruance, it was more of a team effort. "When we write music and work on it, we're actually all in the same room a lot of the time. But the songs vary in how they're written a lot of the time. Sometimes one person will write an entire song, and when we trade parts it's usually a group effort at the arrangement stage."

McKinnon also pointed out that 'Disco Volante' was supposed to beat 'King for a Day' to the punch release date-wise. "We were supposed to get this album out before their album. You can just wonder how much of this is being orchestrated by people behind the scenes at Warner Brothers, saying, 'We'll put a little more emphasis on this.' But it's all speculation on my part, on our part." The sax-blower also finally admitted that the shadow of FNM loomed large on Bungle. "Sometimes it seems like there's a weird kind of opposing energy about it and stuff, and we're pretty aware of it and having to deal with it. It's always been an interesting little dance that we'll do. That two timing son of a bitch! [Laughs] I don't know how much of a weight it is, though. Aw hell, who am I trying to kid? No, seriously though, it has everything to do with how long it's taken to get our shit out."

Released on October 10, 1995, the band opted to produce the album entirely on their own, and was recorded at a variety of studios - Brilliant Studio, Hyde Street Studio, Coast Recorders, and Shotwell Bomb Factory (all located in San Francisco), as well as Mills College Concert Hall (in Oakland). The result was a recording that was the most musically varied and unpredictable of any rock album released that year. Maddeningly, 'Disco Volante' - whose title comes from the name of a yacht in the 1965 James Bond flick, 'Thunderball' (and when translated from Italian to English, means "flying saucer") - received almost no promotion from the record label however. Despite this seeming "sabotage," the album did manage to sneak onto the Billboard Album Charts for a single week (occupying the #113 spot) before vanishing into the abyss. And although 'Disco Volante' was only the second title the group had delivered to their record company, the artist-label relationship had already soured, according to Heifetz. "We're all itching to get off the label, it boggles the mind why they want us at all." Dunn also voiced a similar sentiment, regarding a lack of support from Warners...albeit with some reward - "They just write us the standard check. They don't give a shit what we do, which is great." And lastly, Spruance offered his thoughts. "'Disco Volante' was our renaissance in the Age of Miscommunication. Sure, Warner Bros. didn't do shit. We thought somebody in our camp of one was doing all the communicating. It never started. Then again, we did have a reputation for maintaining a distant relationship with the label."

As far as getting Warners to green light a single or video from 'Volante,' forget it. Heifetz: "We asked them about doing a video and the marketing director, or whatever he is, told us 'We're not going to do a video because we don't see any hits on the record.' He actually said that. Oh thanks guys, thanks for your support."

Featuring an album cover that included a photograph of a woman's eye mostly surrounded by a dried-up viperfish, upon taking a peek inside the CD booklet, it quickly became apparent that the band put quite a bit of effort into the layout and design. But as Heifetz explained, few fans got to experience the full monty - as it turned out the band wanted to use a piece by Czech artist Jiri Trnka, and Trnka supposedly granted permission for them to use it...but it was nixed because Warner Brothers wanted the ownership rights, which the creator declined. What ultimately wound up happening is the band left empty spots in the booklet where the Trnka artwork was supposed to go, and included an address that fans could send two bucks to, for which they would receive the missing bits and they could stick it in at their earliest convenience.

One of the few carryovers from the debut album to 'Disco Volante' was that a few of the members were still hiding their identities behind abnormal aliases - Heifetz was listed as "I Quit," while the most outlandish was Spruance going by "Uncooked Meat Prior to State Vector Collapse." All the rest of the members were listed either by solely their first or last name, or most daringly, Dunn and McKinnon choosing to go by their full first and last names.

Material-wise, 'Disco Volante' is comparable to such releases as 'Angel Dust' and Radiohead's 'OK Computer,' in so much that if listened to from start to finish, it takes the listener on an extraordinary journey. But to Bungle's credit, 'DV' is arguably more unpredictable than either of the aforementioned classics. Instead of kicking things off on a cheery note, Bungle offers the album-opening death metal dirge/downer, "Everyone I Went to High School With Is Dead" - one of three ditties on the album to be 100% composed by Mr. Dunn (the others being "Phlegmatics" and "Platypus"). Up next is an instrumental, "Chemical Marriage," which reflects Spruance's previously mentioned fascination with gypsy music, before we hit the album's first true highlight. "Carry Stress in Jaw" reflects the group's early freeform jazz/metal direction, before leading directly into the unlisted-yet-awesome "Secret Song," which features killer guitar work from Spruance (a kin to a '60s spy movie theme), while Patton sings gibberish lyrics in a "constipated old man" voice. And then...if you were to select a single "must hear" piece of music from 'Volante,' the tremendously-titled "Desert Search for Techno Allah" reflects exactly what it advertises - Middle Eastern sounds with electro-techno, which has to be heard to be truly believed. Out of all the selections on the album, "Techno Allah" is the one that will give your stereo speakers the truest workout (specifically, your sub woofers).

"Violenza Domestica" is a tune sung entirely in Italian (the English translation of the song's title is "Domestic Violence"), with the lyrics appearing to be sung by both vantage points of the bully who is committing the violence, and also of the victim. The next two tracks appear to be the closest to "throwaways" on the album - the strangely melodic "After School Special," as well as "Phlegmatics," which begins with a heavy metal gallop, before "deconstructing" to just voice and one or two instruments. "Ma Meeshka Mow Skwoz" is another highlight - composed entirely by Spruance, the tune combines jazz and surf guitar with some nifty scat singing, as well as musical morsels that sound like something straight out of a 'Bugs Bunny' cartoon (namely the piece that begins shortly before the tune is 50 seconds old).

Some may find the over ten-minute long soundscape, "The Bends," to be just *a tad* indulgent, but it is pretty impressive how the band creates a variety of sonics that sound as if you're in a scuba suit, diving deep into uncharted waters (including a dramatic ending, which sounds as if you're being sucked into a swirling vortex). "Backstrokin" hints at the surf n' spy sounds that the band would explore more thoroughly on their next album, while "the metal" returns with the opening of "Platypus," before detouring into jazz territory, and then ultimately, finishing off on a headbanging note. Finally, 'Disco Volante' ends with another epic - this time, the near thirteen-minute long "Merry Go Bye Bye," which starts with Patton impersonating a hoity toity rock n' roll singer, before continually shifting gears - rapid fire metal, noise, dream-like freeform sounds, random drum whacks, violin scraping, before finishing off with some blaring saxophone skwonking. But be warned - one needs to possess a pretty high endurance to cacophony in order to be able to listen to the complete piece.

Unlike the tour in support of the debut (whose launch didn't exactly coincide with the album's initial release), live dates in support of 'Disco Volante' kicked off only a month after their sophomore effort dropped - taking in the US for the remainder of 1995 (Heifetz: "We're starting in Minneapolis and going in a big loop. The only thing we're missing is everything in the middle. No big sky, no Rockies and Florida, fuck you!"), before embarking on the group's first-ever Euro jaunt in early '96. After a multi-month break, Bungle then did about a month's worth of dates in Australia during October/November. Similarly to their earlier tour, the Bungle members still performed behind masks (albeit more basic ones). As seen on bootleg footage of the band's performance at the Fillmore in San Fran on December 18, 1995, Patton appears to be donning a sheer stocking over his face (a la the "bank robber look"), while Spruance has a 'Phantom of the Opera' mask that obscures only the upper part of his face, Dunn's face is obscured by what appears to be an executioner's hood, while Heifetz sports the most peculiar disguise, which is best described as a huge mop of silver Christmas tree thistle...before replacing it with a wrapped gift box! And the costumes of yesteryear were ditched in favor of regular everyday wear, and with good reason, according to McKinnon - "Last time [the costumes] were just really stinky, and you have to get used to that. Stuff wouldn't be washed for a while, after a while just throw it in the suitcase. Pull it back out, 'Oh. I wore this last night. I think I'll wear it again'!"

Setlist-wise, not much material from the debut made a return appearance - the only tune to regularly appear each night was "Travolta" - while the majority of the set was based on 'Volante' material, as well as the expected batch of off-the-wall covers (Armando Trovajoli's "Casanova 70," the Meatmen's "I Sin for A Living," Loverboy's

"Working for the Weekend," etc.). Looking back on the tour, Dunn sounded pleased, overall. "There are always people who come to our shows with absolutely no clue about what they're going to hear and being disappointed after the show. But in the meantime every now and then we converted some people which made us really proud. Sure the opposite happens as well but we don't care about that. More important are the ones we reach, not the other ones. Things went to a positive direction, especially in Europe."

After 'Volante,' word got out to fans that the band had reconvened to record some of the covers they tackled on the '95/'96 tour. When asked years later about the recordings, Patton responded, "Our drummer's a neurotic freak, and he went and booked a bunch of studio time without really asking the entire band, just because he wanted to look like he was busy doing something. And he booked the studio time and we realized a couple of days before, 'Wait a minute, we don't have any material to record! Well okay, let's record some covers.' We recorded four or five covers, and left it at that - never without any intent of really doing anything with them." When asked how complete the tunes were, the singer described them as "Very skeletal. We'll probably never put them out." Spruance on the other hand, sounded more hopeful about the material's final fate - "I'm sure someday we will go back in and do them." So far, Patton's prediction appears to be the correct one.

Despite not being a commercial hit, 'Disco Volante' certainly succeeded in pleasing Bungle's fanbase (which in a strange twist, seemed to be growing - whereas FNM's US fanbase appeared to have topped off) and establishing the band as one of rock's most truly cutting edge and original-sounding outfits. But with his commitments to Bungle now fulfilled and the band back in hibernation, it was time for Patton to return back to the FNM fold, which as it turns out, was once again experiencing guitar player difficulties.

Chapter 14: Album of the Year

In the classic comedy film, 'This is Spinal Tap,' the fictitious heavy metal band Spinal Tap experience quite a few calamities, including the inability to retain drummers for long periods of time. Just switch "drummers" with "guitarists," and you have a frank evaluation of FNM's situation ever since Jim Martin's departure in late 1993. So it shouldn't have come as an enormous shock that the band experienced yet another line-up shuffle prior to recording their sixth studio effort, 'Album of the Year.' But this time, FNM's guitarist exit was not due to personality clashes nor the unwillingness to tour, as Gould explained. "Dean had been our guitar player and worked great for the tour, but when it came to writing, we found that we worked differently." Fair enough. Menta would go on to perform and record with veteran art rockers Sparks, as well as work as a music editor, composer and sound designer for television and film, and continued work as a writer of music for video games.

So once more, the band decided to go with someone that at least one FNM member had a prior history with - a gentleman by the name of Jon Hudson. Born on April 13, 1968, Hudson (a native of Oakland, California) was a member of the obscure rock band, Systems Collapse (who never issued any professional recordings - only demos - and interestingly, included Will Carpmill in its line-up, the same chap who helped come up with the name "Faith No More" way back when), and was a long-time friend of Gould's (like Menta, Hudson was previously a roommate of Gould's, too).

Patton sounded a bit gun-shy about expressing excitement over FNM's latest addition. "We have another guitarist. I really wish I could say that 'This is the MAN!' and that everything's beautiful, but we've said that three fucking times already. I don't know any longer - it's either us or the guitarists. What I do know is that guitarists stink." The singer continued, "Guitarists have this personality, a 'thing'...they wanna show off and jerk off. In our band there's no room for that. Every instrument has its specific function, and I think we are kind of militaristic about it." Gould also voiced similar concerns - "You start to look like a bunch of assholes. The journalist before said that we seem to be the guys who have the problems: you had so many guitarists and every time you said that he is the right one...but that was right at that point in time. What the hell can we do about it? We just try to make the album sound good in the end."

With a new guitarist now in place, FNM began work on their sixth studio disc overall, and Hudson immediately contributed in the songwriting department, according to Gould. "Kind of 50%. We wrote some songs after he joined and he brought some of his own songs that he worked on for himself and then we started to work on them together. That was really cool." The bassist also explained that stylistically, Hudson's songwriting meshed perfectly with FNM. "Before most of us knew Jon a little better we already spoke the same language when it came to music. It was incredible how his song ideas fit together with FNM. If we wouldn't tell you, you couldn't tell what songs are originally by him." Patton was also willing to pay Hudson a kind compliment - "I think his are some of the best songs on the record."

Recorded at Brilliant Studios in San Francisco, the album was co-produced by Gould and Roli Mosimann, a bloke who previously served as drummer for post-punkers Swans, and had produced numerous albums by one of FNM's favorite bands. Gould: "Roli is the guy who did the Young Gods stuff, and he really added an interesting dimension. He's coming from an angle that we haven't explored before, which is a little bit more on the technology side. There's a little bit of programming, but the songs are still really heavy. The programming just puts the sound in a new light."

Specifically, Gould was the producer of the actual recording process, while Mosimann joined in on the "computer" end of things, as well as the mixing stage. "Until now, every time we did an album, we recorded that on tape and mixed it then - Roli changed our point of view," explained Gould. "He copied all the stuff to the computer and we started to edit it then. We didn't do too much of that...we just really fucked up one song in the computer. Most we did were little things that really improved much. And Roli also mixed the album and his extreme mixing style was really good for us."

Patton also shed additional light on Mosimann's role in the recording. "I think most of the stuff you identified as samples have been things that Roli added, little effects that have been very satisfying for us. We know these songs since we wrote them and what he finally did was something like, 'Yeah, finally it sounds like it should'." And according to Gould, Mosimann added a completely different element than prior producers. "And the things he did were no heavy metal stuff. Andy Wallace is a great producer for the stuff he does, but he never would have mixed the way Roli did. That was a new perspective for us."

Years later, Hudson would look back at the recording sessions and describe them as "Fragmented. I don't know what the other studio experiences were like for Faith No More, I just know that this one was sort of piecemeal. There were a few different stages of making the record. I think the band was having a more difficult time putting this record together. I don't think it was a lack of creativity, I just think people's interests were starting to go elsewhere."

What Hudson was probably alluding to was Patton's obvious on-again/off-again journeys to Bungle-land (and also spending time in Italy to be with his wife), as well as releasing a pair of "ultra-experimental" solo albums (in other words, exceedingly difficult to listen to) - 'Adult Themes for Voice' in 1996 and 'Pranzo Oltranzista' in 1997 - via Tzadik Records, run by his old buddy, John Zorn. Additionally, Bottum had launched his own project, Imperial Teen, an alt-pop band that saw him not behind keys, but rather, behind the mic and with a guitar slung around his neck (the band would release their debut album, 'Seasick,' in 1996). Comparing the band to FNM, Bottum said at the time that the two are "Sort of night and day, pretty much. It seems like the people in Imperial Teen are all of a more similar mindset, the thoughts and ideas flow a little more congruously. Imperial Teen is really important to me because it's more people that are friends that I feel comfortable with. Enough to sing."

But the most publicized project that a FNM band member indulged in during this time was Bordin joining Ozzy Osbourne's band. A long-time Black Sabbath fanatic, this was an obvious dream come true for the heavily-dreadlocked drummer, who performed live with Ozzy in 1996, and then standing in for an ill Bill Ward during Ozzfest's nightly set-closing set by Sabbath in 1997. "I was the guy back in school who had a different Black Sabbath t-shirt for every day of the week," admitted the drummer. "I even once stole a neighbor's car, with a friend, to go and see Sabbath in Anaheim during their 1977 tour. So this really is a great honor for me." Osbourne himself would have nothing but praise for his new timekeeper - "I've always thought he was a great drummer, and having done a few shows with him, he's just a total pro. He's great."

"Very rarely are we all in the same city at the same time," is how Gould chose to describe the sessions. "If we were lucky, there'd be a three-week window and then we'd practice as much as we could and record at the end of the period." The bassist also stated how he felt that 'AOTY' was steadier stylistically than past FNM studio offerings. "We did try to keep a little more consistency because we did realize that not only are we writing it, but people have to listen to it, too. But I think the quality is right up there with anything we've done." Patton added, "It's got more feelings and balance than our previous albums. Possibly it's darker too."

And as with seemingly every new Faith No More release came the obligatory break up rumors, which Gould addressed, and in the process, also pointed out that there was an early batch of songs that wound up going the way of the dodo. "FNM was always a priority for us and we never thought about splitting up. We didn't compose a lot together because everybody was somewhere else to tour etc., but the CD developed bit by bit that way. It was sometimes frustrating when we wrote songs while Mike was away and he didn't like them at all when he came back so we had to cancel them. But looking back I am glad that it turned out to be that way...so now we have only the best songs on the album." He also offered a bit more info surrounding the original - and mostly shelved - tunes. "We wrote something like twelve songs, and of those twelve, we probably axed eight of 'em. They're still around, they're good, but they were leaning a certain way that we didn't want things to lean towards. They were...they were just a little bit too nice. They were pop songs, but there wasn't enough feeling, enough balls."

Regarding the scraped material, Bottum voiced disappointment. "I was really pissed off about it. [Patton's] more inclined to not do something that's a little poppier. The first songs that we wrote, I was really happy with because they were really simple, sort of, effortless. I like that; I don't like tempo changes and time changes. It's just confusing and it doesn't speak to me in any pure way. At the time he kind of wasn't into doing it. I imagine if I really pushed it, I could have got him to do something to those songs. But at the same time, if it isn't effortless for him, then I would really rather he didn't anyway." Gould was just happy the sessions were completed - "This record took a year and a half to make - serious hard work. I mean, the reason I'm the producer is because I've been living with this thing every step of the way. I couldn't rest until this record was finished."

Like FNM's last two releases, I was lucky to hear 'AOTY' earlier than its official June 3, 1997 release date, due to the fact that was I employed at the time by a music publication, and was able to come in very close contact with an advance disc (which also included a pair of tracks that would not appear on the official US release - "The Big Kahuna" and "Light Up and Let Go"). Stylistically, 'AOTY' was not nearly as heavy as the past few releases were - not necessarily a bad thing...just a different thing. Gould would chose an atypical musical comparison of the past few albums, "['Angel Dust'] was like a hurricane coming - a big, ugly storm. 'King for a Day' was like when the storm was hitting you, with all this stuff flying all over the place. And this record...this record is kind of like digging through the wreckage and pulling out bodies afterwards."

'Album of the Year' kicks off with one of the album's hardest cuts, "Collision," and if you listen closely, features Spanish-speaking voices swiped from a shortwave radio. One of the album's best tracks, "Stripsearch," follows, which showcases an outstanding vocal performance from Mr. Patton and includes a very Portishead-like loop at the start. Another standout is the melodic rocker "Last Cup of Sorrow," complete with what sounds like a toy piano tinkering away at certain points.

The other heaviest tune on the album, "Naked in Front of the Computer," was one of three compositions to be entirely penned by Patton (the others being "Got That Feeling" and "Home Sick Home"), and features a very rubbery guitar riff that sounds almost as if someone is detuning the tuning peg as the string is being plucked. Gould explained what the song was about lyrically. "Actually, this song is about email. Patton is kind of obsessed with the idea of how people can communicate and have relationships over the computer without talking or ever meeting. So this is an extreme version of that concept. Funny thing is...the image of someone sitting naked in front of a computer might not have made sense to people a few years ago, but now everybody knows what it means. It's become part of our culture."

Another standout is "Helpless," which once again, combines melody with riffing, and could have easily been selected as a single - due to its killer chorus - and features what sounds like an organ during the verses (the song is also the longest on the album, stretching past five minutes). Musically, "Mouth to Mouth" sounds surprisingly Bungle-esque, due to a Middle Eastern motif throughout. Gould: "This song has an interesting story. Last year I went to Albania. I got an old car, and I drove through the country - a country that's been isolated from the world for like 30 years. So I went in there, and one thing I noticed were a lot of thug-type guys running around in leather jackets with ghetto blasters, but they weren't listening to heavy metal music: it was this loud Arabic music, and it was really inspiring."

The moody rocker "Ashes to Ashes" was one of only two songs that survived the aforementioned "deleted first batch of songs" (the only other survivor being "Paths of Glory"), while "She Loves Me Not" sounds almost like a boy band/soul-pop tune. "Got That Feeling" is the album's most frantic composition, which Gould pointed out, "Basically it's a song about a guy who's a compulsive gambler." One of the more forgettable tunes on the disc is "Paths of Glory," before the band offers a surprisingly bluesy groove with "Home Sick Home."

And finally, the album-closer, "Pristina," has a special lyrical meaning, according to Gould. "Pristina, in Kosovo, is a very heavy place, it has a lot of meaning to a lot of different people, and there is much suffering for it. You can learn more about how the world really works just by observing this small city. When the song came out, Pristina was a dirty little secret, ignored by the media in general. Now it cannot be ignored."

Unfortunately, 'Album of the Year' continued FNM's downward chart slide in their homeland, as it peaked at a meager #41 on the Billboard 200, and like its predecessor, managed to reside on the charts for only a total of eight weeks. And similarly to their previous few releases, in other countries, the album fared far better - hitting #1 in

Australia, New Zealand, and the Czech Republic, and hitting the top-ten in Germany, Finland, and the UK. Also like its predecessor, a total of three singles and videos would be released - "Ashes to Ashes" (which peaked at #15 on the UK singles chart), "Last Cup of Sorrow," and "Stripsearch."

Years later, Gould would look back upon 'KFAD' and 'AOTY,' and explain what he felt the reason was for those two albums in particular not matching the US chart/sales success of 'TRT.' "There is a lot more to the story than you probably know. In fact, up until about ten years ago, 'Angel Dust' was considered our commercial failure. At least by the media and record industry; but not with the fans. We went into the next two albums with the same intentions that we approached 'Angel Dust;' that is, we follow our gut instincts and not pay attention to certain expectations. You must be based in the US, because that is the only place in the world that believes that we received a lukewarm reception... everywhere else those albums were taken for what they were and generally were well-received. As the artists who created these albums, I think that most of us in the band feel these two records were easily on par with all of the other efforts, and a lot of musicians have let me know that both of these albums were a major influence for them." Devin Townsend also points out an element that he felt was lacking in the sonic department - "I did listen to 'King for a Day' and 'Album of the Year,' and there were elements of that I liked, but the guitar was just so dry."

Video-wise, the artsy-fartsy "Ashes to Ashes" was the most forgettable and blah of the bunch, as the band runs through the tune in a run-down building, while Patton sports a superb suit and a beautiful boutonnière (and during the chorus, the band is surrounded by writhing bodies). The "Last Cup of Sorrow" clip was far more interesting, which was the first-ever FNM vid that Patton tried his hand at acting in...alongside a renowned female actress, Jennifer Jason Leigh, best known for her role in one of the all-time classic teen comedy-dramas, 1982's 'Fast Times at Ridgemont High.' As the video's director, Joseph Khan, explains, "It's obviously a riff on Alfred Hitchcock's 'Vertigo.' Hitchcock would have been a pretty badass video director. I was primarily known as an R&B rap director at the time. I'm guessing I got the job because Mike Patton just thought my idea was so weird he had to see how it came out. How many rock stars would want to wear Kim Novak's dress? And I pitched Jennifer Jason Leigh that she would die as Kim Novak and come back to life as Bettie Page. I was my own DP and editor on this, and the tricky thing was I had to force myself to anti-light the interiors with retro cross-shadows. We shot completely in San Francisco on the actual locations Hitch made the movie on. I do not have a Hitch-like cameo in here. I am too Korean to hide myself in this world. I have no idea what that bagel was all about [Bordin noshes on a bagel at the end]. I don't like it either. I was just tired and loopy and it seemed like a good idea at the time."

Another standout video clip was for "Stripsearch" (directed by Philip Stolzt), which was filmed on location in Berlin, Germany, and features a screenplay by Gould. Again, Patton does a surprisingly good job acting - as a gentlemen who turns out is hiding a terrible little secret...until he finds himself in deep doo-doo at what appears to be an inspection at an airport or indoor border-crossing. The clip also features a "zoom in" effect towards the end, which was utilized in quite a few rock videos of the era (most notably Beck's "Devils Haircut"). When I asked Patton if he would ever consider accepting a role in a film (a couple of years after the "Last Cup" and "Stripsearch" clips), he responded, "I've gotten a couple of stupid offers - maybe if there was a good one I'd consider it. But literally, it was like, come on this dumb ass TV show which nobody's ever heard and play a rock musician. And that's all I need...'this is your life!' I don't know, it's not an ambition that I have, but if it happens, I probably wouldn't be opposed to it." In 2005, Patton would eventually make his acting debut in the eccentric (and heavily David Lynch-influenced) flick, 'Firecracker,' co-starring the late Karen Black, and directed by Steve Balderson.

The album cover of 'AOTY' features a very un-rock n' roll image of an elderly fellow accepting flowers from a child, while aboard a train. The man in question is said to be Czechoslovakia's first president, Tomáš Garrigue Masaryk, who was also a philosopher and a supporter of Czechoslovak independence, and served in office from 1918 through 1935. Also, 'AOTY' was the first-ever FNM album not to include the lyrics printed inside the packaging (in its place were more photos of Masaryk).

The 'AOTY' tour began in Europe during the spring (prior to the album's release), before hitting Euro festivals during the summer, and spending all of September and nearly the first half of October in North America. Opening the US leg would be a then-unknown Limp Bizkit. Looking back, Bottum was not impressed. "I had no interest in the sound of Limp Bizkit. It was not how I wanted to be represented at all. Not to be snotty at all but that guy [rapper/singer Fred Durst] had a really bad attitude. He was kind of a jerk. I remembered he called the audience faggots at one show when they booed him. Not a good scene."

Limp Bizkit's Wes Borland appears to agree with Bottum's assessment of the opening band not connecting with FNM's audience. "That was a hard tour for us. That was the hardest tour we ever had, because Faith No More's crowd *really* wanted to hear Faith No More, and they weren't so interested in the opening act. It was a huge honor to be on that tour, but we didn't have the best crowd response on that tour. We actually got booed off the stage...Limp Bizkit's been booed off the stage two times - one time was at the Electric Factory in Philadelphia opening for Faith No More, and the other time was when I was not in the band and they had an incident on the Metallica tour in Chicago [during 2003], where they got booed off because of Fred making comments about the radio DJ Mancow." Borland also recalls there was not much socializing between the two bands on tour - "No, we didn't. The band was kind of off and on their own. Patton was making 'Adult Themes for Voice' during that tour - that crazy four-track record. So he was sort of locked away in his little world of wherever he was doing that. But later, I got to meet Patton and talk with him and hang out with him a couple of times, and I really like him a lot. He's always been kind to me."

It was on September 19th that I soaked in my sixth FNM performance overall, which would take place once more at Roseland in NYC. I was able to somehow score entry into the "VIP area" of the venue (which is located to the side of the crazed crowd, and elevated), so I was able to observe the full show without an obstructed view - until some drunk lunkhead opted to stand up directly in front of me, jump around, and bellow the lyrics to "Epic." Also of note, the entire band - except for Bordin - performed in dress shirts and ties that evening. The new songs sounded swell in a live setting, while a few tunes that I had never witnessed performed live before served as a tasty treat - "Ugly in the Morning" and especially "Midnight Cowboy" (the latter of which featured Patton playing a mini keyboard-like instrument powered by a tube that he blew air into). I also recall at one point Patton asking the audience what they ate that evening, and when one such participant declared "a hot dog," the singer retorted with a hearty "FUCK YOU!" "We Care A Lot" served as a fitting set-closer as well, which looking back, is surprising that the quintet didn't utilize more often as a grand finale at their concerts.

After the US, FNM finished the year off with dates in New Zealand, Australia, Japan, Europe, and their first-ever date in Russia (on November 23rd, at Malaja Arena Luzhniki, in Moscow), before wrapping it all up on December 10th, at the L'Aéronef, in Lille, France (FNM would also reconvene for a trio of festival shows in April of 1998 - one in Spain and two in Portugal).

At some point, the band also found time to re-record a pair of classic tunes from aforementioned art rockers Sparks - "This Town Ain't Big Enough for Both of Us" and "Something for the Girl With Everything" - that both groups would collaborate on together, and would appear on Sparks' 1998 release, 'Plagiarism.' Bottum: "The Sparks project ranks for sure as one of my favorite FNM chapters. It stemmed from the fact that Billy and I had been uber fans of that band since we were really little. Like ten years old. We mentioned our obsession in an interview for Seconds Magazine at some point in the '90s, and Russell and Ron [Mael, Sparks' co-founding brother team] saw that. They sought us out and asked if we'd be interested in collaborating. We all happened to be in Munich at the same time so we set up a meeting. The destination was their choice. We met at a cafe on the edge of an equestrian center for teenage girls. We sat and drank tea, inside, while watching young girls being trained on horses. Completely bizarre. Ron and Russell said it was their favorite place for tea." Interestingly, Dean Menta would supply guitar for a song on the same album - albeit not either of the tunes featuring his former employer (a composition entitled "Funny Face").

During the 'AOTY' era, Patton was asked if he could imagine life without FNM. His response? "I can imagine it, put it that way. This isn't the only piece of green grass, if you know what I'm saying."

Interesting. Very interesting.

Chapter 15: Split

Although it seemed inevitable that this day would come, when "the news" hit on April 20, 1998, it was still unsettling. As an official press release stated:

After 15 long and fruitful years, Faith No More have decided to put an end to speculation regarding their imminent break up...by breaking up. The decision among the members is mutual, and there will be no pointing of fingers, no naming of names, other than stating, for the record, that "Puffy started it." Furthermore, the split will now enable each member to pursue his individual project(s) unhindered. Lastly, and most importantly, the band would like to thank all of those fans and associates that have stuck with and supported the band throughout its history.

Gould would also go on to issue his own official statement:

I personally would like to thank all of you folks who've done such a fantastic job in keeping us alive, and growing with us through our changes, but especially in helping make our band available to people through the Internet, because I'm absolutely convinced that without all of your help we would have been ignored (especially in the States).

Seeee ya,
Bill

One reason why the news came as a surprise when it did was due to the fact that FNM had just performed three dates only two weeks earlier. But allegedly what took place was FNM was offered to open up shows for Aerosmith on the band's summer 1998 of Europe, but had to bow out, due to the fact that Bordin had committed to playing in Ozzy's group once more, as part of that summer's US Ozzfest tour (whose dates were running concurrently with the Aerosmith ones). Instead of getting a fill-in, FNM finally decided to call it a day, and ride off into the sunset.

Later the same year (November 24th, to be exact), the first of several FNM "best ofs" was issued, titled 'Who Cares a Lot?: The Greatest Hits,' (which was a double CD set - one of hits, one of rarities), while a video compilation, 'Who Cares a Lot?: The Greatest Videos,' would be released on February 23, 1999.

A year after the split was announced, Patton sounded relieved. "I'm definitely glad it's over. It was a great thing while it lasted, but it really had to end. I think if it had continued it would have gotten really ugly. No fistfights or bloody noses or anything like that, but the music would have been substandard. So the line must be drawn there." When I interviewed Patton a few years further down the road, he still felt putting FNM to rest was the right thing to do. "I think it was the right time to turn off the lights before we became a pathetic band. Creatively, we hit the wall as a band and it was important to some of us that we end it with integrity."

It also sounded like the feeling was mutual for Bottum. "Initially I think it was kind of a relief when we first broke up. I was trying to do Imperial Teen and I was only able to give it half of what I should have and it was kind of the same with FNM. I was going back and forth and not committing either way. The vibe was that way with most of us in the band. It's a long and difficult haul to do what we did. Billy and I had been friends since we were like ten years old. To follow the course of what it takes to get success with a band...the touring, the business, the artistic decisions, the proximity factor, the growing up...it's an awful lot to ask of young men. It was like fifteen years of really hard work. Really, really hard work. I mean, great times and super amazing achievements but it was a huge chunk of our lives that was very trying. By the time we broke up it was a relief. Mixed with anger. We weren't getting along that well at that particular point."

And despite the press often focusing on all the negatives over the years, Bordin made it a point to clear up any misconceptions - "We loved this band. This band was our fucking lives. So for people to say, 'It's a bad story' or 'They didn't care' is bullshit. Don't believe the fucking hype."

In the wake of FNM's retirement, Gould went on to form his own record company, Koolarrow, which has issued a wide variety of acts over the years (including Brujeria, Hog Molly, and Dubioza kolektiv, among others), and performed/recorded with Jello Biafra, as part of the group Jello Biafra and the Guantanamo School of Medicine (2009's 'The Audacity of Hype'). Bottum would continue recording and touring with Imperial Teen (issuing such subsequent releases as 1998's 'What Is Not to Love,' 2002's 'On' and 'Live at Maxwell's', 2007's 'The Hair the TV the Baby & the Band,' and 2012's 'Feel the Sound') as well as scoring several films (2005's 'Adam & Steve,' 2007's 'Kabluey,' 2009's 'What Goes Up,' and 2010's "Hit So Hard' and 'Fred: The Movie').

Bordin would continue with his role in Ozzy's band, supplying the beat on various tours, and appearing on three studio albums - 2001's 'Down to Earth,' 2005's 'Under Cover,' and 2007's 'Black Rain,' as well as a concert recording, 2002's 'Live at Budokan.' Bordin was also involved in a controversial project, when the original bass and drum work (courtesy of Bob Daisley and Lee Kerslake) on Ozzy's first two classic solo albums, 1980's 'Blizzard of Oz' and 1981's 'Diary of a Madman,' was stripped away and replaced with re-recordings of their parts by Bordin and then-Ozzy bassist Robert Trujillo in 2002. Thankfully, this ridiculous maneuver was later corrected in 2011, when both titles were reissued once again with the original bass and drum tracks back where they belonged. Additionally, Bordin played drums on Jerry Cantrell's 2002 solo effort, 'Degradation Trip,' and in 2003, it came to light that Gould, Hudson, and Bordin had attempted to put a post-FNM project together, which had fizzled before finding a singer or issuing any recordings.

Patton also kept an extremely tight schedule post-FNM, including the formation of a new outfit comprised of several renowned gentlemen.

Chapter 16: Fantômas

With Faith No More fully deleted from his schedule planner, Patton's first "palate cleanser" was an all-new group he had assembled, Fantômas. A "super group" if you will, joining Patton in the project would be Melvins guitarist Buzz Osborne, Slayer drummer Dave Lombardo, and the singer's old pal/Bungle mate, Trevor Dunn, on bass. Dunn would later reflect on how the line-up was pieced together - "[Patton] was trying to decide who was gonna play drums and guitar, and he said he just looked at his record collection and thought of his favorite players and his favorite bands, and he thought, 'Fuck it, I'm just gonna call Dave Lombardo and Buzz Osborne and give it a shot.' And they were both into it. So actually that move in itself was inspiring to me, like, 'Wow, you can just do that! You can call your heroes and jam with them'."

Before releasing a drop of music (and this was before the creation of such helpful items as YouTube, so no one had a bloody clue as to what they sounded like), the quartet set out to introduce their sounds on unsuspecting live audiences. When word got out that the band would be playing the Knitting Factory in NYC on July 1, 1998, of course, I was in. From first glance at how the band's instruments were set up on the tiny-ish stage, you could tell that this was not going to be your average/ordinary rock n' roll show, as the drums were on the far side of "stage right," while a bank of various effects were set up on "stage left" (which as it turned out, was where Patton would be working from that evening).

Going into it, you'd think that a band as out there as Bungle would have prepared you for rock music that had little to do with traditional song structures. Well, Fantômas made Mr. Bungle sound like a top-40 pop act. I would later learn that the material performed that night would comprise their self-titled debut, but to the audience's ears, it sounded as if they were just improvising much of the set. I recall at one point there being a break from all the racket, and the audience was granted a spot of quiet - during which various members of the crowd started heckling, including one chap who yelled out something to the effect that he strongly felt that Dunn resembled distinguished renaissance man Corey Feldman. All the while, the band members stared straight ahead, oblivious to the hollering.

Unable to find a suitable record label to take the project on, Patton did the only logical thing - form his own company with pal Greg Werckman (who had previously worked for Alternative Tentacles), dubbed Ipecac Records. And their first-ever release was…the self-titled debut by Fantômas, on April 26, 1999. One of the contributing factors for putting out the record himself was because Warner Brothers (who had first dibs on it) decided to pass. As Patton explained, things had changed quite a bit in record company land - "This is how it works: If you're smart, you record your record as cheaply as you can. You realize these huge advances are your fucking money; it's just like some big money lender giving you the money. You're never going to get out of the hole. So, unless they're waving a huge amount of money at you that you know you're never going to pay back, you take it and party. If not, you do it yourself, you don't give it up. If they're not waving enough money to make you blink, fuck 'em."

You certainly have to give Patton (who penned all the material himself) credit for concocting an album that sounded like nothing else before it - as each tune (which went by different numbered "Pages" rather than traditional song titles) seemed to be a soundtrack to some sort of comic book. While an interesting listen from beginning to end - it's also admittedly a challenging one to stick with (Patton sings no words at all, just guttural sounds and screams). A few of the ditties stick out more than others - the best of the bunch being "Page 19" (which features Patton perfectly replicating a shaker-type instrument with his voice) and "Page 21" (which again includes vocals utilized in an out-of-the-ordinary manner).

It turns out that a specific album inspired the music that Patton penned for this debut…which one of Fantômas' members played on many a moon ago. "I just wanted to start a hardcore band that plays very short tunes that don't really have a set beginning or ending, that's part of one big song…I see it as thirty hardcore tunes; that's what we played tonight. With this music, the less is better. OK, I'll give an example: Slayer- 'Reign in Blood.' The best metal record, in my opinion, ever made. Thirty-two minutes. In, out, you're gone. That's what I'm going for." Osborne also confirmed another inspiration for Patton's Fantômas songwriting - "He has come up to from a lifetime of reading nothing, but comic books. He doesn't really go much farther than that, you know. Sometimes he watches a little TV, like major TV movie type stuff, and gets things from there, 'cause those are always very sick and twisted."

Years after the release of the debut, Lombardo was very complimentary towards Patton and his whole Fantômas experience. "When you work with other musicians you learn their method of operation, how they learn the songs, how they come together in a studio and practice these pieces. Working with Patton showed me a whole other side to music I knew existed but I had never experienced. And when I experienced it, it was amazing. What that was is the art of improvising; the art of creating music that is very, not unconventional, but not traditional. There's a lot of metal bands [and] bands in general [saying], 'Oh we don't sell out, we don't create mainstream music.' But really, technically, a lot of metal bands follow the metal format and that in a way is kind of a mainstream within its own genre. So you step out of that and create something that has a very small genre. I mean not genre; very small fanbase, and then exploring those ideas in the avant-garde side of music. I mean, that takes a lot of guts and a lot of creativity and a lot of work. He's just amazing, I cannot say [enough good] stuff about him, there is so much to say. I could go on forever!"

It was also around this time that Devin Townsend had the opportunity to meet Patton for the first time. It was not as satisfactory as he would have liked it to be. "I only had one interaction with Patton, and it was like, super awkward. I don't know what the relationship would be like if I actually met the guy, but absolute rabid respect for him and everything he does. It was at some festival I guess maybe 15 years ago. Fantômas was playing, and I know Dave Lombardo, and Mike Patton was out there. Having been such a big influence on me, I kind of walked up, and sheepishly was trying to say, 'Hey, my name is Devin and you're a big influence on my life' or however it came across. But I think he was either predisposed or in the middle of a conversation or something. So the vibe I got from him was very much like, 'Yeah, yeah, yeah - just don't bother me.' [Laughs] So I was just like, 'Whoa! OK, *I'm out'.*"

But Fantômas was not the only project Patton had been working on since FNM's break-up - he and the Bunglers were hard at work on a new studio set.

Chapter 17: California

As it turns out, it took Mr. Bungle the same amount of time to follow up 'Disco Volante' as it did their debut - four years. Prior to the release of their third album (which would be go by the title of 'California'), Trey Spruance dropped a few hints as to what to expect. "There are a lot of song-ish elements on this album that are missing on our previous records. Those elements on this album will be welcomed by many and hated by many others. Some fans may get mad because we're not playing 'experimental' music. We don't really care. We've made a pact to trust our musical instincts and not worry about people's expectations. We could keep putting out 'weird' records and be pretty comfortable, but that would get a little thin. We want the freedom to try new things and have fun."

With Bungle now trying their hand at less unpredictable and more focused (from a songwriting standpoint) material, it left little room for saxophonist Theo Lengyel, who exited the band. "I miss him," admitted Heifetz. "He added a huge chemical imbalance that helped us on the road. He hates us and rightfully so. The music changed, plain and simple. Very little call for saxes, trombone, or flute. He was an original member. I'm not. Makes me feel a bit like a union-buster. He once shit in a goldfish bowl on stage [on New Year's Eve '89]."

When I once interviewed Patton about the material on 'California,' I asked about what led to the band finding themselves finally taking a stab at the traditional verse-chorus-verse format. "Whenever we make a record, it's focused. We end up going for a certain thing and streamlining all our chaotic ideas into a thread that follows a certain pattern. Sometimes that sounds like chaos to other people, but it makes sense to us. The difference with this record [is that] we kind of did it in a song format. There's more songs on this record that follow a linear pattern that have verses and choruses. That just happened naturally. We threw our ideas up against the wall and the ones that stuck were more, at least in our eyes, 'poppy.' Poppier-kinda tunes. It just happened."

While certain styles that made 'Disco Volante' such a delicious delicacy reared their head again at various points on 'California' - exotic

Middle Eastern bits, heavy metal, noise blasts, etc. - another crucial element was added. Spruance: "It wasn't until four or five years ago that I realized how great some of [Brian] Wilson's Beach Boys stuff is. You know when you're a kid, you love the Beach Boys - then you turn 'cool' and you have to hate them. It took me a while to get over that. For Brian Wilson - and I feel this way too - there isn't a difference between production and songwriting. They're one and the same. In the late '60s, the idea that the studio could be used as a compositional tool was almost like an epidemic. That idea has gradually faded, though, and now you hear a lot of things that are just production or just a great song. When you hear a marriage of the two, it's such a refreshing experience."

And since Spruance was looking to use the recording studio as a "compositional tool," 'California' was recorded at four different studios - Coast Recorders, Division Hi-Fi, Forking Paths Studio, and Different Fur Studios - while the band utilized several 24-track machines and more than 50 analog tracks. And like 'Volante,' 'California' was produced solely by the band, with no help from outsiders. According to Heifetz, the reason was simple - "We know our music better than anybody." But as Patton explained it, there was little time to waste in the studio this time around. "There are parts on our second record that were improvised. But on our first album and our new album everything is note for note. Camping out in the studio is cost prohibitive."

Released on July 13, 1999, the title of 'California' was chosen because an earlier idea for the title wasn't going to fly. Patton: "The record sounds like a picnic with an occasional hailstorm, so we figured 'California' would work. We were going to call this 'In Technicolor', but for obvious copyright reasons, we couldn't." By chance, the Red Hot Chili Peppers had released a new album around the same time with a very similar title - 'Californication.' "More than anything, that title really sums up sonically what's going on the record," added Patton. "It's very pleasant at times, and then there are a lot of little disasters that come up and present themselves, then blow over and go away like a storm. I would tend to explain it more like that, rather than, 'Oh, California is this very deceptive place; it's bright on the outside and a really dark place on the inside.' I mean, let's let the Chili Peppers do that." Cover image-wise, 'California' featured a retro silhouette doodle of a man and woman running merrily alongside a palm tree, on a mostly white cover - which resulted in the only Bungle album cover that seemed to truly tie in with the theme of the album's musical contents.

And the contents were oh-so-enjoyable. Instead of starting the album off with a bang or a blast as they had on their previous records, the listener is treated to the soothing sounds of "Sweet Charity," which is equal parts Hawaiian music and the band's aforementioned rediscovery of the great Beach Boys. Written entirely by Patton, the tune also serves as a vocal tour de force. "There's a shitload of vocals, way more than I'd ever done before with Mr. Bungle," explained the singer. "The layering and stuff like that, not just with the vocals, but all the instruments...like, if someone were going to try and remix 'Sweet Charity,' I'd pray for them. One track alone is a harmony vocal, then all of a sudden it's a glockenspiel for two notes, then it turns into a hand drum, and then it turns into a guitar part that lasts for 30 seconds. It's a disaster."

The down-and-dirty rockabilly rocker, "None of Them Knew They Were Robots" follows, which was one of two compositions on the album that featured lyrics penned entirely by Spruance (the other being "Golem II: The Bionic Vapour Boy"). Another mellow breather is offered up, "Retrovertigo," which was penned entirely by Dunn (as was another tune, "The Holy Filament"), which then leads to one of the album's best tracks, "The Air-Conditioned Nightmare," that sounds like a warped tune from an early '60s teen-beach-party flick...with some metal guitars thrown in for good measure. Bungle's longtime Middle Eastern music fixation carries on with "Ars Moriendi," which was the other tune on the album penned entirely by Patton. Around the time of the album's release, the singer explained how he went about showing Bungle his tunes. "I demo everything. I demo almost everything I do. I kind of have a home studio. Most people wouldn't call it that, but it works for me [Laughs]. Doing it that way makes working with these guys real easy. And when I give them a tape...it's usually a little garbled and funky. But they know what I mean, cause we've known each other for so long. It's nice not having to go through the whole translation process."

We then arrive at one of Bungle's best-ever ballads, "Pink Cigarette," which is equal parts Burt Bacharach and Beach Boys. As Heifetz explained, "Beach Boys and Brian Wilson have been in our heads for years. I tried to get these guys to do something from the Beach

Boys about ten years ago. They didn't go for it. How can you not be influenced, at least slightly, by Brian Wilson if you have squeezable melodic intentions?" The aforementioned Spruance composition, "Golem II," is full of funky keyboard sounds and peculiar vocals, which leads into the aforementioned Dunn composition, "The Holy Filament," which features some sweet angelic vocals throughout. A '50s doo-wop goof, "Vanity Fair" is a fun listen, before ending things with "Goodbye Sober Day," which would become a favorite of Patton's on the subsequent tour - "'Goodbye Sober Day' is fun to play live. 'Cause we re-arranged it, it's a different arrangement. That excites me."

Regarding any tracks that may have slipped through the cracks from the 'California' sessions, Spruance did mention some leftovers. "There are a couple of things we recorded and there are still some things from 'Disco Volante' too. But we still have yet to release a single. But when we do, we'll have a bunch of b-sides and we'll throw them on there. Or it might be a tour EP. We'll get 'em out there sooner or later. Originally we were gonna have earlier stuff come out on later albums, but we scrapped that idea, cause there's so much music it's just ridiculous. So now that we're more focused and playing as a band more often, we'll just put out more stuff." To this day, this material maddeningly sits lonely somewhere on a shelf, quite possibly having accumulated several layers of dust.

As with its predecessor, 'California' would only manage a one-week residency on the Billboard 200 Charts (at a mere #144). The reason for this paltry showing? The finger can easily be pointed - or more appropriately, *flipped* - at Warner Brothers, who put hardly any effort into promoting the album. "Bad," is how Spruance described Bungle's relationship with the label. "It's always been pretty bad. It's never really changed. Whether we do a weird album like 'Volante,' or a straight-ahead-ish one like this, the problems are always different, but they're always there. It's just really screwy. They keep us for pure numbers. Because first of all, they don't spend a dime on us, but at the same time, we don't end up going into debt. A lot of the bands you hear a lot about for a year or so, and then they're gone. Their money doesn't get recouped, so they get dropped. 'Cause Warner doesn't cut bands, but it cuts personnel very often. So for us, we don't get dropped or cut because we have a strong fanbase and cult following that they don't know anything about and did nothing to foster, so when the cuts come, we make it. They scratch their heads and say, 'What are we gonna do with this band?...I don't know'."

Patton discussed the possibility of Warners finally getting off their keysters and - shockingly - actually doing their job and releasing a single from the album. "They talked about releasing a single but I don't know if they'll really do it. In fact, I think they probably won't. They wanted to remix a song, and that idea isn't completely distasteful to me, as long as we can choose who would remix it. And it turns out that none of the people that we wanted to do it could do it. So we'll see, I don't know. They were talking about three different songs - 'Retrovertigo' was one which would be pretty easy, 'Sweet Charity' maybe, and 'The Air-Conditioned Nightmare.' I'm not holding my breath man, you shouldn't either."

Ultimately, not a single stinking single would be issued, which was absurd, now that Bungle was offering up more easily-digestible material. "You wanna hear irony?" asked Patton. "You're telling me how straight and palatable it is. With this record, we were closer to being dropped from our label then we have ever been. Figure that one out. If you put it all down on paper, we're not fuckin' No Doubt or Limp Bizkit. We'll never be that. I don't think we'll ever make sense to them. There's gotta be something they are hanging onto. I'm not sure."

The album does have its share of admirers however, including Coheed and Cambria's Travis Stever. "I enjoyed Mr. Bungle. Not as much as Claudio [Sanchez, Coheed's singer/guitarist] did, however. Mr. Bungle was something I wasn't familiar with at all, and heard them through Claudio and our friend, Pat Sayers. They were very into the first couple of records. Funny enough the record I am most familiar with is the later record, 'California.' I really liked that record and yet again, by that time, the people I knew who were into Mr. Bungle didn't enjoy that record as much, and felt it had lost something. That is the classic case with bands and know it happens with Coheed all the time. Someone will get turned on to the band for one of our newest records and someone will turn to that same kid and say, 'Oh man, that record sucks. I like the first two albums before they blah blah blah'."

As a result of no label support, Bungle had to make up for the lack of effort by hitting the road - *hard*. In fact, the supporting tour for

'California' was by far the most extensive tour that Bungle would undertake of their entire career. Beginning in July 1999, Bungle would tour the US for the remainder of the year - including an "Evening with Mr. Bungle" trek later on, which saw the band play two sets (with an intermission) in the middle. In early 2000, the band toured the US once more as part of the Snocore Tour (on a bill that also included System of a Down, Incubus, and Puya), before hitting Australia in March, and then visiting Europe in August and September.

Also, it should be noted that this was the first-ever Bungle tour where the band members did not perform "masked" or in costumes. Patton: "The most glaring reason for that is - I remember being on stage once during our last tour, which was, God only knows, like three or four fuckin' years ago. And having this incredibly tight latex mask on, where I could hardly breathe, which has got its charm and all, but here I am trying to play a piano part on an Ennio Morricone cover. I just thought to myself, 'What do I think I'm trying to do here?' I just gave it up. I can't even come close to playing this shit if I'm gonna be torturing myself on stage like that'."

I had the pleasure of catching two separate Bungle performances on the tour in support of 'California' - August 3rd at the Bowery Ballroom and on November 9th at Irving Plaza. The Bowery performance saw most of the band dressed in Hawaiian shirts and Patton sporting a lei, while the rest of the stage followed the "surf" theme. Having never experienced Bungle live before, it was hard not to be extremely impressed with how well they pulled off their complicated material so effortlessly, and made me wonder why the heck I had waited so long to catch the band live and in the flesh. The Irving Plaza show was during the "Evening with" portion of the tour, which again, saw the group following a similar fashion sense as the earlier show I attended. I also recall during the intermission, a screen was lowered from the ceiling of the venue, and a '60s surf movie was shown (sans the film's dialogue, as the venue opted to play music over it), in which a masked surfer rides in on an airplane, and then hits the waves. The biggest responses of the night were spirited renditions of two tunes from the debut album, "Travolta" and "My Ass is On Fire," which got the moshers moshing and Spruance banging his head - with his lone long braid-dreadlock in the back of his head swinging wildly.

Despite having not toured in three years, Bungle's fanbase came out in droves for the tour. And even the band members were bowled over by the demand from the fans. Patton: "I mean, we hadn't made a record in four years or toured in five [actually three, but continue...], and we're still selling out shows. It's like, 'How the hell is this happening?' I ask that question, but I don't know if I really want to know. I just want to keep doing it. I just don't know where these fans are coming from, really, but it seems like they're getting it, and that's what's important."

When I interviewed Patton not long after the Bowery performance, I asked if the band was planning on playing bigger venues at later dates on the tour. He sounded a tad frustrated with the lack of faith from promoters. "We're kinda on a strange level where we're always building up for the next time, but the next time never comes. We find ourselves playing the same venues, for the same amount of money, for the same people. So it's a little strange. I would think that we could have done it [play a larger venue such as Roseland when the band hit NYC on the tour], but I think that our agent is a bit conservative - he would rather look like a cool guy selling out a club than take a risk. And you know, there would be a bit of a risk there, but I think that in the future that's the kind of risk that we'd want to take. It gets old playing the same places over and over again."

I also couldn't resist asking Patton what his thoughts were when fans hollered moronic comments during performances (for some reason, any project that Patton is involved in always seems to attract obnoxious yellers). "Well, I try to block it out. I better not let it annoy me or I'd be tearing my fuckin' hair out! Because it happens every night in every city of every fuckin' band I've ever played in. I have to block it out. It just kind of makes you wonder what kind of life these people lead. What's going on at home."

In the past, a wide variety of covers (some recognizable, some oh-so-obscure) were a major part of the band's setlist. And this time around, renditions of "Taboo Tu" (Arthur Lyman), "Begin the Beguine" (Cole Porter), and "Tower of Strength" (Frankie Vaughan) were tackled. However, according to Spruance, Bungle was focusing on their own material more than ever before. "You know, actually there aren't that many [covers] this time, simply because getting the new songs off this record together live has been a bitch. It took me over a month and a half working on the samples, programming and routing. Getting it all set up so three people can control it was pretty gnarly. So that ended up eating up a major, major chunk of our rehearsal time. From the time we finished the record, we only actually rehearsed for three weeks before starting the tour. So when it came time to put together the show, we revived a couple of old ones and threw in only a few new ones. We wanted to focus more on our music this time around, 'cause with three albums, there's just that much more shit to play now."

It was also during this tour that a public brouhaha boiled over between Bungle and the Red Hot Chili Peppers. As Patton explained, "We've had some recent, well, not really run-ins, but encounters with them. Strange encounters. I mean, the Chili Peppers is something I hadn't really thought of in years. And I'll go ahead and tell you this. Why not? I haven't told anybody else yet. We were looking at booking some Mr. Bungle shows in Europe this past summer, some big festivals, which is something we'd never done before. We figured it'd be a good thing: We'd get to play in front of a lot of people who wouldn't otherwise hear us. Our agent was in the process of booking these festivals, and it was becoming apparent that we'd landed some pretty good ones - one in France, another one in Holland, some big-name festivals. Turns out someone's holding a grudge! [Laughs] We were booted off several bills, including a really big festival in Australia, specifically because Anthony Kiedis did not want us on the bill. He threatened to pull the Chili Peppers if Mr. Bungle was on the bill. Now, rationalize that one! That's so fucking pathetic! I mean, this guy's selling a million records! We are not even a speck of dust on this guy's ass! What's the fucking problem? It's unbelievable."

Patton went on to admit that because of this, Bungle lost a considerable chunk of change. "Absolutely! When it happened once, we kind of shrugged it off and laughed and said, 'That's really sad. Let's get on with our lives, no big deal.' But with the one in Australia, they basically reached into our pockets and robbed us. It's a pretty pathetic thing." When asked what started this animosity, the singer explained, "It's basically some kind of old grudge. I think what happened was that ten years ago, Faith No More was really big in Europe and enjoying a lot more notoriety than the Chili Peppers were. That pissed them off, or him, or whatever, and they started talking shit about us in the press way, way back then. And we laughed it off - 'What's this guy's problem?' - and it went away. Then, lo and behold, there's still poison in the air!"

But at their 1999 Halloween performance at Clutch Cargo's in Pontiac, Michigan, Bungle got some sweet revenge. Hitting the stage dressed as the Peppers (Patton shirtless with a blond wig a la Kiedis, Dunn shirtless with his hair done in mini-braids a la Flea, touring member James Rotondi also shirtless and wearing shorts held up with suspenders a la John Frusciante, Spruance dressed as "The Ghost of Hillel Slovak," and Heifetz with a backwards baseball cap a la Chad Smith, and all sporting the exact "tattoos" on their bodies as the Peppers members), Bungle covered a total of four Peppers tunes that night - kicking off the first set with a medley of "Around the World" and "Give It Away," and then opening the second set with a medley of "Scar Tissue" and "Under the Bridge."

Other than the little Chili Peppers hiccup, everything had finally come together for Bungle, as it appeared as though the band had become a full-time proposition. When asked if it wouldn't take long for the band to issue "album number four," Patton responded, "It better not, I can't wait that long. I think that's one thing...this band has been a band for 15 years, and it's pathetic that we've only made three records. There's no excuse in the world that is good enough to justify that. I'm ashamed of it, and I'm going to do my best to change it."

Spruance also sounded hopeful about Bungle's future, with the goal being new albums issued at a brisker rate. "Well the thing that's nice now is that we're all in the same boat. Like, I've got my side thing [Secret Chiefs 3] and they've got theirs [Fantômas, etc.], so we're all going at the same pace now and it's gonna be a lot easier to schedule stuff. And I know I said that last time around, but hopefully - I think so. I mean, we have new management now and everything's coming together and just seems ready to go."

Sadly, there would be no bright nor fruitful future for Bungle.

Chapter 18: Bye Bye Bungle

After the tour in support of 'California' concluded in late 2000, fans waited patiently for rumblings concerning new Mr. Bungle music. And waited...and waited...and waited. Patton launched another new project, Tomahawk, with then-Melvins bassist Kevin Rutmanis, former Jesus Lizard guitarist Duane Denison, and former Helmet drummer John Stanier (issuing a fine self-titled debut in 2001 and a sophomore effort, 'Mit Gas,' in 2003). Additionally, Fantômas issued two more albums during this time ('The Director's Cut' in 2001 and 'Delìrium Còrdia' in 2004). Spruance continued issuing albums with Secret Chiefs 3, which also included Dunn, Heifetz, and McKinnon in its ranks from time to time ('First Grand Constitution and Bylaws' in 1996, 'Second Grand Constitution and Bylaws: Hurqalya' in 1998, 'Book M' in 2001, and 'Book of Horizons' in 2004) and were all released via the guitarist's own label, Mimicry. All fine and dandy, but what about Bungle? It was time to take matters into my own hands, and ask Patton about the elephant in the room in 2004 via an email Q&A. His response was not what yours truly and Bungle fans throughout the world were happy to hear.

"I'm at a point now where I crave healthy musical environments, where there is a genuine exchange of ideas without repressed envy or resentment, and where people in the band want to be there regardless of what public accolades may come their way. Unfortunately, Mr. Bungle was not one of those places. We could have probably squeezed out a couple more records but the collective personality of this group became so dysfunctional. This band was poisoned by one person's petty jealousy and insecurity, and it led us to a slow, unnatural death. And I'm at peace with that, because I know I tried all I could."

While Patton did not disclose who the "one person" he mentions above was by name, it could very well have been aimed at Spruance. Years later, the guitarist was asked about Bungle's disappointing dissolution and his relationship with Patton. "As time wears on you find out who your friends are, and who they aren't. Mike and I always had the best working relationship imaginable. Really very, very good and fruitful. There are other things in life we see differently. I don't think those things are irreconcilable at all. But when you get used to having things your own way, and certain people around you resist the 'natural order' of becoming subordinate to you, you may start nursing resentments. Even lashing out at them and calling them egomaniacs etc. for not assuming the position. I think in my case it was too painful for Patton to realize that where there are no subordinates there is no insubordination. Like most of us, Mike tends to begin the process of deciding whether or not he can afford to discard a person's point of view altogether, rather than facing certain difficult facts of life. So to answer your question, there was never any big mess between he and I specifically."

"The general dysfunction coming from being expected to silently endure more and more of this emerging top-down/top-dog order-barking thing he'd taken to just ended up getting really tiresome for everyone involved. In a band, strong personalities need to know where to draw the line on this kind of stuff. Anyway, since it wasn't going to happen, I was the idiot who started to draw that line. I admit I had more emotional involvement in the process than would be necessary for a non-robot, having poured comparatively ridiculously copious doses of my blood into the project. Patton's subsequent resentment towards me is a fairly predictable outcome. You don't stand up to him and stay off the shitlist. A bummer, yeah, but it's essentially a self-protecting reflex action - something I don't really feel a need to hold against him too much. He has his way. It won't change. And after all why should it? This method works well for him overall - who am I to question it? I dare say it's even part of his charm (we are a nation of pathological narcissists after all!). Whatever. Really, I feel fondly about the time we spent making music together, and feel we did some great things. And, while I am diametrically opposed to it on a human level, over time I do appreciate the clarity of his cut and dry approach: how black and white it makes things. You're either in the club, or out of the club. Unfortunately, I have to say I do prefer life as an excommunicate from that kind of 'friendship.' I know he prefers it that way too. I'm sure both of us would agree it was a good run, though."

Mr. Bungle, rest in peace.

Chapter 19: Reunited

Ever since their split in 1998, with each passing year, it appeared as though the "legend of Faith No More" continued to spread. The same mainstream media outlets that shunned or slammed the band in the past were forced to give credit to the group, when countless (admittedly stinky) nu metal and rap metal bands began name-dropping Faith No More as a prime influence in what seemed like every bloody interview. Gould: "It is very cool to see even though it didn't seem to work at the time. If you look at it in the long term, our gut instincts were correct. It's super cool to see - to make an influence like that."

As a result, the various former members of Faith No More had been asked about the possibility of a reunion from time to time in interviews. In 2006, Patton had this to say - "If I personally stood to make three million dollars after taxes I would consider it. Really! Why bother unless it is for stupid money? At this point it would not have anything to do with the music. Most of these reunions are sad cash ins, but to each his own." Gould also gave his thoughts about the possibility of a reunion - "I think the only thing that would make me interested in it is maybe to do it in a club in Bakersfield without telling anybody - for 50 bucks! Then I would do it. If it was a human thing between human beings, I would do it. If we couldn't do that, I don't think there would be any reason to do that. I think it would be fake."

Then, on February 25, 2009, the following statement was issued to the media:

Faith No More has always stood out as some sort of unique beast; part dog, part cat - its music almost as schizophrenic as the personalities of its members. When it all worked, it worked really well, even if the chemistry was always volatile. Throughout our 17 years of existence, the mental and physical energy required to sustain this creature was considerable and relentless. Though amicable enough, when we finally split, we all followed paths seemingly destined to opposite ends of the universe.

Yet during the entire 10 years that have passed since our decision to break up we've experienced constant rumors and requests from fans and promoters alike. Nevertheless, for whatever reason, none of us kept in regular touch, much less to discuss any possibilities of getting together.

What's changed is that this year, for the first time, we've all decided to sit down together and talk about it. And what we've discovered is that time has afforded us enough distance to look back on our years together through a clearer lens and made us realize that through all the hard work, the music still sounds good, and we are beginning to appreciate the fact that we might have actually done something right.

Meanwhile we find ourselves at a moment in time with zero label obligations, still young and strong enough to deliver a kickass set, with enthusiasm to not only revisit our past but possibly add something to the present. And so with this we've decided to hold our collective breaths and jump off this cliff...BACK, GOD FORBID, INTO THE MONKEY CAGE!!!

We can only hope that the experience of playing together again will yield results erratic and unpredictable enough to live up to the legacy of FNM. Who knows where this will end or what it will bring up...only the future knows. But we are about to find out!

FAITH NO MORE are:
Mike Bordin, Roddy Bottum, Bill Gould, Jon Hudson and Mike Patton

While FNM fans worldwide were obviously extremely pleased by this announcement, those hoping for a reunion of the classic 'Angel Dust' line-up were understandably disappointed. A few years later, the man who had been snubbed gave his side of the story, and frustratingly, it sounded like it was close to taking place at one point. Jim Martin: "For some time during 2008, I had been receiving information with increasing frequency that 'we' were booking a reunion tour, festivals, Europe. I was informed that yes, the promoters were selling it as the original line up. In February 2009, Roddy called and said they were just beginning to think of putting something together, and just now feeling out everyone, and what did I think? I said yes, I was interested. I also told him I knew the tour was already booked, they were on the eve of announcing it, and it was time to sign the deals. I told him to send over the contracts so I could review them and started pressing management for details. Several days later, I was able to get management on the phone who told me they decided to use someone else...I know it's odd, no, you didn't miss anything. It happened just like that. In an effort to preclude any sloppy misinformation, I made the announcement that I would not be participating in the rumored reunion dates several days before they made their announcement."

Bottum gave his thoughts on this close call with Martin. "Y'know, initially I thought that Jim was the obvious choice too but honestly, Jon had as much if not more of a role in the FNM band than Jim did. It was a tough call. We reached out to Jim initially but it just felt like his head was in a different place. We kind of went on to grow together and create together for a long, long time after Jim left and we all developed a way of being together and playing together that Jim honestly wasn't a part of. It felt more representative to do shows with Jon than it did to do shows with Jim. Later on down the road we tried to get him on board to play but we couldn't come to an agreement of how it would go down. I think we all wanted to explore that. It's sad it didn't ever happen."

Looking back on the initial rehearsals after the reunion announcement, the keyboardist recalls there was "A crazy nervous weird energy. So much time had passed between our last show and that time. There was a lot going into it. I basically put all my stuff in my Prius and drove it up to the Bay Area so I had a lot of time to dwell on it. It all kind of came down to muscle memory. It was weird. My fingers were like disconnected from my head and just played the parts magically. I didn't think it would be emotional but it was. I honestly got a little teary about it. It's SO much time that we all put in together, it really is an intense force of nature, connecting like that and creating music. Sorry, it sounds corny, but it's a really special communication."

Unlike the days of 'Angel Dust' where it seemed like the members of FNM were actually searching out journalists to offer odd comments, this time around, the band decided to shun the press altogether, and let the performances and music do the talking. The ensuing tour (dubbed "The Second Coming Tour") would kick off on June 10, 2009, at their old stomping grounds, the Brixton Academy (now going by the name of the O2 Academy) in London, and two days later, handed in a solid performance as one of the headliners at the Download Festival (several songs of which were later aired throughout the world, including VH1 Classic in the US). FNM spent the rest of the summer touring Europe and Israel (including performances at various renowned festivals, including Roskilde, Pukkelpop, Reading, etc.), and then hit Mexico and South America in October and November.

Come 2010, FNM committed to further dates, including New Zealand and Australia in February and March, before finally offering US fans a handful of dates in April (the 12th through the 14th at San Francisco's Warfield and a performance on the 17th at the mammoth Coachella Music and Arts Festival in Indio, California - the latter of which saw a brief appearance by actor Danny DeVito mid-set). The Warfield performances proved special for the band, as on the final night, none other than Chuck Mosley replaced Patton on vocals for a four-song encore (the first time he appeared on staged with the band in 22 years), which included renditions of "As the Worm Turns," "Death March," "We Care A Lot," and "Mark Bowen," and then both singers dueted on a set-closing rendition of "Introduce Yourself."

"[Having Chuck there] was weird," recalled Gould. "Funny. Great. Soundcheck was great, we were laughing, he was just so out there. I grew up with him, way before FNM. He was like an older brother to me, and he saved me from listening to a lot of bad music. And when we got rid of Chuck, we were probably at the most opposite ends of the spectrum. So it was really great to come back as friends. And the music is a lot different with him in it, I really like it. It's more simple, a little darker, a bit goth in a way. We were trying to get Jim to do it too but he didn't want to do it. He thought about it for a couple of days and came back with a real big 'No!' Jim was all business, and sometimes the business isn't the point."

Speaking of Martin, the guitarist later commented on his reluctance for a "one-off" performance with FNM. "I know the fans want the real thing, and I was prepared to have a real dialogue about doing a run together. Unfortunately, it didn't happen. As for a random appearance, I do not feel that would do anyone justice."

Come June, three US east coast dates were announced - a deuce at the picturesque Williamsburg Waterfront (on the 2nd and 5th) and one at the Mann Center for the Performing Arts in Philly (on the 3rd). As you could probably have guessed by now, your humble author was indeed present for the first night in Brooklyn.

For those who aren't familiar with the Williamsburg Waterfront venue, it is outdoors, and behind the audience is the East River, and then across it is a spectacular view of lower Manhattan. On a sunny and warm day, fans were first treated to a set by human beatbox and master of vocal sounds, Rahzel. I was familiar with Mr. Rahzel's talents from catching a set a few years earlier by a short-lived Patton project, Peeping Tom, which included Rahzel in its ranks. Armed with just a microphone, Rahzel kept the crowd entertained with a variety of sounds a kin to the magnificent "Man of 10,000 Sound Effects," Michael Winslow. At one point, Rahzel asked the crowd what they were currently listening to, and started mimicking a few of the artists that were shouted out. For reasons unknown, Rahzel ignored my request of "GG Allin."

Up next was anti-comedian Neil Hamburger, who handed in a perfectly executed and confrontational stand-up act (which would have made the genre's forefather, Andy Kaufman, mighty proud) - that included jokes about the Red Hot Chili Peppers, among other topics, and also continuous throat clearing (and spitting the regurgitated contents into a cup), which sounded absolutely sublime cranked through the mega-decibel soundsystem.

Then, finally, FNM time. Keeping in line with their knack for picking/perfecting covers of other artists, the band started things off with a smooth and sultry cover of Peaches & Herb's 1979 hit ballad, "Reunited" (which saw Patton enter with the aid of a walking cane), before segueing into the long-lost ambitious title track from 'The Real Thing.' Up until that point, the crowd was on its best behavior, but by the time "From Out of Nowhere" was unveiled (with Patton holding a megaphone up to his mic and selecting the "siren" sound effect), the audience went berserk - the moshers started moshing, and the surfers started surfing. As a result, I retreated towards the back to observe - bringing back a sense of déjà vu to the Roseland '92 show.

As I had been tracking FNM's setlists on the reunion tour up until this point, I was happy to see tunes that had been neglected during the mid-late '90s tours making a comeback, such as "Land of Sunshine," "Surprise! You're Dead!", and "Cuckoo for Caca," all of which made appearances that evening. Also added to the setlist was another new cover selection, the theme song from the 1981 film, 'Chariots of Fire.' At one point, Patton told the crowd that we were foolish for looking at the band during the performance, as the real beautiful sight was the sunset happening behind us, as the sun was slowly sinking behind the tall skyscrapers of Manhattan. All in all, a fine performance, and proof that the band could still deliver the goods in concert - not something that is always a sure thing when bands reunite after an extended period of time. Immediately after the mini-US east coast leg of the tour, FNM revisited Europe for two and a half weeks of festival appearances, before closing the year with a pair of performances at the Hollywood Palladium in Los Angeles, California (including a standout moment at the December 1st performance, which saw Ron and Russell Mael of Sparks join FNM on stage for a rendition of "This Town Ain't Big Enough For Both Of Us"...as well as none other than Dean Menta jumping in on guitar), and two more shows in Santiago, Chile.

Much of 2011 was taken off from the band, except for four South American performances during November - in Argentina, Uruguay, Chile, and Brazil. The Chilean performance at the Maquinaria Festival on November 12th proved to be another standout, as the group performed the 'King for a Day' album in its entirety for the first time...with Trey Spruance on guitar. Included in the set were such treats as "Star AD" (performed for the first time ever live, with a horn section, to boot), while a rendition of "Just A Man" featured a choir. And as a treat for hardcore followers, the encore included the obscure 'KFAD' era b-side, "Absolute Zero" (also the first-time ever performed on stage).

Bottum would later give his thoughts on the one-off reunion with Spruance - "I love Trey, he's such a sweetheart and so amazingly talented. So much of our reunion thing was about letting water just go under the bridge. Not that I had any bad water with Trey but to see it all come around full circle and know that we were all enjoying it meant a lot to me. The only changes we really made were by adding two guitars to a song or two and adding the choir to a couple of songs and I think we added some brass to a song...sorry, I forget the names of songs a lot but you get the idea." The appearance of Spruance and Patton on the same stage obviously got the attention of Mr. Bungle fans, as the duo had apparently settled their differences enough to the point that they were able to share the same stage again. Could this lead to a rebirth of Bungle? I guess all we can do is remain patient and keep our peepers peeled.

And as with previous FNM tours, Patton did his best to give the fans something special to remember each performance by. Whether it be complaining about a foul odor emanating from the crowd (June 13, 2009 at the Greenfield Festival in Interlaken, Switzerland), having a female audience member teach him how to do the "Kolo" (July 11, 2010 at the Exit Festival in Novi Sad, Serbia), getting dropped by the audience while crowdsurfing (July 16, 2010 at the Gurten Festival in Bern, Switzerland), methodically "eating" a fan's shoelace and gagging it back up (August 16, 2009 at the Sziget Festival in Budapest, Hungary), or exposing his johnson (February 20, 2010 at the Exhibition Ground in Brisbane, Australia), the singer certainly aimed to please. And Gould appreciates that "anything-goes" stance - "Even we don't know what's going to happen. And that's how we like it. I mean, Patton, he's not young you know. He hurts himself…that kind of adrenaline, it's really important to have that. You don't feel it. That's part of the fun. It's a tribal thing, an animal thing. People need that. It can't be all business, like oh go check out a band because they are 'up and coming,' as if it's like buying a stock."

House of Pain's Everlast caught several performances of The Second Coming Tour, and walked away thoroughly impressed. "I just saw them on that last run in Europe - [House of Pain] did a few festivals with them. As far as rock n' roll shows are concerned, Mike Patton is God. He can do no wrong, man. That guy came out in like a fuchsia pimp suit with gaiters on, and immediately climbed a stack of speakers and dove into the drummer!" [Laughs] Additionally, Everlast made a worthy observation while comparing the modern day FNM line-up to the line-up of yore - "As many [shows] as we might have played together when I was young, it's hard to remember those times - I was a lot wilder back then. I actually *watched* their shows this time, so I enjoyed them more than ever. That last run I saw them on, it was funny, because a couple of the guys aged and didn't hold it down as well. Like it looked like Mike Patton and the drummer who has the dreads…the rest of the guys kind of looked like a high school faculty staff a little bit." [Laughs]

Finally, The Second Coming Tour ground to a halt in 2012, after a final European leg, which included two performances in Russia, at the Creation of Peace Festival in Perm and Stadium Live in Moscow. The latter show on July 2nd featured a cameo appearance from the all-female masked band, Pussy Riot (who had touched off a worldwide "freedom of speech debate," when three of its members would eventually be sentenced to prison after an uninvited performance in Moscow's Cathedral of Christ the Saviour Church), just before the set-closer, "We Care A Lot," during which Patton and Bottum donned Pussy Riot masks, in tribute. "We've always encouraged art forms that provoke," explained Bottum as to the reason FNM invited the all-female group on stage. "We've made a career of doing just that with our music. We recognized that Pussy Riot provokes intellectual thought and thought it would be an interesting addition to the show." And then...the final tour performance was at the exact same location that it all began three years earlier - the O2 Academy in London, England, on July 10th.

With soundboard recordings from the tour circulating amongst fans, it was clear that a killer official live album and/or DVD could easily be assembled, to which Bottum responded about the possibility of such releases, "Who knows? We recorded a whole bunch of shows when we played live over the past three years. Some of the recordings sound really superb. We haven't really talked about releasing anything live."

In early 2013, Patton gave this not-so-promising-sounding update as to if there will be any more dates added to the reunion trek. "It's sort of petered out. We're also maybe a little too conscious for our own good. Meaning there's a lineage of bands that maybe did some nice things and then needed the cash and got back together and basically just sprayed diarrhea over their entire body of work. We're very worried about that. We don't want to overdo it." However, Gould sounds more optimistic regarding if there will be additional Faith No More performances at some point in the future. "I personally can't see us not doing anymore shows again, I just don't see it. There's no point in not to do it. Why quit now? I think it's just this tour...we did this tour and that's what we decided to do. And we did it. We accomplished this goal, it worked out for all of us, and then we look at each other and say, 'Hey what do you want to do now?' And I think that's how it's got to be."

And lastly, the bassist offered his thoughts on the possibility of a seventh FNM studio album. "Hasn't been discussed. It's the elephant in the room. It's in everybody's mind but everyone is afraid to talk about it. That's the reality. All I can do is offer my own opinion, and I'm just 20% of the band. But my thing is, it's like having a really great plate of food and throwing it on the ground. Everything is great for doing it and if we did it, it's going to be great. It's going to be because this is the best energy ever. And people have done a lot of other things since then that could bring a lot more to it than before. But that's my take on it. I've got to let it go with that because if it's meant to be, it's meant to happen."

Chapter 20: Shit Terrorist

The tales of Mike Patton's nutty actions over the years are so abundant that they could quite possibly fill an entire book - with full details and thorough analysis of each and every exploit. And there was a very tough decision to be made in the creation of this book - carefully spread these tales of folly throughout, or give them their own special chapter? After much deliberation, a verdict was reached...go with the latter option.

As the man himself once said, "A lot of pieces written about us, selectively edit together all the vile and disgusting stuff, which is fine, 'cause nobody wants to read about us making coffee. But I don't think we buy into a lot of the myths of what we're doing. We just lived with that for three months [the G n' R tour], and saw so much of it...the whole idea that there has to be something outrageous and abnormal is washed up and gone. I mean we do our own thing, like I don't use toilets - I just don't. It's not a wild rock n' roll thing; it's a hobby - shit terrorism. I did a shit on the bench outside Charles and Diana's palace, but that didn't cause any rumpus. It could have been anyone's shit really. The consistency wasn't so good. It wasn't a prizewinning trophy."

"Shit terrorism" or "shit terrorist" are phrases that were linked to the singer quite a bit (especially in the UK press) back in the days of yore. And with good reason - Mr. Patton enjoyed having fun with his feces. As Kim Thayil recalls about his former tour mate - "Mike Patton's thing, he was kind of obsessed with scatological issues in relation to his pranks, and his scatological manifestation of his pranks was in defecation...he liked shitting in funny places. He liked to shit and hide it somewhere in the cafeteria, or shit in the parking lot of a hotel behind some car, or just go and shit on a hood of a car." Or as Patton himself once confessed to an interviewer, his "interest" had grown beyond just pranks - "Sometimes a shit-eating video is so much cooler than watching two people kissing. Do you know what I mean?"

Journalist William Shaw once attempted to get to the bottom of the origins of Patton's fecal fixation, and was rewarded with a bit of insight...and a bonus tale of revenge. "Mike says it stems from a childhood fear of invasive insects in the bathroom. But the singer has turned his aversion to the WC [water closet] into a form of scatological terrorism. Without batting an eyelid, he recounts a story about a meanie club owner who locked Patton and the rest of Mr. Bungle up in his club because he claimed they owed him money. He left the man a special gift in the club's microwave oven. 'It started out being a problem, but now it's more of a weapon than anything,' Patton says."

But enough of this doo-doo talk...for now at least. Another topic that Patton offered quite a few tidbits about during his FNM career was his sexual habits, which were quite dissimilar from the usual debauched tales of rock stars. "I could tell you a nice juicy one from my childhood," Patton once said. "I remember my mum was a daycare helper, she babysat kids. We could always go play in the front yard, me and all the kids she looked after, and I distinctly remember I used to hump things all the time, in front of everyone, I didn't care. And I remember on the front lawn I was laying on the ground and just humping the earth, in front of everyone. And of course I didn't know it was something you were supposed to do in private. My mum was panicking, I used to call it 'my tricks' and I'd announce it when I got home from school. I'd say, 'OK mum, I'm going to do my tricks,' and I'd turn on the TV and find some program with girls in it and I'd just lay on the couch...it was like a normal thing like having a snack or something. I may have a lot of sexual hang ups but masturbation's not one of them!"

Ah yes, we mustn't forget another topic that Patton had a fondness for discussing early on in interviews - choking the chicken. "I talk so much about masturbation in interviews because I go on the defensive as soon as journalists start asking about groupies. It's much easier relating to yourself on tour than it is to someone you've just met. Maybe I should say I've grown beyond it and now I'm into farm animals. Too many journalists still believe the rock n' roll myth. From my side it's definitely not like that. A lot of bands are doing it, but they must have had insecure childhoods - maybe their parents dropped them on their heads."

Whereas countless rock musicians who tour the world see it as a golden opportunity for potential "romantic encounters," Patton looked at it as something that may have affected him negatively. "I can't explain a whole lot about sex life, except for the fact that it isn't bountiful. I think meeting people is great. But on a sexual level it's much easier to get bored I guess...I don't know...I've had a lot of mechanical sex...I wouldn't say that I'm seriously into S&M. I mean, come on, having somebody pee on you wearing a Darth Vader suit. It's great and everything. But take a few steps back and you have to laugh. I don't know what happened to me. Maybe I went through puberty or something. I'd say touring as much as we did - becoming a stimulation junkie, developing a very high threshold for pain and a very low attention span - would tie anyone in a knot." A much safer outlet for his sexual desires back in the "pre-internet days" seemed to be the then-popular phone sex lines. "You don't call a 970 number because you want to talk. That's not why I try it. I don't know why. I've always had a problem with interaction. I'm just not that good at it."

And unlike some celebrities who cheerily respond to letters penned from fans, Patton admitted to answering only one such letter. It didn't go good. "She started sending gifts and somehow twisted around the idea that I wanted to dominate her, you know? She called me her master...she said, 'I'll do anything for you. I'm your devoted slave'." And there were at least three other "misadventures" with female admirers. "Recently, a girl chained herself to me with handcuffs after a gig, just because I refused to talk to her. I politely declined, though. I am a well-bred boy. I don't want to be too specific, but...it got pretty ugly. I've got some letters, really creepy, man...written in blood, with devil's horns drawn on them. And last year a perfect stranger hired a private detective to follow me. All very interesting from a distance, but not when it happens to you."

Something else that you wouldn't spot in your average Patton interview were any Nikki Sixx-ian tales of snorting and/or shooting every substance that came into view. Although he did admit to having one vice. "I'm not a big drug taker, but I'm hooked on coffee and I never get enough sleep." Another time, he used coffee to fend off sleep - "I did this experiment, depriving myself of sleep just to see how long I could go." Supposedly, when he reached the third day sans sleep, he came across televangelist Robert Tilton on the tube (probably via Tilton's infomercial-esque religious show, 'Success-N-Life'). "I made a vow of faith to [Tilton]. You promise to send him $100 and he sends you all these neat things. He sent me anointing oil, prayer cloths, posters, books - and I never sent him any money. And I do feel guilty about it, too!"

The singer once talked about another drug - which he failed to mention by name, but was of the "herbal health food" variety - that he and a few of his mates had indulged in. "You mix it with water to make you go to sleep, but if you have too much, this other thing kicks in. It's like drinking a six-pack of orange soda and sitting in the back of a hot car. It's a nauseating, piece of shit high, and most people end up vomiting. But it's fun 'cause you never know what's gonna happen. Three of us took it one day, and we ended up sleeping with our bodies in positions they should not have been in."

And it was while on tour - and more specifically, on the concert stage - that Patton soon realized he could get away with much more than the Average Joe ever could. "It's nice to have a place to go and not be held totally responsible for your actions," he once said about performing. Another time, he gave an example. "On our last tour I jumped into the crowd and broke this kid's nose. I tried to get him medical aid but he said he'd rather have a t-shirt. It's bad. What do you tell his parents? The other day I met a guy who had a scar over his eye, just like mine. I asked him how he got it and he said: 'You did it to me, but it's cool'." The singer also saw himself as two different personalities - one on-stage, and the other off-stage. "I just don't want to be a pop star and supply you with scandals and sensations. I separate my job as a musician from my private life. I don't want people to write about what's in my fridge or in which bed I'm sleeping. I'm a shy and introverted guy...I'm sometimes very reserved when it comes to human relations. I'm scared of showing my inner feelings. On the other side it's pretty easy for me to go wild on stage. I play that role like an actor."

Watch just about any concert-length bootleg performance of Faith No More or Mr. Bungle from way back when, and you're almost certain to come across several clever on-stage comments from the frontman. But on one occasion, he may have "bantered" a bit too far, according to Gould. "His parents came to see the show once. And Mike was onstage, saying how he'd fucked his mother last night while his father watched. Our old producer Matt Wallace was sitting with them, and he asked them what they thought of his comments like that, and his dad said, 'Well, where the fuck do you think he learned to talk like that'?" The apple doesn't fall far from the tree, eh?

And it was that exact "What is he going to do next?" vibe that made Patton's performances with FNM and Bungle so unpredictable and yet so worthwhile. But according to Vision of Disorder's Mike Fleischmann, he wound up on the losing end when he attended a Patton performance with John Zorn and Ikue Mori in August 1996. "My friends and I were such big Patton fans that in the late '90s, we bought tickets to see him and John Zorn at the Knitting Factory in NYC. They came out onstage, and Zorn started squawking his saxophone at a really high pitch. Patton started squealing and screaming, and they had a woman on keyboards just banging incoherently on the keys. I tried to bear with it, but it became too painful and I had to put my fingers in my ears. I felt better when I turned around and saw other pained looks in the crowd with hands covering their ears. At one point, Zorn singled out a member of the crowd who was smoking a cigarette, and yelled something like, 'You better put out that cigarette...or I'll put it out for you!' At another point, during a quiet section, one of my friends sarcastically yelled out 'Epic'! - a request that the performers ignored. 15 more minutes of the same noise and I gave up and waited outside for my friends. As I was walking out, there was a line of people awaiting their next set. A guy yelled out to me, 'Yo dude! Do they do any Bungle?' I think I just made a disgusted face and kept walking - I didn't wanna say anything bad to the others who had bought tickets."

Patton's tendency of going just a tad far on stage can understandably rub some the wrong way, including Madball's Mitts. "That was something that bummed me out about him. This isn't just something in an interview, if he ever wanted to debate me on it, I would tell him to his face - I was always almost downright offended by the way that that guy sings on his live show. He's got these songs on the record that have beautiful vocal melodies, and then he gets up there, and he's just like...'BLAH!!!' Screams his head off, and almost mocks his own vocal lines. Now, I don't know how to interpret that - is that because he's bored of singing it? Well, if he's bored of singing it the way it was recorded, I don't care, because I paid money to hear that fucking song. I'm not bored with it. Your fans want to hear the songs. If you had to do it over again, would you go back and scream your fucking head off, like a screaming baby over those songs? Is that what you originally intended? Or, are you just trying to be obnoxious? I never respected that guy's live performances, because I think his live performances mock his fans. I think it's disrespectful to the fans of his band, the way he does his stuff. And it's not like the guy's not talented - he's got an unbelievable voice, and he writes unbelievable vocal lines. I just always thought that it was really disrespectful and he's kind of mocking his fans, the way he would get up there and just scream like a screaming infant."

"He just seems like he's trying to go on that GG Allin tip," continues Mitts. "Like, 'Let's see who I can piss off, and let's see how obnoxious I can be.' My interpretation of that is for some reason, I feel that Mike Patton has inspired this army of loyal diehard fans, that no matter what he does, they think it's brilliant. I just don't see it. Maybe it's just lack of vision on my part. In my head, I somehow imagine the scenario that that guy's out there, just trying to see, 'Well, what can I do that people won't like?' He's trying to find a way to scare those people away, but they don't do it - they just think everything he does is brilliant."

But according to HIM's Ville Valo, it is this daredevil artistic sense that makes Patton such an exceptional singer and compelling performer. "It sounds effortless and it also sounds at the same time like he doesn't give a fuck - while he's still loving what he does. And that's a really odd combination - you have great performers who are not necessarily great musicians. And very rarely do those two things come together. And again, the sense of 'enigma' - nobody really understands what the hell that dude is about. All the records he's making are really left-of-center and some of them you might like, and some of them you might hate. It doesn't really matter - the point is he's treading his own path. And that's what makes the whole thing special - at least in my ears and eyes."

It seemed as if Patton was never at a loss for an interesting tale when he sat down with a journalist, including another lesson in revenge...albeit a rather messy one. "You wanna know a great way to get even with somebody? My particular vengeance was against a business that had fucked me over really bad. So one morning, see, I woke up, ate an entire burrito, drank a half-pint of rum, downed some castor oil, then drank some Ipecac syrup, which takes about a half hour to work. Then I walked down to this business, and I'd timed it perfectly. Nothing is more repulsive, and no one would ever think you'd go through so much trouble! This place had a nice, clear counter and no janitor, either. It kinda backfired, though, because I took too much castor oil, which coats the stomach, so not a lot of food came up. But a lot of blood did, though!" Too bad iPhones and other discreet recording devices didn't exist at the time, as the gag certainly would have worked wonders with 'Jackass' and 'Tosh.0' devotees if launched into cyberspace.

And while we're on the subject of modern day television programming, years before the show 'Oddities' made it hip to have an interest in whackoid artifacts, Mr. Patton would gush about a display at Glasgow University that he would visit while on tour, which featured a variety of "pickled" human body parts - "It has got everything from two-headed goats to giant human genitals pickled in jars and I just love it. It is really all beautiful stuff. A doctor friend of mine - who works in Glasgow - arranged the previous visits for me. I had to put on a white coat and pretend that I was a visiting student in order to get in. I plan to do the same this time but I just hope that no one will recognize me as that could turn out to be very embarrassing." He would continue, "Some people think that I am a pervert because of my unusual tastes, but I'm not. I collect medical specimens and pictures from all over the world in same the way (sic) other people collect stamps. It's just my hobby."

Another time, a journalist spoke of several books that Patton had proudly acquired. "The first, a pictorial collection of embalmed bodies lying in their states of grace, is titled 'Sleeping Beauty.' An assassinated family, featured therein, is being considered for the sleeve of the next single, 'A Small Victory' [which ultimately, didn't make the cut]. The second book, which the singer extracts from a carrier stowed in his claustrophobic bunk, strikes fear and loathing into my breast. The attractive scarlet Jackson Pollock-esque jacket does not prepare me for the photographs inside, cataloguing the work of a performance artist who decorates naked members of his audience with the organs of ritually slaughtered animals. There are group shots of people up to their elbows in bloody entrails, smearing goat guts over a living naked form. Close-ups of male genitalia, dressed with fresh brains, still seeping mucus: 'Some people would feel guilty owning this book, unless they have the correct reason,' says Patton. 'I don't know why I own it. It's fucked up, but I like it. Discovering this kind of thing comes out of boredom. You just start getting really curious. And the further away you get, the more exciting it is. It's that way with sex, with art and with music for me. After a while you just have to know what the next step is."

Interestingly, for a gentleman who was always very honest and forthcoming in interviews, one topic that Patton refused to give many details about was his marriage during the '90s, as he once scolded an interviewer who dared ask a question pertaining to the subject - "There comes a point in interviews, where a line has to be drawn. And I'm drawing that line now. Understand me? Perhaps we should have drawn it earlier." Even his own band mates were befuddled by Patton's reluctance to discuss his significant other during the interview. Gould: "So, you just asked him if, now he's married, he plans to have any kids? Ha! Ha! I'm not making any excuses for the guy but he really doesn't like talking about himself. Did you ask him if he'd done anything creative with his shit recently? He wouldn't have liked that. All that stuff just tortures him; but he did it, he should learn to live with it. Y'know? All that business with shit is what he's best known for."

And while his bizarre behavior is what probably provided the majority of headlines in the rock music press, there is no denying that Patton is certainly one of the most talented - and arguably, most diverse - vocalists that listeners of popular music have ever heard. And it turns out that is an opinion shared by House of Pain's Everlast - "What *can't* he do? Seriously, the dude's range is bananas. I mean, he's got to be eight octaves. I've heard him hit crazy high notes, and then that motherfucker sings the lowest low, or even come out and sound like somebody from one of these death metal bands - and sound *better* than any of them. A whole other time we did some festivals together, he was doing this thing with Rahzel - it was just him and Rahzel with microphones, no instruments. And it was just bananas. He's got one of them things - it's super-talent. Beyond human in ways." Kyuss' John Garcia offers this short-but-sweet compliment - "One of the best rock n' roll singers I believe of my generation. Absolutely one of the best."

While countless renowned rock singers have experienced throat problems over the years - who never came close to pushing their voices to the limits that Patton does on a nightly basis while on tour - you have to wonder if he follows a special regimen to keep his voice up to snuff.

Patton once explained, "I've lost my voice maybe once in the last ten years. I've found out that the more you abuse your voice the better, or the less it hurts in some ways. I find that if I take two or three days off in the middle of a tour, I get a sore throat. The more days I do in a row, the better it is for my voice. I don't have the chance to get sick."

With such a wide variety of voices he has utilized for his various musical projects, it makes perfect sense that Patton does not discriminate when it comes to music listening. "I used to have records by Elton fuckin' John. Oh, and by Sade. Billy and I once spent our last penny on a ticket for a Sade concert. And we had to borrow some money on the spot to buy a poster as well. I still like her, by the way. And what a babe! Hey, FNM is a potpourri of very different, very bizarre musical tastes. When we play a record at home, one day it's Henry Mancini, the next day Slayer."

I also once had the opportunity to ask Patton about who some of his favorite singers were, to which he responded, "Oh God, this is a toughie. Too many. Um, singers I like - Sammy Davis Jr., Shooby Taylor, Mel Blanc, Diamanda Galas, uh...Franz [Treichler] from the Young Gods I think is a great singer. Who else could I say...an incredible Italian vocalist, Demetrio Stratos, who influenced me a lot."

OK, I agree - we've wandered off the original topic for far too long. To the best of my knowledge, Mike Patton is the only public figure "courageous" enough to openly discuss his interest or fetish in scatology. As the man himself once admitted, "I have kind of a problem, I don't like to use toilets - ever." And while Patton first began being tied to the subject circa the 'Angel Dust' era, Kim Thayil recalls a related story that possibly stretches back to the Faith No More/Soundgarden/Voivod tour.

"I think we were playing the Aragon Ballroom with Faith No More. I remember going to the bathroom and Faith No More was on stage. I was taking a piss, and all of a sudden, Mike ran into the bathroom - he was all sweaty. He ran into the shower, and I was laughing. I go, 'What the fuck are you doing? Aren't you guys on stage?' I can still hear the band, but there's no vocals - maybe a guitar solo. He's in the shower, he ran out, he smiled at me, and then ran back onstage. Then, after the show, our tour manager comes up, and he's like, 'Someone took a dump in the fucking shower. Some of the employees say they saw *you* in the bathroom.' I go, 'Yeah, I took a piss! Mike Patton ran down off the stage! It must have been Patton - *that's* what he was doing in the shower!' We ended up learning that was his 'thing.' I think Mike Patton influenced Matt Cameron into doing some similar things. This is all shit that Mike Patton and Matt Cameron did - they'd take dumps into a bowl or a plate, and then undo the vents in a hotel room, then put the plate or bowl into the vent, then re-screw the vent screen back on, so that the room I guess would be inundated with a certain 'perfume,' and the employees would have a hard time figuring out what the origination point was for that foul odor. They'd eventually take off the vent screen and find Mike Patton's 'prize.' And I know Matt Cameron did that a couple of times because he learned that from Patton."

Patton once spilled the beans about another tactic he utilized, that also involved hotel rooms and unsuspecting victims who occupied the rooms after he did. "When I was staying in a hotel room once, I took a shit, rolled it into a ball and put it in the hair dryer so that the next guest to dry their hair would get hot shit in their face. Ain't that rock n' roll?" Other charming stories reported in the press about Patton included chewing on a tampon that was left on stage by a member of L7, doing #2 in an orange juice carton, resealing it, and tucking it away on L7's tour vehicle, and last but not least, urinating in a shoe on stage and then consuming the collected contents.

By the time Soundgarden hooked up once again with FNM on the aforementioned G n' R Euro tour, Thayil recalls that Patton had wholeheartedly embraced another bodily function. "There's something else he would do - he would drink lots of water and Coke or coffee, and some diuretics, and hold it in. Then he'd pee and fill up...I think Guns N' Roses had water jugs on stage. We didn't really use that, I just had beer. But those guys had things that could squirt water. And Patton would fill it up with piss and then throw it into the crowd. I think he collected like a milk jug full of piss - he was doing this for a few days. I believe that's the case. He filled up a jug full of piss and I remember the Soundgarden guys talked about it and the crew guys were like, 'Oh my God! Do you see what he's doing!' Ben [Shepherd, Soundgarden bassist] would say, 'Fuck! He's got a fucking jug full of piss and he said he's going to throw it into the crowd!' I guess he did - I think he swung the jug full of piss into the crowd. And somebody told me he was going to take a shit on stage...or maybe he did. This is not apocryphal - it may be anecdotal, but it's not apocryphal. I never saw this happen, but I heard that that happened - I didn't hear that was a plan, I heard that happened from crew guys and band guys on that tour, that he tried or just dropped his pants and took a dump on stage. But the stage was grated. Guns N' Roses had a stage with grating, so if you spilled anything, it fell through, just so you couldn't slip on the thing."

Roddy Bottum tells a classic story from the same tour in the 'Video Croissant' release [and later reappeared in the aforementioned home video, 'Who Cares a Lot?: The Greatest Videos']. "We had a particularly good show in Seville, in Spain. The audience was really into us, but someone threw a plastic bottle up on stage at one point, so we kind of encouraged it. We kind of all speak a little bit of Spanish, so we're saying 'Más! Más! Más cosas!' [English translation - 'More! More! More things!'] And people are throwing plastic bottles and cans at us. The sky was filled with plastic bottles and cans. At one point, someone took an Evian bottle and urinated in it, put the cap back on, and threw it on stage. So we had the bottle on stage - it was on stage - and we were all talking about it. We're saying, "Wow, someone peed in this bottle and threw it on stage," and it's sitting there on stage. And at one point in the set, Mike Patton took the bottle, stood up on Axl's monitor, unscrewed the cap, *and poured it over his entire head.* Drenched himself with urine."

Dean Menta also has similar memories of Patton "amusing himself" with bodily functions - "The peeing, the pooing, the drinking the pee, the peeing in the shoe and drinking. The peeing in a cup and handing it to a young girl in the front row who I think assumed it was water and guzzled it. Things of that nature." But perhaps it was a quote from Gould about his singer's peculiarities that boggles the mind the most - "I can't tell you some of the worst things he's done, until the statute of limitations runs out."

Lastly, Thayil offers some parting thoughts on the Shit Terrorist. "I do have to emphasize that it's hard to consider a scatological obsession with feces as being witty. I actually think it's somewhat dull, as far as wit goes. But it is amusing that a person would be amused by that. It's sort of like a meta-amusement. And I think we all had fun at the idea that this guy was amusing himself by doing that shit."

No pun intended with that last sentence, Kim?

Chapter 21: Tributo

TRAVIS STEVER: The best way I can describe the influence is through a story. I fell off on Faith No More once 'Angel Dust' came out. I only had given a couple of songs a chance. Big mistake. One day I was hanging with Claudio at my grandmother's house in Pearl River, New York. We were only fourteen or fifteen, and he had some tapes to listen to as we sat around. One of the tapes was 'Angel Dust.' It had been out a year or maybe even more by then, and Claudio was all about it. He was about to put it on and I said I only heard a song or two from that record, and didn't think it would be good. He quickly replied with, "Fuck no - this album is great" or something along those lines, and put it on. I was hooked. To this day, it's my favorite Faith No More record, and I can thank him for that moment of showing me the light. And that carried on for years to come.

Claudio and I would drive along through our teens and early twenties blasting 'Angel Dust,' 'King for a Day,' and the very underrated 'Album of the Year.' They were a part of our youth and musical upbringing, so of course it influenced the music we created. I remember the first time Claudio showed me a demo of a song he had written for Coheed, called "Al the Killer." I was so excited about that song because of the Faith No More feel I felt it had. There are many more songs that we have done through the years that have had a guitar part or vocal melody that I will say, 'Oh shit - there's that Faith No More influence.'

JOHNNY CHRIST: Yeah, there's definitely some influence - vocal arrangements and everything like that. The Rev was very inspired by Mr. Bungle and Faith No More - and also Oingo Boingo - when he wrote songs like "A Little Piece of Heaven." There was definitely some influence there.

VILLE VALO: I think it was a combination of bands [that proved to be influential from the early '90's]. It was the reunited Bad Brains, it was Jane's Addiction, definitely - 'Nothing's Shocking' and 'Ritual.' And then

Faith No More. And it all happened at the same time. All the bands sounded really unique and the cool thing about it was that it wasn't like a big trendy thing, that all of a sudden 15,000 bands wanted to sound exactly the same. You couldn't because all those bands were so unique - the way of performing and doing what they did was un-copy-able. I think that's what makes it special and still makes it hold up.

MICHAEL FLEISCHMANN: FNM and Bungle had a huge impact. They changed the heavy music game in my book. They showed everyone that there are no rules to this. You bring who you are to your music and play it the way you want. Bands that take chances are so much more interesting to follow. No two FNM or Bungle albums sound alike or like anything else you've ever heard. Billy Gould was a huge influence on my bass playing - style-wise and sound-wise. The more you listen to FNM you realize the majority of their songs are built around these incredible bass grooves. Some of them are so simple. Take two classic songs - "We Care A Lot" and "Epic." Both of them are built on top of Gould just rhythmically hitting his open E sting - he barely needs a left hand. But at the same time, he can also gallop like Steve Harris ("Surprise! Your Dead!") or put a totally different spin on the art of slapping ("Crack Hitler," "Woodpecker from Mars"). He softens his sound for a funky feel on "Evidence," and even takes a solo on "Kindergarten." He's just such a creative, diverse player.

MAX CAVALERA: Amazing. They did some of the most cool stuff ever. 'Angel Dust' is one the masterpieces of rock, of all time. It's so furious sometimes, and then it gets super-melodic. And schizophrenic at the same time. And the album title 'Angel Dust' is a great record title, also. Everything about it was great.

JEFF WALKER: I'm not an uber-fan. I would say they're one of the world's most overrated bands - but then, I would say that about my own band, as well! I was definitely a fan, around the time of 'The Real Thing' and 'Angel Dust.' I kind of lost interest after 'Angel Dust.' Cool dudes - they were Carcass fans [at a FNM performance at London's Marquee in 1992, Patton, Gould, and Bottum were all attired in Carcass shirts]. That was a cool connection we had. I've always been a big fan of Billy Gould's bass playing. Really cool band.

Why? [In response to being asked why he feels FNM are overrated] I just think they were - I can't really quantify it. They're definitely a good band, they've got some great songs. But the kind of adulation that they cause from people, it's just really bizarre...they're definitely a bunch of great musicians and a great singer. They had some cool songs. But I've never found them as eclectic or experimental as people try to make out - I think Billy Gould and Mike Patton in their careers later have been, but I don't think with Faith No More. I'm not dissing them, because I'm a fan of those records, but like I said, I just lost interest later.

TRAVIS STEVER: They are two very different entities [FNM and Bungle]. Sometimes they would cross in sound. "Star AD" from 'King for a Day' - with its horns and craziness - has a "Bungle feel." But for the most part, they were two very different but unique sounds. I feel like they both respectively paved the way for a lot of bands and acts to go in totally different directions. I remember someone saying that Faith No More is the reason bad nu metal exists. Well, a lot of those bands people speak of just took an element of their sound and ran with it. They are missing everything else that makes Faith No More so original.

EVERLAST: Tons of them [have been influenced by FNM]. You already mentioned Rage...there was a whole nu metal scene for a while. I mean, Korn definitely stole some stuff. Any of those bands. Any band that started post-that era definitely had some influence.

MITTS: I think they definitely influenced what later became that '90s sound of nu metal. Just having a lot more groove to it. I think that the Chili Peppers, Faith No More, and Fishbone definitely brought a new angle to heavy music as the '90s went on, and you hear that in that whole '90s sound.

KIM THAYIL: What they were doing, definitely their influence went all over the place. Mike Patton's vocal versatility to this day is having its influence, with Mr. Bungle and Fantômas, but also with Faith No More.

JOHNNY CHRIST: What Mr. Bungle did is a little out there, but I think it definitely inspired a lot of musicians to continue writing that way. And with Faith No More having some mainstream success, it definitely influenced a lot of musicians that are out there today.

MICHAEL FLEISCHMANN: What sets both bands apart obviously is the diversity they bring to the table and how effortlessly and natural they are able to make it sound. No one even comes close in my book.

JOHN GARCIA: I have absolutely mad respect for that band. I still listen to them. Every once in a while, I'll throw on 'Angel Dust' for sure, absolutely, all their records, and my wife and I will kick back and reminisce.

WES BORLAND: Faith No More was definitely the move for me into being completely open-minded about weird music. I think it's weird enough to where it doesn't sound dated. It's its own thing and it sounds like Faith No More, but it doesn't sound like it was trying to copy anything else. So I think even though certain music reminds you of certain times in your life when you hear it, it was so different from everything else going on then. Actually, a lot of music from that period of time was so different.

Like, I remember going to Lollapalooza over a two-year period [1992-1993], and seeing Primus, Rage Against the Machine, Ministry, and Red Hot Chili Peppers - there were all these bands that didn't sound alike, that were all kind of appealing to all these people at the same time. If you listened to Tool, you probably liked Primus - but they were nothing alike. And if somebody liked Primus, you could assume they probably liked Faith No More - but they didn't sound anything alike. It was a really interesting time, where all the bands that all my friends liked were all different from each other, in an extreme way. It's not like, "Yeah, I listen to Slayer and Megadeth, and bands that are more narrowly similar." That was an odd time if you think about it, and I don't feel like it's that way now. I feel like there are these very separate genres of music, where people are like, "I listen to *this* kind of thing, I listen to *this* kind of thing."

DEVIN TOWNSEND: There's few things that are going to be rendered obsolete, just by the technological aspects of it - keyboard sounds or production values. But the rap thing as well, the song "Epic," I probably share the impression of that song that I'm sure a lot of the band does, and a lot of the people who were introduced to it do. It doesn't do it for me. But still, it's great. It's nostalgia, so it's hard for me to be objective about it.

JEFF WALKER: I don't bother going back and listening. I mean, how does it hold up? The thing is with any song that you love when you're younger, it evokes memories of the time and place. So it still delivers on that basis, because 'Angel Dust' is almost a classic album now to some people. It does transpose you to another time and another place. I occasionally pick out the odd song once in a while and listen to it. 'Angel Dust' stands up, I think. All their stuff stands up - there's stuff I listen to from my childhood that just sounds horrible and it's better left in the memory. But I think with Faith No More, what you remember and when you listen to the CD is one and the same. That shows its strength - that it's lasted.

MICHAEL FLEISCHMANN: FNM albums are timeless for me. They have entered into my "classic" category - they are like fine wine. Bungle, you have to be in the right mood for. Their music can be intense!

MITTS: I think it holds up pretty good. There's certain records in my life that from 20 years ago if I go to put it on nowadays, I'm just like, *"Eh."* But if I put on 'Angel Dust' or 'King for a Day,' I can still put those two on. 'The Real Thing,' maybe I played that out a little much. It's a great record, I just personally don't see a need to go back and revisit that record. But 'Angel Dust' is one that I can pretty much listen to at any time in my life, and 'King for a Day,' as well.

JASON NEWSTED: For me, I just had the first few records. So that holds up. I still actually play 'Introduce Yourself' a lot, believe it or not. I have 'Introduce Yourself' on a CD in my little house in Florida, and I only have a handful of CD's there, so that gets played a lot. It takes me back to that place in Mabuhay that night, because that was a song that really caught me. "Introduce Yourself" was really their big thing from the stage. When that happened, the whole crowd is in it. You are in that song and I'll never forget that. That takes me to a special place. I listen to that one more than any of their other records, for sure.

VILLE VALO: I was in a club and they were playing 'Angel Dust' - it's such a big part of my life and growing up, that it always sounds good to me. It's not as if I would say, "This sounds passé" or "I don't like this snare drum sound" or whatever. It was great then and such a milestone in me becoming a bit more of an "adult" than I was, that I wouldn't change a thing. The only thing I would change is the fact that I would have loved to see them play. That would have been great, because I heard great things about them. But at that time, in the part of the world I was living, there was not a lot of international acts coming through. So we just had to follow every snippet on MTV, if possible.

JOHNNY CHRIST: It's still awesome. When I have my iPod on shuffle, when some of those songs come up, it's really fun to listen to again and they still hold up. Absolutely.

TRAVIS STEVER: I am going to go sit in my yard right now, drink beer, and listen to 'Angel Dust' (I recently re-bought it on vinyl), and then I will follow it up with Mr. Bungle's 'California,' and love every minute of it. So that's how it holds up in my world.

Sources

All quotations are taken from the author's interviews, except as noted below.

PRELUDE
Wallace: "They were really...the whole thing." (*Classic Rock*, October 2006)

CHAPTER 1
Patton: "More than anything...joke's on us'!" (*Classic Rock*, October 2006); **Patton:** "When a master...fuckin' chocolate éclair!" (*Music Express*, August 1992); **Bordin:** "Our time isn't...fucked as ever." (*Rolling Stone*, September 1990); **Gould:** "I don't see...a mass scale." (*Rolling Stone*, September 1990); **Patton:** "Actually, it's kind...the line somewhere." (*Faces*, 1990)

CHAPTER 2
Gould: "Before the Animated...that made sense." (faithnoman.com, 2012); **Wims:** "We were all...on the EP." (faithnoman.com, 2012); **Gould:** "I really liked...Worthington, and Bordin." (faithnoman.com, 2012); **Gould:** "The first thing...Faith. No Man." (*Classic Rock*, October 2006); **Bordin:** "My grandfather came...I'm a real mongrel." (*Smash Hits*, September 1990); **Bordin:** "I grew up...and left us." (*Metal Maniacs*, December 1992); **Bordin:** "I have a...put on microphones." (*Smash Hits*, September 1990); **Bordin:** "I learnt how...little bit further." (*HM*, November 1995); **Morris:** "Bordin ended up...drummers would have." (faithnoman.com, 2012); **Bordin:** "I don't particularly...ourselves as well." (faithnoman.com, 2012); **Morris:** "The original name...of the name." (faithnoman.com, 2012); **Gould:** "It was a little...was very appealing." (*Classic Rock*, October 2006); **Gould:** "Pretty horrible shows." (*Classic Rock*, October 2006); **Bordin:** "[Gould] saw a...he had to." (*Classic Rock*, October 2006); **Gould:** "I had pneumonia...that record deaf!" (*Classic Rock*, October 2006); **Bordin:** "We all just...was

'No More'." (*Classic Rock*, October 2006); **Carpmill:** "Mike Bordin and...motto, 'Always Faithful'." (faithnoman.com, 2012); **Gould:** "No reason, we...No Man days." (faithnoman.com, 2012)

CHAPTER 3
Gould: "I don't think...People hated it." (*Spin*, December 1990); **Gould:** "We had this...from that party." (*Faces*, 1990); **O'Brien:** "They had a...ended with FNM." (faithnoman.com, 2012); **Bottum:** "She was around...pop sorta stuff.'" (*Reflex*, June 1992); **Bottum:** "Liked to sing...adorned with flowers." (*Classic Rock*, October 2006); **Gould:** "She was a...after a while." (*Classic Rock*, October 2006); **Bordin:** "When we started...be gotten at." (*Metal Maniacs*, December 1992); **Gould:** "We played clubs...that musical freedom." (*Monitor*, Spring 1991); **Bottum:** "We were established...wanted to go." (*Public News*, January 1992); **Gould:** "He had a...a band thing." (*Classic Rock*, October 2006); **Mosley:** "They had three...was good enough." (clevescene.com, 2009); **Mosley:** "The thing I...really stupid stuff." (*Classic Rock*, October 2006); **Bordin:** "I was with...him to do'." (*Classic Rock*, October 2006); **Gould:** "Jim and Mike...can play guitar'." (*Classic Rock*, October 2006); **Martin:** "People say that...this before rock." (*NME*, June 1992); **Martin:** "My influences to...fascinates all life." (faithnomoreblog.com, 2012); **Martin:** "We had this...the Bell Tolls'." (*Classic Rock*, January 2005); **DiDonato:** "Cliff and Jimmy...tape back over." (*Classic Rock*, January 2005); **DiDonato:** "At times, Jim did not care...Cliff was doing and vice versa." (*Classic Rock*, January 2005); **Wallace:** "I always liked...the band properly." (*Classic Rock*, October 2006); **Wallace:** "At the time...to have that." (*Classic Rock*, October 2006)

CHAPTER 4
Martin: "We burned a...the Paganism behind." (*Classic Rock*, October 2006); **Wallace:** "Everybody kind of...going to do." (*Classic Rock*, October 2006); **Gould:** "'Just play it...that's what happened." (*Classic Rock*, October 2006); **Mosley:** "I probably 'mental...out right there." (*Classic Rock*, October 2006); **Mosley:** "I could croon...do much else." (clevescene.com, 2009); **Mosley:** "Rapped over the...hear a melody." (clevescene.com, 2009); **Mosley:** "When it came...out of me." (clevescene.com, 2009); **Bottum:** "I still like...of the time." (*Reflex*, June

1992); **Gould:** "The star was...order through disorder." (faithnoman.com, 2012); **Gould:** "Well, yes there...little of that." (faithnoman.com, 2012); **Gould:** "I think that...lot of Run-DMC." (*Classic Rock*, October 2006); **Gould:** "We got in...fucking money whatsoever." (*Classic Rock*, October 2006); **Martin:** "We traveled across...of my beard!" (*Classic Rock*, October 2006); **Mosley:** "One of the...updated the lyrics." (*Classic Rock*, December 2010); **Mosley:** "I always like...our own song." (*Classic Rock*, December 2010); **Mosley:** "When we had...song coming out." (*Classic Rock*, December 2010); **Martin:** "We were traveling...in 56 days." (*Classic Rock*, October 2006); **Fieldy:** "That shit just...rock my world." (*Guitar World*, January 1997)

CHAPTER 5

Perry: "When Faith No...to be there" (Advert, unknown); **Gould:** "By the time...for this roadie." (*Classic Rock*, October 2006); **Keneally:** "The headliner came...was so impressed." (keneally.com); **Keneally:** "The night after...to no end." (keneally.com); **Martin:** "It was bestowed...some funny times." (faithnomoreblog.com, 2012); **Gould:** "There was a...attacked him again!" (*Classic Rock*, October 2006); **Gould:** "The upshot of...without firing them'." (*Classic Rock*, October 2006); **Mosley:** "I've never been...don't touch anymore." (*Classic Rock*, October 2006); **Mosley:** "I said, 'I...can you do?" (*Classic Rock*, October 2006); **Bottum:** "At the time...we were doing." (faithnomoreblog.com, 2013); **Mosley:** "I've always talked...last 20 years." (*Classic Rock*, December 2010); **Mosley:** "I regret making...to fire me." (faithnomoreblog.com, 2012); **Gould:** "We had considered...it really well." (*Monitor*, Spring 1991); **Gould:** "We were friends...a musical connection." (*Classic Rock*, October 2006); **Bottum:** "Mike Bordin really...cup of tea." (*Classic Rock*, October 2006); **Martin:** "We auditioned about...and cookies type." (*Classic Rock*, October 2006); **Patton:** "That was really cool and atmospheric" (*Kerrang!*, June 1997); **Patton:** "There's a core...guys in college." (*Virtually Alternative*, September 1999); **Dunn:** "We had all...same corner together." (*Georgia Straight*, March 1992); **Lengyel:** "Well, it really...kind of shit." (*Daily Texan*, December 1995); **Patton:** "I had no...completely lost." (*Circus*, November 1990); **Patton:** "I've only had...my extra payment." (*Smash Hits*, September 1990); **Patton:**

"Hippies and loggers." (*Music Express*, August 1992); **Spruance:** "I'm frightened by...was a Satanist." (*Kerrang!*, 1991); **Patton:** "FNM played in...of Mr. Bungle." (*Music Express*, August 1992); **Patton:** "Eureka is a...San Francisco again." (*Circus*, November 1990); **Patton:** "When I first...record store, *wow...*" (*Circus*, November 1990); **Spruance:** "It was a...records or whatever." (*Metal Forces*, 1991); **Patton:** "I was in...I doing here'?" (*Creem*, July 1992); **Gould:** "I have to...stand a chance." (*Select*, March 1995)

CHAPTER 6
Bordin: "The music was...what we are." (*Classic Rock*, October 2006); **Gould:** "I think sometimes...which was lucky." (*Monitor*, Spring 1991); **Patton:** "It was strange...anything I do." (*Reflex*, June 1992); **Patton:** "It was no...doing a project." (*Q*, May 1995); **Patton:** "The studio had...couple hours later." (*Kerrang!*, May 2005); **Wallace:** "He was singing...Faith No More." (*Classic Rock*, October 2006); **Martin:** "What happened was...getting more ideas." (*Classic Rock*, May 2005); **Gould:** "An Indian name for the drug DMT" (AOL Cyber-Talk, November 1994); **Gould:** "The way we...song is different." (*Monitor*, Spring 1991); **Bottum:** "Seems to be...role in interaction." (*Classic Rock*, May 2005); **Patton:** "Jello shots, Hermetic...junkie jibber jabber." (*Classic Rock*, May 2005); **Patton:** "I think I...sleep deprivation experiments." (*Classic Rock*, May 2005); **Gould:** "That song was...the set altogether." (*Classic Rock*, May 2005); **Patton:** "Believe it or...YOUR responsibility now!" (*Kerrang!*, May 2005); **Patton:** "I think we...quite measure up." (*Kerrang!*, May 2005); **Martin:** "That song was...a pop hit." (*Select*, September 1990); **Gould:** "There's a record...on my bass." (*The Real Thing Bass Guitar Transcription Book*, 1990); **Patton:** "Oh man, I...the fucking thing." (suicidegirls.com, 2006); **Ziman:** "I remember, the...were so feisty." (movieweb.com, 2010); **Bottum:** "It's good we...horribly upbeat song." (*Select*, September 1990); **Bordin:** "We didn't come...clique or group." (*Spin*, December 1990); **Bordin:** "We're not a...acid-head dirtbags." (*Spin*, December 1990); **Patton:** "It's awful I...shit, it's pathetic." (*Virtually Alternative*, September 1999); **Gould:** "We got a...to kill you!" (*Faces*, 1990); **Patton:** "The best shows...the most inspiring." (*Oor*, August 1992); **Bottum:** "At that point...is pretty flattering!" (*Reflex*, June 1992); **Welch:** "They were the...them a

chance." (*Guitar World*, January 1997); **Show Review:** "The only thing...rap shit?' attitude." (*The Probe*, 1991); **Patton:** "I think the...and getting drunk." (*Reflex*, June 1992); **Cameron:** "That was probably...from the lights." (*Classic Rock*, Summer 2005); **Bottum:** "I remember playing...people were aghast." (*Classic Rock*, May 2005)

CHAPTER 7

Patton: "Of course I...OKAY, I'M SORRY!" (*Kerrang!*, May 2005); **Bottum:** "I think it...what he did." (faithnomoreblog.com, 2013); **Patton:** "Goddamn. It's not...my hat back." (*Spin*, December 1990); **Patton:** "Masturbation is a...always something missing." (*Spin*, December 1990); **Patton:** "The only difference...while she watched." (*Spin*, December 1990); **Patton:** "Masturbation is like...I can't untie." (*Spin*, December 1990); **Patton:** "It all comes...as I can." (*Guitar For the Practicing Musician*, September 1992); **Patton:** "Puffy's the only...an Avon ad." (*Guitar For the Practicing Musician*, September 1992); **Martin:** "I remember it...he was famous..." (faithnomoreblog.com, 2012); **Bottum:** "One of the...launched into 'Easy.'" (*Spin*, December 1990); **Perry:** "At a recent...look suitably mortified)." (*Select*, September 1990); **Martin:** "We felt a...feeling of affection." (*Select*, September 1990); **Bottum:** "I think that...just didn't satisfy." (faithnomoreblog.com, 2013); **Patton:** "I really want...torture that fucker." (*Circus*, November 1990); **Bottum:** "We actually were...was very real." (faithnomoreblog.com, 2013); **Bottum:** "We went out...front of him!" (*Reflex*, June 1992); **Patton:** "It's very hard...with those things." (*Guitar For the Practicing Musician*, September 1992); **Gould:** "We were told...lucky. Nobody died." (*NME*, June 1992); **Patton:** "Every once in...uh, too long!" (*Reflex*, June 1992); **Bottum:** "The funny thing...away with it." (*Select*, September 1990); **Patton:** "You don't spend...to deal with." (*Music Express*, August 1992); **Patton:** "Yeah, South America...of in hiding." (*The Face*, August 1992); **Patton:** "Once Roddy and...what just happened." (*BAM*, February 1993); **Bottum:** "The other day...gotta happen sometime." (*Select*, September 1990); **Martin:** "Big money is...swirling around us." (*Select*, September 1990); **Bottum:** "To me that...mouth) and silence." (*Creem*, July 1992); **Patton:** "The only thing...go home sometimes." (*Faces*, 1990)

CHAPTER 8

Patton: "In Mr. Bungle...one collective 'it'." (*Faces*, 1990); **Patton:** "I'm gonna need...from those bastards." (*Circus*, November 1990); **Spruance:** "It's funny, FNM...to work with." (*Kerrang!*, 1991); **Dunn:** "Actually, we just...blew us away." (*The Probe*, 1991); **Spruance:** "Zorn could lend...brought that out." (*Kerrang!*, 1991); **Patton:** "Pinched my ass...for Naked City." (*Kerrang!*, 1991); **Spruance:** "As extreme and...Zappa, of course!" (*Kerrang!*, 1991); **Patton:** "I haven't really...answer for that." (*The Onion*, 1999); **Spruance:** "People will buy...the used bin!" (*Kerrang!*, 1991); **Patton:** "Real art has never been shown on MTV." (*Spex*, August 1992); **Heifetz:** "I didn't know...still that stupid." (westnet.com/consumable, 1999); **Dunn:** "Expect a really...what we're doing." (*Georgia Straight*, March 1992); **Dunn:** "I have both...seeing the country." (*Georgia Straight*, March 1992); **Patton:** "Pretty much, that...that on me." (*Virtually Alternative*, September 1999); **Patton:** "I heard the...was bent over." (*Music Express*, August 1992); **Patton:** "Hey, it was...out the audience?" (*Music Express*, August 1992); **Dunn:** "Actually, to tell...nobody came up." (*Georgia Straight*, March 1992); **Dunn:** "We're into big...cartoon or something." (*Sounds*, February 1991); **Bottum:** "I've seen them...I'd ever have." (faithnomoreblog.com, 2013); **Welch:** "We liked that...I was younger." (songfacts.com, 2013); **Welch:** "Bungle, just the...costumes and stuff." (songfacts.com, 2013); **Welch:** "The song called...To.' So many." (songfacts.com, 2013); **Dunn:** "After our last...the sound system." (*Daily Texan*, December 1995); **Patton:** "Thanks for not...they're beautifully erotic." (*Sounds*, February 1991)

CHAPTER 9

Wallace: "There were times...the band members." (*Rolling Stone*, May 1992); **Patton:** "Everything this time...bitter and deceptive." (*Rolling Stone*, May 1992); **Gould:** "People who were...this time around." (*Rolling Stone*, May 1992); **Bordin:** "Jim wasn't stoked...fuck is that'?" (*Classic Rock*, October 2006); **Patton:** "We came into...album that way." (*CMJ New Music Monthly*, April 1995); **Martin:** "My publicized 'not...pissed everyone off." (faithnomoreblog.com, 2012); **Patton:** "It sounded like...except for Jim." (*Guitar For the Practicing Musician*, September 1992); **Wallace:** "He kept referring...band was furious."

(*Classic Rock*, October 2006); **Gould:** "I did play...side of things." (faithnomoreblog.com, 2012); **Bottum:** "Yeah, there's not...to expand technologically." (*Music Express*, August 1992); **Bordin:** "We worked on...kind of interconnected." (*Metal Maniacs*, December 1992); **Gould:** "When we did...a real advantage." (*Hot Metal*, 1992); **Wallace:** "He was into...for?!' Crazy shit." (*Classic Rock*, October 2006); **Patton & Gould:** [Patton takes a...cultural icons! Heroes!" (*Creem*, July 1992); **Patton:** "Last time around...on this record." (*Rolling Stone*, May 1992); **Patton:** "This time it's...that at all." (*Creem*, July 1992); **Patton:** "I drove around...great for inspiration." (*Circus*, 1992); **Patton:** "A grotesquely positive...frame of mind." (*Reflex*, June 1992); **Bottum:** "Mike wrote those...drug he does." (AOL Cyber-Talk, November 1994); **Patton:** "I also wrote...as I could." (*Metal Hammer*, January 1995); **Bottum:** "It was one...of that sample." (faithnomoreblog.com, 2013); **Patton:** "RV means recreational...average redneck mentality." (*Oor*, August 1992); **Gould:** "'Smaller and Smaller'...of the others." (faithnomoreblog.com, 2012); **Patton:** "We decided to...with Wolves' aesthetic." (*Music Express*, August 1992); **Bottum:** "I think at...on that one." (AOL Cyber-Talk, November 1994); **Patton:** "One thing I've...Sinatra, Jackie Gleason." (*Music Express*, August 1992); **Patton:** "There's this one...addicted to that." (*Creem*, July 1992); **Bottum:** "What'd you think?...job is done." (*Music Express*, August 1992); **Bottum:** "They weren't really...loud, obnoxious girls" (*Public News*, January 1993); **Martin:** "I was surprised...in the past." (*Guitar For the Practicing Musician*, September 1992); **Bottum:** "Yeah, they just...went really well." (*Public News*, January 1993); **Patton:** "'Crack Hitler' is...disco - bad! Horrible!" (*Reflex*, June 1992); **Patton:** "'Jizz' means sperm...of the lyrics." (*Oor*, August 1992); **Gould:** "I went through...and 'Spanish Eyes'." (faithnomoreblog.com, 2012); **Bottum:** "I think that...even for us." (faithnomoreblog.com, 2013); **Gould:** "We really don't...didn't really work." (faithnomoreblog.com, 2012); **Gould:** "Warners spent the...close as possible." (faithnomoreblog.com, 2012); **Gould:** "It's two beautiful...the balance thing." (*Creem*, July 1992); **Patton:** "We were delighted...we like best." (*Oor*, August 1992); **Gould:** "Roddy had the...was the cover." (faithnomoreblog.com, 2012); **Bordin:** "It has nothing...then really soothing." (*Metal Maniacs*, December 1992);

Bottum: "We were going...of the record." (*Music Express*, August 1992); **Patton:** "It's the same...rest it's boring." (*Oor*, August 1992)

CHAPTER 10
Patton: "Better than I thought...best like that." (*Oor*, August 1992); **Cameron:** "That's when Faith...in my life." (*Classic Rock*, Summer 2005); **Bottum:** "It's like, seriously...without their permission." (*The Baltimore Sun*, July 1992); **Patton:** "These are the...do is eat..." (*Details*, September 1992); **Gould:** "G n' R and...experience first hand." (*NME*, June 1992); **Gould:** "Touring with Axl...I have Axl!" (*Rip*, December 1992); **Gould:** "We wouldn't do...to know myself!" (*Hot Metal*, 1992); **Patton:** "I always feel...lowest common denominator." (*The Face*, August 1992); **Patton:** "I wouldn't go...something. I think." (*Details*, September 1992); **Patton:** "I've seen Axl...what? It's mine!" (*Spex*, August 1992); **Patton:** "To take a...thousands of people." (*Details*, September 1992); **Patton:** "A juicy tidbit...do with it." (*Rip It Up*, July 1992); **Gould:** "Every band in...big kinda sucks." (*Rip*, December 1992); **Bottum:** "Besides, I'm getting...coupla car mechanics..." (*Rip*, December 1992); **Gould:** "There was a...the riot happened." (*Classic Rock*, October 2006); **News Article:** "The Montreal police...the transit system." (*New York Times*, August 1992); **Martin:** "[Patton] had some...to lose interest." (*Classic Rock*, October 2006); **Martin:** "Number one thing...it hurt us." (faithnomoreblog.com, 2012); **Gould:** "We got busted...obviously, we hadn't." (*Classic Rock*, October 2006); **Martin:** "Axl Rose and...We became estranged." (*Classic Rock*, October 2006); **Patton:** "We care about...for months now." (*Bravo*, July 1995); **Bottum:** "All moments from...Guns N' Roses tour." (*HM*, December 1995); **Gould:** "For these gigs...of Motor Vehicles." (*Details*, September 1992); **Patton:** "Our manager sent...to boost sales." (*Sky*, December 1992); **Bordin:** "I honestly never...12-year-olds." (*Select*, August 1993); **Patton:** "We wanted them...I love that." (*Sky*, December 1992); **News Article:** "Patton enjoyed the...would let them'." (*Buffalo News*, October 1992); **News Article:** "A spokesman for...soon as possible." (*Buffalo News*, October 1992); **Patton:** "The October festivities...love with her." (*Oor*, July 1993); **Bottum:** "When we first...she was shocked." (*The Advocate*, June 1993); **Bottum:** "I'd like to...there? So many." (*The Advocate*, June 1993); **Bottum:** "Kids who are...positive role models."

(*The Advocate*, June 1993); **Bottum:** "My singer and...were up to." (*The Advocate*, June 1993); **Bottum:** "Which rock stars...Cobain, of course." (*The Advocate*, June 1993); **Bottum:** "I don't know...issues regarding such." (*Classic Rock*, October 2006); **Gould:** "I found out...felt personally insulted." (*Q*, May 1995); **Gould:** "It was hard...couple of years." (*Q*, May 1995); **Patton:** "Well it was...die. Fuck you'!" (*Select*, March 1995); **Bottum:** "Yeah, I got...and our business." (faithnomoreblog.com, 2013)

CHAPTER 11

Bordin: "Who knows what's...I know nothing." (*Select*, August 1993); **Gould:** "I think it...to shift again." (*Select*, August 1993); **Bottum:** "I think everyone...40 pop single." (*Select*, August 1993); **Martin:** "Take into consideration...long it takes." (*Select*, August 1993); **Patton:** "'Cause he's 66...gonna die soon." (*Smash Hits*, September 1990); **Unnamed FNM roadie:** "Jim Martin is...hours to shit." (*Select*, August 1993); **Martin:** "The main thing...bury your bone" (*Select*, August 1993); **Martin:** "There's no way...Perhaps a lifetime..." (*Select*, September 1990); **Bordin:** "We really gave...but time-wise." (*Metal Hammer*, January 1995); **Gould:** "Jim had a...we were doing." (*Metal Hammer*, January 1995); **Patton:** "We voiced our...like fucking children." (*M.E.A.T.*, May 1995); **Patton:** "You fuck someone...playing, not fighting." (*Metal Hammer*, January 1995); **Martin:** "I actually felt...leave my body." (*Classic Rock*, October 2006); **Mosley:** "I thought [firing...thing was gone." (rollingstone.com, August 2009); **Gould:** "Jim was a...for whatever reason." (consequenceofsound.net, October 2010); **Martin:** "There has been...chose the latter." (faithnomoreblog.com, 2012)

CHAPTER 12

Patton: "I got married...doesn't get easier." (Loveline, July 2006); **Bordin:** "He was a...play with him." (*Metal Hammer*, January 1995); **Gould:** "It's weird. Geordie...a record out." (*Metal Hammer*, January 1995); **Patton:** "I was actually...for the music." (*Metal Hammer*, January 1995); **Patton:** "Trey came in...like being reborn." (*M.E.A.T.*, May 1995); **Spruance:** "Well, I've played...weren't really interested." (*The University Reporter*, January 1996); **Gould:** "I had a...from the start."

(*Bass Player*, August 1995); **Patton:** "He's a dry...to work with." (*Metal Maniacs*, August 1995); **Bottum:** "I think we...the same producer." (*VAJ*, June 1995); **Bordin:** "Andy really helped...how we sound." (*The Island Ear*, June 1995); **Gould:** "We usually record...nothing to do." (*Axcess*, March/April 1995); **Gould:** "We had these...care of it." (*Axcess*, March/April 1995); **Bordin:** "So the day...sparks and everything." (*Axcess*, March/April 1995); **Gould:** "Once we ran...in the studio." (*Axcess*, March/April 1995); **Patton:** "Probably I can...A Day,' probably." (*Virtually Alternative*, September 1999); **Gould:** "Roddy wasn't really...just wasn't there." (*Classic Rock*, October 2006); **Bottum:** "I was friends...gone with it." (*Classic Rock*, October 2006); **Bottum:** "I knew the...to stop them." (*Select*, March 1995); **Bottum:** "My first impulse...important to me." (*Select*, March 1995); **Spruance:** "It was at...'What the fuck'?" (*Classic Rock*, October 2006); **Patton:** "Doing the record...really satisfying shit." (*M.E.A.T.*, May 1995); **Gould:** "Some bands, like...built like that." (*Bass Player*, August 1995); **Bordin:** "Instead of putting...or lighter feel." (*Metal Hammer*, January 1995); **Patton:** "This time we...a pop record." (*Metal Hammer*, January 1995); **Bordin:** "[Patton] definitely has...we're still here." (*Metal Maniacs*, August 1995); **Patton:** "Kurt? God no!...Welcome to America." (*Metal Hammer*, January 1995); **Gould:** "The guitar solo...growing as musicians." (*Faces*, June 1995); **Bordin:** "That song is...past five years." (*Metal Maniacs*, August 1995); **Patton:** "I think we're...make that distinction." (*Metal Maniacs*, August 1995); **Bordin:** "It's just a...we loved it." (*Metal Maniacs*, August 1995); **Patton:** "Just picture a...what it's about." (*Metal Maniacs*, August 1995); **Bordin:** "He was uncomfortable...something like that." (*Metal Maniacs*, August 1995); **Patton:** "It's like a...G n' R music." (*CMJ New Music Monthly*, April 1995); **Gould:** "There's also some...of it, too." (*Faces*, June 1995); **Spruance:** "If it is...more mediocre music." (*The University Reporter*, January 1996); **Gould:** "Radio will say...will want it!" (*Kerrang!*, July 1995); **Gould:** "I tried to...who we are." (consequenceofsound.net, October 2010); **Patton:** "No idea, we've...that special anyway." (*Oor*, July 1993); **Gould:** "We have been...cool factor though." (westnet.com/consumable, April 1995); **Gould:** "I'm proud of...car ever sold." (*San Francisco Chronicle*, February 1997); **Gould:** "The b-sides that...in my life!" (*Live Wire*, May 1995); **Patton:** "The video is...a video is." (*Huh*, April 1995); **News Article:** "Wiry in his...Cowboy'-type hustler." (*CMJ New Music Monthly*, April 1995); **News Article:** "Mike Patton looks...be quite beat." (*Metal Hammer*, January 1995); **Gould:** "I think he...hard fucking work." (*Faces*, June 1995); **Bordin:** "He spent this...everybody likes him." (*The Island Ear*, June 1995); **Menta:** "A friend asked...of the band." (*Bravo*, July 1995); **Menta:** "Talked shit behind...they always did." (*Classic Rock*, October 2006); **Patton:** "Maybe we could...were more familiar." (*Creative Loafing*, May 1995); **Bottum:** "In Chile, one...a whole lot." (faithnomoreblog.com, 2013)

CHAPTER 13

McKinnon: "I'm not really...whole lot different." (*Daily Arts*, November 1995); **Dunn:** "When coming together...song. Hard work!" (*Visions*, April 1996); **McKinnon:** "I think [side...good for it." (*Daily Arts*, November 1995); **Dunn:** "We all live...whole time together." (*Visions*, April 1996); **Heifetz:** "We really need...what's going down." (*Rave*, October 1996); **Spruance:** "We really have...working together on." (*Rave*, October 1996); **Spruance:** "Well, within the...blow your mind." (*The University Reporter*, January 1996); **Spruance:** "University libraries are...of our asses." (*The University Reporter*, January 1996); **Spruance:** "That's what's so...usually the shit." (*The University Reporter*, January 1996); **McKinnon:** "The band gets...was pieced together." (*Georgia Straight*, March 1992); **Dunn:** "After that, we...this record done." (*Daily Texan*, December 1995); **McKinnon:** "A lot of...it on them." (*Georgia Straight*, March 1992); **Spruance:** "When we write...the arrangement stage." (*Rave*, October 1996); **McKinnon:** "We were supposed...on our part." (*Daily Arts*, November 1995); **McKinnon:** "Sometimes it seems...our shit out." (*Daily Arts*, November 1995); **Heifetz:** "We're all itching...us at all." (*F*, December 1995); **Dunn:** "They just write...which is great." (*The University Reporter*, January 1996); **Spruance:** "'Disco Volante' was...with the label." (westnet.com/consumable, 1999); **Heifetz:** "We asked them...for your support." (*F*, December 1995); **Heifetz:** "We're starting in...Florida, fuck you!" (*F*, December 1995); **McKinnon:** "Last time [the...wear it again'!" (*Daily Arts*, November 1995); **Dunn:** "There are always...especially in Europe." (*Visions*, April 1996); **Patton:** "Our drummer's a...anything with them." (*Virtually Alternative*, September 1999); **Patton:** "Very skeletal. We'll...put them out." (*Virtually Alternative*, September 1999); **Spruance:** "I'm sure someday...and do them." (*Snap Pop*, July 1999)

CHAPTER 14

Gould: "Dean had been...we worked differently." (spin.com, January 1997); **Patton:** "We have another...militaristic about it." (*Beat*, March 1997); **Gould:** "You start to...in the end." (*Zillo*, May 1997); **Gould:** "Kind of 50%...was really cool." (*Zillo*, May 1997); **Gould:** "Before most of...originally by him." (*Zillo*, May 1997); **Patton:** "I think his...on the record." (*Zillo*, May 1997); **Gould:** "Roli is the...a new light." (*San Francisco Chronicle*, February 1997); **Gould:** "Until now, every...good for us." (*Zillo*, May 1997); **Patton:** "I think most...like it should'." (*Zillo*, May 1997); **Gould:** "And the things...perspective for us." (*Zillo*, May 1997); **Hudson:** "Fragmented. I don't...to go elsewhere." (*Classic Rock*, October 2006); **Bottum:** "Sort of night...Enough to sing." (*Herald Sun*, June 1997); **Bordin:** "I was the...honor for me." (*San Francisco Chronicle*, May 1996); **Osbourne:** "I've always thought...pro. He's great." (*San Francisco Chronicle*, May 1996); **Gould:** "Very rarely are...of the period." (*San Francisco Chronicle*, February 1997); **Gould:** "We did try...anything we've done." (*San Francisco Chronicle*, February 1997); **Patton:** "It's got more...it's darker too." (*Beat*, March 1997); **Gould:** "FNM was always...on the album." (*Intro*, May 1997); **Gould:** "We wrote something...feeling, enough balls." (*Keyboard*, September 1997); **Bottum:** "I was really...he didn't anyway." (*Herald Sun*, June 1997); **Gould:** "This record took...record was finished." (*Keyboard*, September 1997); **Gould:** 'Angel Dust'] was...out bodies afterwards." (*Keyboard*, September 1997); **Gould:** "Actually, this song...of our culture." (*Keyboard*, September 1997); **Gould:** "This song has...was really inspiring." (*Keyboard*, September 1997); **Gould:** "Basically it's a...a compulsive gambler." (*Keyboard*, September 1997); **Gould:** "Pristina, in Kosovo...cannot be ignored." (reocities.com/SunsetStrip/palladium/5113/archive_billyqa.html, July 1998); **Gould:** "There is a...influence for them." (songfacts.com, 2012); **Khan:** "It's obviously a...at the time." (vimeo.com, 2012); **Patton:** "I've gotten a...opposed to it." (*Virtually Alternative*, September 1999); **Bottum:** "I had no...a good scene." (faithnomoreblog.com, 2013); **Bottum:** "The Sparks project...place for tea." (faithnomoreblog.com,

2013); **Patton:** "I can imagine...Interesting. Very interesting. (*Metal Hammer*, June 1997)

CHAPTER 15
Press Release: "After 15 long...throughout its history." (old.fnm.com/news, April 1998); **Gould:** "I personally would...Seeee ya, Bill" (old.fnm.com/news, April 1998); **Patton:** "I'm definitely glad...be drawn there." (*The Onion*, October 1999); **Patton:** "I think it...it with integrity." (*Classic Rock*, October 2006); **Bottum:** "Initially I think...that particular point." (faithnomoreblog.com, 2013); **Bordin:** "We loved this...the fucking hype." (*Classic Rock*, October 2006)

CHAPTER 16
Dunn: "[Patton] was trying...jam with them'." (invisibleoranges.com, March 2011); **Patton:** "This is how...blink, fuck 'em." (*Exotic*, November 1998); **Patton:** "I just wanted...I'm going for." (*Exotic*, November 1998); **Osborne:** "He has come...sick and twisted." (*Jyrki* TV Show, 2000); **Lombardo:** "When you work...go on forever!" (geeksofdoom.com, May 2011)

CHAPTER 17
Spruance: "There are a...and have fun." (*Guitar Player*, March 1999); **Heifetz:** "I miss him...Year's Eve '89]." (westnet.com/consumable, 1999); **Patton:** "Whenever we make...It just happened." (*Virtually Alternative*, September 1999); **Spruance:** "It wasn't until...a refreshing experience." (*Guitar Player*, March 1999); **Heifetz:** "We know our...better than anybody." (westnet.com/consumable, 1999); **Patton:** "There are parts...is cost prohibitive." (*HUMP*, July 1999); **Patton:** "The record sounds...reasons, we couldn't." (*CMJ New Music*, August 1999); **Patton:** "More than anything...Peppers do that." (*The Onion*, October 1999); **Patton:** "There's a shitload...It's a disaster." (*The Onion*, October 1999); **Patton:** "I demo everything...whole translation process." (*Snap Pop*, July 1999); **Heifetz:** "Beach Boys and...squeezable melodic intentions?" (westnet.com/consumable, 1999); **Patton:** "'Goodbye Sober Day'...That excites me." (*Virtually Alternative*, September 1999); **Spruance:** "There are a...out more stuff." (*Snap Pop*, July 1999); **Spruance:** "Bad. It's always...I don't know'." (*Snap Pop*, July 1999);

Patton: "They talked about...you shouldn't either." (*Virtually Alternative*, September 1999); **Patton:** "You wanna hear...I'm not sure." (*Instant*, September 1999); **Patton:** "The most glaring...stage like that'." (*Instant*, September 1999); **Patton:** "I mean, we...that's what's important." (*The Onion*, October 1999); **Patton:** "We're kinda on...and over again." (*Virtually Alternative*, September 1999); **Patton:** "Well, I try...on at home." (*Virtually Alternative*, September 1999); **Spruance:** "You know, actually...to play now." (*Snap Pop*, July 1999); **Patton:** "We've had some...problem? It's unbelievable." (*The Onion*, October 1999); **Patton:** "Absolutely! When it...pretty pathetic thing." (*The Onion*, October 1999); **Patton:** "It's basically some...in the air!" (*The Onion*, October 1999); **Patton:** "It better not...to change it." (*Virtually Alternative*, September 1999); **Spruance:** "Well the thing...ready to go." (*Snap Pop*, July 1999)

CHAPTER 18
Patton: "I'm at a...all I could." (rollingstone.com, December 2004); **Spruance:** "As time wears...good run, though." (markprindle.com, 2007)

CHAPTER 19
Gould: "It is very...influence like that." (*Classic Rock*, October 2006); **Patton:** "If I personally...each his own." (*Classic Rock*, October 2006); **Gould:** "I think the...would be fake." (*Classic Rock*, October 2006); **Press Release:** "Faith No More...and Mike Patton (fnm.com, February 2009); **Martin:** "For some time...made their announcement." (faithnomoreblog.com, 2012); **Bottum:** "Y'know, initially I...didn't ever happen." (faithnomoreblog.com, 2013); **Bottum:** "A crazy nervous...really special communication." (faithnomoreblog.com, 2013); **Gould:** "[Having Chuck there]...isn't the point." (consequenceofsound.net, October 2010); **Martin:** "I know the...do anyone justice." (faithnomoreblog.com, 2012); **Bottum:** "I love Trey...get the idea." (faithnomoreblog.com, 2013); **Gould:** "Even we don't...buying a stock." (consequenceofsound.net, October 2010); **Bottum:** "We've always encouraged...to the show." (faithnomoreblog.com, 2013); **Bottum:** "Who knows? We...releasing anything live." (faithnomoreblog.com, 2013); **Patton:** "It's sort of...to overdo it." (*The Believer*, January 2013); **Gould:** "I personally can't...got

to be." (consequenceofsound.net, October 2010); **Gould:** "Hasn't been discussed...meant to happen." (consequenceofsound.net, October 2010)

CHAPTER 20

Patton: "A lot of...a prizewinning trophy." (*Sky*, December 1992); **Patton:** "Sometimes a shit...what I mean?" (*Q*, May 1995); **Shaw:** "Mike says it...anything,' Patton says." (*Details*, September 1992); **Patton:** "I could tell...one of them!" (*Raw*, June 1990); **Patton:** "I talk so...on their heads'." (*The Face*, August 1992); **Patton:** "I can't explain...in a knot." (*NME*, June 1992); **Patton:** "You don't call...good at it." (*Details*, September 1992); **Patton:** "She started sending...your devoted slave'."; **Patton:** "Recently, a girl...happens to you." (*Nieuwe Revu*, May 1995); **Patton:** "I'm not a...get enough sleep." (*The Face*, August 1992); **Patton:** "I did this...I could go." (*Music Express*, August 1992); **Patton:** "I made a...about it, too!" (*Music Express*, August 1992); **Patton:** "You mix it...have been in." (*Sky*, December 1992); **Patton:** "It's nice to...for your actions." (*M.E.A.T.*, May 1995); **Patton:** "On our last...but it's cool'." (*Sky*, December 1992); **Patton:** "I just don't...like an actor." (*Bravo*, July 1995); **Gould:** "His parents came...talk like that'?" (*Select*, March 1995); **Patton:** "You wanna know...blood did, though!" (*Music Express*, August 1992); **Patton:** "It has got...be very embarrassing." (*The Sun*, April 1997); **Patton:** "Some people think...just my hobby." (*The Sun*, April 1997); **Patton:** "The first, a...next step is." (*NME*, June 1992); **Patton:** "There comes a...drawn it earlier." (*Select*, March 1995); **Gould:** "So, you just...best known for." (*Select*, March 1995); **Patton:** "I've lost my...to get sick." (*Exotic*, November 1998); **Patton:** "I used to...next day Slayer." (*Nieuwe Revu*, May 1995); **Patton:** "Oh God, this...me a lot." (*Virtually Alternative*, September 1999); **Patton:** "I have kind...use toilets - ever." (*Details*, September 1992); **Patton:** "When I was...rock n' roll?" (*The Face*, August 1992); **Bottum:** "We had a...himself with urine." (*Video Croissant* home video, 1993); **Menta:** "The peeing, the...of that nature." (*Classic Rock*, October 2006); **Gould:** "I can't tell...limitations runs out." (*Select*, March 1995)

37529617R00119

Made in the USA
Lexington, KY
05 December 2014